MOTOR CYCLE CAVALCADE

IXION

of *The Motor Cycle*

MOTOR CYCLE
CAVALCADE

With thirty-two pages of photogravure illustrations

ILIFFE & SONS, LTD.

LONDON, BIRMINGHAM, COVENTRY, MANCHESTER AND GLASGOW

Published for " The Motor Cycle " by
Iliffe & Sons, Ltd., Dorset House, Stamford Street,
London, S.E.1

First Published 1950

Printed in Great Britain at The Whitefriars Press, Ltd., Tonbridge,
Kent, and bound by Adams and Harrison, Ltd., Biggleswade, Beds.
(BKS 832/50)
Photogravure illustrations by Sun Printers Ltd., Watford, Herts.

CONTENTS

PREFACE

MOTOR CYCLING IN THIS COUNTRY began on a very tiny scale in 1896. Since the original pioneers were grown men at that date, it is obvious that few of them can still be alive. The archives of the sport and pastime have never been complete. *The Motor Cycle*, the first journal continuously and exclusively devoted to such topics, was not founded until 1903. During the blitzes of World War II, many factories and offices were destroyed. It follows that records are already patchy.

This situation inspired certain enthusiasts to apply pressure to me, as the only professional writer among the survivors of the earliest days. They asked me to attempt to recapture the atmosphere of those distant years, and to dovetail it into the continuous sequel, before much of our story faded into the mists of time. Such was the genesis of this volume.

Any attempt to compress the story of fifty-four years into 100,000 words on a statistical basis would have been tedious to a degree. My assignment, therefore, was to aim at a judicious mixture of salient and representative facts and figures with sufficient personal experience to make the dish palatable. This factor explains the slightly unusual format of the book.

An old man's memory is apt to play strange tricks, and, in the absence of so many records, absolute accuracy cannot be guaranteed. I have, in fact, been astonished to discover how little some companies know of their own past. Great pains have been taken to verify important facts. I bear the sole responsibility for any inaccuracies.

Warm thanks are due to practically every firm in the industry for their kind assistance. Obligations to individuals are too numerous to catalogue, but I must name five. Geoffrey Smith, Editorial Director of *The Autocar* and *The Motor Cycle*, is mainly responsible for this publication. Arthur Bourne, genial Editor of *The Motor Cycle*, has never been too busy to help me with his shrewd advice and comprehensive knowledge. Roy Morton, chief of *The Motor Cycle* Technical Information Department, has again proved himself to be the kindest of walking encyclopædias. A. F. Johnson has most generously risen from honourable retirement to tackle the arduous job of covering half a century with suitable illustrations. No thanks can do justice to his help. Major H. R. Watling, of the British Cycle and Motor Cycle Manufacturers' Union, has furnished much information, and allowed me to make free use of the brochure written by the late Eric Walford for the Union, in which much pioneer history is preserved.

It cannot be emphasized too strongly that the opinions here printed are my own, and are not necessarily shared by my publishers.

PREFACE

If my personal experiences, and some of the machines which I
have known best, bulk too large in these pages, I regret such over-
emphasis, but I could devise no other method to prevent the
narrative degenerating into a tedious parade of dry facts and drier
figures.

IXION.

London: 1950.

NOTE

Readers will meet certain repetitions throughout the volume. As
this will serve in part as a book of reference, such repetitions are
unavoidable if some chapters are to be complete in themselves.
For example, the development of variable gears figures alike in
touring, trials and racing.

CHRONOLOGY

1884
Edward Butler built the first motor tricycle.

1885
Gottlieb Daimler built the first motor bicycle at Kannstatt.
Karl Benz built a three-wheeled carette at Mannheim.

1892
J. D. Roots' water-cooled tricycle with two-stroke engine.

1894
J. H. Knight's tricar with water-cooled four-stroke engine.

1895
Colonel H. C. L. Holden's four-cylinder, water-cooled motor bicycle.

1896
The Motor Car Act dispensed with the man carrying a red flag in front of mechanically-propelled road vehicles, and raised the speed limit from 4 m.p.h. to 12 m.p.h.
Debut of the Beeston motor tricycle

1897
About this date De Dion Bouton (of Paris) built practicable motor tricycles of the single front wheel type. Weighing about 90 lb, they had a 120 c.c. engine rated at ½ h.p. and sold at £50.
Eight motor cycles were exhibited at the Stanley Cycle Show in the Agricultural Hall, Islington.

1898
Allard and Ariel motor tricycles were staged at the Crystal Palace Show.
Simultaneously Enfield and Eadie sold similar machines with De Dion engines.
Accles, Turrell and Dennis also built a few tricycles.
Debut of the Beeston 1¾ h.p. motor bicycle.
Six motor bicycles were exhibited at the Stanley Show.

1899
The Rover Co. began experiments.
F. R. Simms produced low-tension magneto ignition.
One motor cycle exhibited at the Stanley Show.

1900
The famous 1,000 Miles Reliability Trial. The entries included two quads, four tricycles and two front-wheel-driven Werner motor bicycles. Of this octet, five were British (Ariel and Enfield quads; two Ariel tricycles; one Motor Manufacturing Co. tricycle).
One motor cycle exhibited at the Stanley Show.

1901
The Singer Co. began to market its famous " motor wheel " bicycles and tricycles, embodying the Simms low-tension ignition.
115 motor cycles were exhibited at the Stanley Show, of which 105 were motor bicycles, mostly " assembled " types with French or Belgian engines.

1902
E. H. Arnott, captain of the Motor Cycling Club, rode a French Werner motor bicycle from Land's End to John o' Groats in 65 hr 45 min.
214 motor cycles at the Stanley Show.

1903
The Auto Cycle Club (forerunner of the Auto Cycle Union) was founded as the motor cycle committee of the Automobile Club of Great Britain and Ireland (later the R.A.C.). With the late F. Straight as secretary, it organized its first 1,000 miles trial, spreading the mileage over 14 days of short out-and-home runs, for example, from the Crystal Palace to Brighton and back.

Speed limit raised from 12 m.p.h. to 20 m.p.h. with reduced limits of 5 m.p.h. and 10 m.p.h. at selected danger points.

375 motor cycles at the Stanley Show.

First sidecar marketed under the name of the Liberty sociable attachment.

First issue of *The Motor Cycle* published in Coventry (March 31).

Fierce controversy on the relative merits of mechanical *v.* automatic inlet valves.

1904

M.C.C. organize first 24-Hour London-to-Edinburgh Run, and inter-club Team Championship.

21,521 motor cycles registered by midsummer.

Trailers ousted by tricars and fore carriages.

Experiments with 3-inch tyres begun (the standard size was still 28 × 2 inches).

Britain exported 488 motor cycles in six months.

Speed of $76\frac{1}{2}$ m.p.h. attained by a 110-lb machine in France.

1905

28,000 machines registered in the British Isles.

Début of the first horizontally-opposed twin-cylinder engine (originally the Fe, later known as Barter, Fairy, and finally Douglas).

High-tension magnetos become popular.

3 h.p. Triumph driven 200 miles per day for six consecutive days.

1906

Royal Commission reports on road construction with special emphasis on dustlessness.

The new high-tension magnetos raise the standard of reliability.

1907

First Tourist Trophy Races in the Isle of Man over a short course in the Peel-Kirkmichael area.

Brooklands track opened on April 6.

1908

First motor cycle races on Brooklands track (April 18).

1909

T.T. Races reorganized, and freed from fuel limit.

British Motor Cycle Racing Club founded.

Scottish Six Days' Trial inaugurated.

The late Ivan B. Hart-Davies rides a $3\frac{1}{2}$ h.p. single-gear Triumph (weighing 196 lb) from John o' Groats to Land's End in 33 hr 22 min.

Vogue of adjustable belt pulleys.

A 500 c.c. Trump-J.A.P. established the classic one hour track record at 48 miles.

The Road Board and Road Fund constituted by Parliament.

1910

Registrations totalled 86,414.

First Olympia Show.

3,418 machines exported.

Morgan Runabout marketed.

Powell and Hanmer introduce the first motor cycle lighting dynamos.

First London-to-Exeter winter run.

1911

Tourist Trophy Races switched to the present " mountain " course of 37 m 1,290 yds. Junior race instituted.

Countershaft gears (with either all-chain or chain-cum-belt transmissions) come to the fore.

V. Surridge (Rudge) raises the 1 hour track record to 60 miles.

1912

Variable gears standardized by many leading manufacturers.

Kickstarters come into favour.

Petrol price, 1s $2\frac{1}{2}$d per gallon (previous minimum price, 9d).

1913

180,000 machines registered, including many two-strokes.

16,850 machines exported.

1914–1918

First World War.

1920
As the industry completed the switch to peacetime manufacture, through boom and slump, the all-chain drive with countershaft gear box became accepted as standard on full roadster models.

1921
100 m.p.h. reached by D. H. Davidson on a 1,000 c.c. Indian.
500-mile motor cycle races at Brooklands for the first (and last) time.
373,000 registrations.

1922
100 m.p.h. first attained by a 500 c.c. machine (Douglas, ridden by C. G. Pullin).
H. Le Vack (998 c.c. Zenith-J.A.P. laps Brooklands at 100 m.p.h.

1923
Manx " amateur " races organized over T.T. course.
World's fastest land speed on two wheels by C. F. Temple at 108·48 m.p.h. on a 996 c.c. British Anzani.

1924
First 100 m.p.h. by a 350 c.c. machine (W. D. Marchant, on a Chater-Lea).

1928
First speedway meeting at High Beech, near Epping.

1929
Chromium plating begins to supersede nickel plating.
British riders on British machines won the five leading Continental Grand Prix events in France, Belgium, Germany, Spain and Holland respectively.

1930
The Road Traffic Act and the Highway Code come into force.
Third party insurance made compulsory.
Speed limit abolished.
T.T. circuit first lapped in less than 30 min by W. L. Handley (Rudge).
J. S. Wright (O.E.C.-Temple-J.A.P.) sets up new world fastest speed at over 150 m.p.h.

1931
A 346 c.c. New Imperial demonstrates reliability by covering 15,600 miles in 25 days on Dutch soil.

1932
New scheme of motor cycle taxation adopted by Parliament, with reduction to 15s per annum for engines of less than 150 c.c.
Ernst Henne on a German B.M.W. of 750 c.c. covers the flying kilometre at 151·86 m.p.h.

1933
Olympia Show included a B.S.A. with fluid flywheel and preselector gears.

1934
Ernst Henne raises the world record to 152·901 m.p.h.
Speed limit of 30 m.p.h. in built-up areas imposed.
Driving tests for learners imposed on April 1.

1935
Italian Guzzi machines win both the Senior and the Lightweight T.T.
Hour record raised to 114·092 m.p.h. on Montlhéry track by J. Guthrie (Norton).

1937
First motor cycle Show at Earls Court.
World record raised to 169·8 m.p.h. by the late Eric Fernihough on a blown Brough Superior.
The industry backs the National Physical Laboratory in investigating the source and character of noise emitted by four typical makes.
Henne (B.M.W.) regains the world record at 174 m.p.h.

1938
Supercharged German D.K.W. two-stroke, ridden by Kluge, wins the Lightweight T.T. at phenomenal speed.
Taruffi (500 c.c. Gilera) covers 121·234 miles in one hour.

11

A team of French army officers achieve a possibly more practical feat on Montlhéry track, near Paris, by riding a Gnome et Rhone motor bicycle 30,988 miles at an average speed of 68 m.p.h. in 19 days.

1939

Brooklands track finally closed. (Last B.M.C.R.C. meeting thereat on July 15, 1939.)

Petrol rationing.

Lamp power restricted by masks.

1939-1945

Second World War.

1940

Extension of white lines on roadway to facilitate driving in blackout and fog.

Compulsory immobilization of parked machines.

All army officers up to the rank of brigadier to undergo a course in motor cycling.

All signposts removed.

1941

Army motor cyclists taught at special schools with tests on the same lines as pre-war one-day trials.

Popularity of autocycles among the civilian public.

Development of light models for commando and airborne troops.

Home Guard find motor cycles invaluable.

1942

Acute rubber shortage, but no rationing of motor cycle tyres.

1946

Industry in process of conversion from war production.

53,486 motor cycles exported. Total value of exports (including parts), £3,790,335.

Sunbeam introduce an " in-line " two-cylinder with shaft drive.

1947

T.T. Races revived after the 1939-1945 suspension. Run on low-octane, ration petrol, known as " Pool."

Douglas introduce a horizontally-opposed two-cylinder set across the frame, with torsion-bar rear suspension.

55,367 motor cycles exported. Value of exports (including parts), £5,037,550.

1948

First post-war Motor Cycle Show at Earls Court. Main features: vertical, parallel twin-cylinders, with telescopic front forks, hydraulically damped; and many sprung rear suspensions.

Velocette stage a revolutionary, silent " everyman " model, with 150 c.c. water-cooled, horizontally-opposed two-cylinder engine set across the frame, lever starting and shaft drive.

75,136 motor cycles exported. Value (including parts) £7,359,137.

1949

Clear tokens of an incipient boom in motor-assisted bicycles. None was staged at Earls Court, but both British and Continental samples found an increasing market during the year.

65,269 motor cycles exported. Value of exports (including parts), £6,861,202.

*   *   *   *   *

Note—The tendencies evident in the gradual return towards peace motoring conditions after the war are identified and valued in the letterpress of this book. At the date of writing, the bulk of the industry's output is still earmarked for export. All that can wisely be said is that the early post-war years witnessed a further and substantial extension of the popularity of motor cycling under innumerable handicaps.

PART I—FOREGROUND

CHAPTER 1

IN THE BEGINNING

I N SOME SIDE CHAMBER of the Temple of Fame, niches may be reserved for the names of men who rank as pioneers in man's minor activities. Therein may be commemorated the first two motor cyclists, Edward Butler and Gottlieb Daimler.

Butler, an Englishman, is an enigma, of whom practically nothing is known. If he had been born twenty years later, he might have become as famous and wealthy as Henry Ford. A psychologist might infer that he was an introvert, with few friends, who toiled laboriously at his quaint hobby in an atmosphere of derision, and was nagged by his wife for wasting money on unprofitable experiments, and making a mess of her house, until he eventually died, poor and frustrated. But his brain had all the qualities of a great inventor. He foresaw the future of the petrol engine in road transport long years before anybody else, excepting only his German counterpart. He was hemmed in by every conceivable handicap. The law limited the use of power vehicles to a speed of 4 m.p.h. and, even at this crawl, they must be preceded by a man with a red flag. Apparently he had little money, for he seems to have made every component of his machine with his own hands—probably he worked for wages, and experimented in his scanty leisure.

He was not able to base his model on the pedal bicycle, for in 1884 the safety bicycle did not exist, and only a lunatic could think of adding an engine to the high " penny-farthing " type of bicycle. But nothing could daunt his enthusiasm. We do not know how many crude attempts proved futile before he at last constructed the motor tricycle which will always keep his memory green.

It was an amazing vehicle, quite incredibly modern in certain items, far more modern than some designs which sold well years later, when the roads were freed by the Emancipation Act of 1896 and capital was available in large quantities for inventors.

The tricycle was of the single stern-wheel type. A neat little chair with side rails was slung between the two front wheels. Two convenient vertical tillers with a radial motion operated the steering. The twin-cylinder engine was horizontal, with one cylinder on each side of the rear wheel. Long and curiously curved connecting rods operated cranks near the rear hub, connected by chains to the

13

spindle. The ignition was electric, the carburettor had a float feed, the rotary valves were driven by chain. There was a hot spot to warm the mixture, and a hollow rear mudguard contained the cooling water for the cylinder jackets, while its position furnished an admirable header for thermo-syphon circulation. The epicyclic reduction gear between the cranks and the rear spindle had a ratio of 6 to 1. Before starting the engine, the driver depressed a pedal which jacked up the rear wheel on two small rubber-faced rollers. Later Edward Butler designed a second tricycle with vertical cylinders, but this was never made.

It is sad to think that this brilliant experiment probably never travelled on the road. We can only hope that some kindly farmer allowed Butler to test it in a flat meadow, or that a village squire gave him the run of his park. We know that it attracted some attention from C. T. Crowden, of Leamington, a younger man than Butler, who many years later became works manager of Lawson's Great Horseless Carriage Company. Presumably, when liberal legislation proved so tardy in its coming, Crowden lost interest and a disillusioned Butler returned dismally home to listen to his wife's " I told you so! " Nevertheless, his tricycle was an intellectual *tour de force* with few parallels in the long story of engineering progress.

Gottlieb Daimler, of Kannstatt, in Germany, built several motor cycles, of which the first was made scarcely a year later than the Butler tricycle. He suffered from no such legal handicaps as hampered Edward Butler, for he could freely drive his experiments on the road with no speed limit. Daimler was an extrovert, with very vigorous dreams of fame and wealth and power. His wife was presumably docile in the German fashion, whereby a frau obeys her husband, and confines her activities to " kitchen, kids and kirk ".

I suspect that Daimler began his experiments with comparatively large and heavy three- or four-wheeled chassis. Perhaps it gradually dawned on him that" one thing at a time " is a sound rule, and that no chassis would be valuable until he produced a dependable engine. Maybe, after wasting time and money on building chassis, and on having them towed back to his workshop, he decided to concentrate on engines. Be that as it may, he never took any real interest in the motor cycle as such, but used it as a mobile test bench for his engines, scrapping the motor cycle frames as soon as he had developed his engine to roadworthiness. Nevertheless, Daimler designed some very ingenious motor bicycles. It is even possible that he has some claims to figure as the accidental inventor of the safety bicycle with two wheels of small and equal diameter.

His 1885 bicycle had such wheels, although they were of the artillery pattern with wooden spokes and rims, and of approximately 30 inches diameter. The front fork was an inverted vertical U of strip steel. The frame consisted of a steel girder, sloping sharply backward from the head of the front fork to the rear hub. Midway down its length two pendant steel hangers formed the engine supports. The handlebar was set about a foot behind the front fork, which it operated by a belt running over two horizontal pulleys. Twisting the handlebar had the effect of winding up a cord, cotton-reel fashion; this applied the brake and furnished a free-engine device, based on shifting the jockey pulley which tensioned the belt drive! The tall, vertical engine was slung in the narrow gap between the close-coupled wheels, and was an accurate prophecy of 1900 practice, for it had an enclosed crankcase and mushroom valves. The total effect reminds one more of a child's hobby horse than of a cycle.

His later machine (see photogravure supplement) was roughly similar, but its frame was a duplex girder. The curious hood over the engine was Gottlieb's temporary idea of a good saddle, being apparently suggested by the contours of a horse's back!

As soon as Gottlieb had produced an engine which could be trusted to run, he hastily scrapped these crude and uncomfortable motor cycles, and designed a series of four-wheeled chassis to accommodate his successive engines. His trips on either of these hobby horses must have been as uncomfortable as they were precarious. Born in 1834, he lived until 1900, and acquired both wealth and reputation before his death. The famous Mercedes factory sprang from his experiments, and was constructing a splendid 40 h.p. car as early as 1903. It took its name from the beautiful daughter of Herr Jellineck, who exploited Gottlieb Daimler's brainwaves commercially.

In Britain, a stagnant period separated these pioneers from the practical engineers who stepped into their shoes from 1896 onward when a 12 m.p.h. speed limit rendered road experiments possible. Nevertheless, even in our hidebound country, men were not lacking to challenge a moribund law, or to anticipate its repeal. From 1874 onward, J. H. Knight, of Farnham, was indefatigable. He began with a steam tricar in 1874. His 1894 model was a $\frac{3}{4}$ h.p. steam tricycle, with tiller steering, a single front wheel, a four-stroke engine, and a two-speed gear.

In 1885, Karl Benz, of Mannheim, drove a three-wheeled vehicle, belonging rather to the car than the cycle sphere, albeit it was sometimes called a " tricycle ". It had an ingenious transmission. The countershaft was driven by flat belts, with a loose pulley for a free-engine position and fixed pulleys of varying diameters for the gear ratios; its final drive was by chain. I drove one of these about 1898, but refuse to accept it as a motor cycle. Meanwhile, in 1892, J. D. Roots developed a genuine tricycle, the true ancestor of that large fleet of petrol-engined tricycles which, under such names as De Dion and Ariel, occupied the " cycle " field from about 1897 until the first motor bicycles appeared.

The Roots trike was a true " cycle ", with two large stern wheels and a smaller steering wheel in front, all of the wire-spoke, steel-rim, spidery type. It had a cycle frame, cushion tyres, and was absolutely devoid of springs. The engine was most ingenious.

Located behind the rear axle, it drove by naked gearing and was an inverted water-cooled two-stroke, using tube ignition. The water reserves were carried inside the frame tubes. One imagines that if our road laws had been revised in 1892 instead of in 1896, Britain might have started the motor epoch on level terms with the French, the Belgians, and the Germans. Very little development was required to make the Roots design saleable.

Of course, the opposition to reform of the road laws was immensely formidable. In the concluding decades of the 19th century, Britain was by emphasis a horsey nation. Railroads had previously encountered furious and organized opposition, and they had never sought permission to use the public roads. But these new monstrosities bluntly demanded the same road rights as the horse and the pedestrian. They smelt. They were incredibly noisy. They dripped oil. They stirred up the dust. They pounded vulnerable waterbound road surfaces.

The nobility and gentry kept horses for utilitarian transport, they rode and hunted for pleasure. The farmers bred horses, and earned much of their living by feeding horses. The towns and the inns based their trade on horse traffic. A posting house on a main road drew a handsome income from horsed traffic. The advent of the railroads had been resisted. The pedal cycle had been resented, and " cads on castors " were still trapped and fined for speeding.

Violent opposition had met the introduction of a few steam road vehicles for heavy transport in the northern factory districts, and steam trams were only tolerated in hilly counties where horses could not haul heavy loads up the steep gradients. Every magisterial bench was staffed with horsey people. Parliament was a council of horsemen. The only wonder is that the Emancipation Act passed Parliament as early as 1896. The engineers of the country had hardly expected so early a reform, and they were caught napping.

It would be an exaggeration to say that France, Germany and Belgium had stolen quite so long and splendid a start as one might expect, considering that Daimler and Benz had put practical vehicles on the road some ten years previously. But a further four years were wasted before British engineers got down to their new opportunities. In 1896 they knew a good deal about stationary gas engines, but not a man-jack of them had any real acquaintance with the petrol engine.

Moreover, every necessary component, small or large, had to be designed by the user, or imported from abroad. Nowhere in this country could one buy an English axle or wheel or coil or carburettor or tyre or hub or sparking plug or contact-breaker or brake parts or any other conceivable component of a car or motor cycle, still less an engine, or a propeller shaft, or a piston, or a valve, or a piston ring, or a cam, or any suitable gears!

By contrast, the French traders were tumbling over each other to book orders for all these essentials, even if deliveries were slow

16

and small. We cannot wonder that production moved at a snail's pace and, for some years, consisted almost exclusively of rather inferior tricycles, the Ariel alone excepted. The first cars to sell over here were mostly French or German—the De Dion, the Panhard, the Benz, and so forth. The majority of the early motor cycles had foreign engines—the De Dion, the Minerva, or the Kelecom. Assemblers raced across the Channel, and inveigled some foreign factory to sell them engines with an English name cast on the crankcase.

It would also be an exaggeration to assume that Continental streets and roads were already crowded with cars and motor cycles. But petrol-engined vehicles were at least familiar sights in all the major Continental countries. In part, they were the newest hobby of the wealthy. In part, they were amusing scientific toys for wealthy amateurs, their position corresponding to that of radio receivers and television sets in the earlier phase of those yet unborn industries.

The foreign cyclists and cycle industries were welcoming them with open arms. No cycle trader could grow very fat on sales of a machine which cost little and lasted for years. The new trade catered with far costlier commodities, and involved luscious commissions, not to speak of almost constant maintenance service at high fees. Never perhaps were the rich so " soaked " as in the early days of the motor movement on the Continent.

Other handicaps beset the British pioneer quite apart from technical ignorance and the utter lack of component parts. The patent situation was obscure. Many foreigners had hastily registered alleged " master " patents in this country. One gentleman claimed to hold such a lien on every imaginable form of spray carburettor. Another advanced a similar strangle-grip on gear boxes. No Briton could safely design and market a motor vehicle until he knew where he stood with regard to such patents, and his lawyers hesitated to advise him until the courts had given a ruling.

Again, vast capital would obviously be required for so immense a venture as the gradual motorization of our traffic. The company promoter ran riot in the land. Both rogues and honest men of poor judgment complicated the organization. Such difficulties go far to explain why the cycle factories and the cycle retailers bulked so large at this period. Many small cycle retailers were first-class mechanics, and actually designed and assembled many of the machines which they retailed. It was no great matter for one of them to buy an engine abroad, modify his familiar cycle frame to suit, and offer a motor cycle under his personal transfer. At least two of the best machines of the period were so produced while the would-be car manufacturers were bogged down by the patent laws and financial operations.

For the moment the Continental view of motor cycles was that the tricycle was king. Several motor bicycles had appeared at various periods, notably the Hildebrand-Wolfmuller, a light open-framed design, not unlike the Scott in appearance. This had been hawked round Britain, and ridden by M. J. Schulte, of the Triumph Co., on the Coventry track as far back as 1895. That shrewd judge pooh-poohed it, and bided his time.

About the same date Colonel H. C. L. Holden had constructed a four-cylinder water-cooled motor bicycle with connecting rods coupled direct to cranks at the rear hub. A few were sold between 1899 and 1902. But their owners got no pleasure out of them. A plausible gentleman, E. J. Pennington, arrived from America and further confused British engineers by absurd claims for impossible engines.

So the French motor tricycles dominated the motor cycle section of the market from 1897 to 1901. The De Dion was the most famous, and therefore the most widely copied. The Ariel was probably the best to be produced in any number, though I found one built by an Ashford retailer which was even better. None of the tricycles was even remotely tolerable by modern standards. The dual effects of a rigid front fork and the massing of most of the weight astern rendered them tail-heavy and uncomfortable. The three wheel-tracks generated much vibration on the poor roads of the period. Lack of an emergency gear on most models limited the climb. Naked gear drives created a frightful noise as the teeth wore.

The advent of the motor bicycle was rather unworthily heralded by the import of the front driven Werner from Paris in 1898. From that date onward, crude as the Werner was, the tricycle was doomed. Those who formed our expert cycle industry leapt eagerly at the motor bicycle, perceiving how easily the pedal cycle might be converted into a light, fast roadster with excellent climbing powers. They were destined to learn that the conversion was by no means as simple as it looked. Indeed, they did not complete the job until 1920, although by about 1911 they had evolved a type which was utterly reliable, if a trifle awkward in thick traffic and on single-figure gradients.

Thus was a new industry born after a prolonged and difficult confinement.

CHAPTER 2

DAWN OF A CENTURY

THE INTRODUCTION OF A MORE LIBERAL speed limit of 12 miles an hour, and the abolition of the shabby cicerone with his red flag late in 1896, did not immediately unleash any very feverish activity in the British motor cycle world. England had at the time but a single motor cycle—the Holden, of which an 1897 model is on view at the Science Museum, South Kensington.

It is not definitely known whether Colonel Holden designed it for sheer fun, or with an eye to War Office orders. It was an extraordinarily ambitious design, and housed the first four-cylinder petrol engine ever seen on the roads of the world. The " flat four " engine lay horizontally beneath the frame, and a lilliputian rear wheel was directly driven by the connecting rods. All three frame panels were filled by petrol, water and accumulator tanks. It had a skew-driven oiler, and handlebar throttle control. The magnates of the cycle trade did not flock to purchase its patents, perhaps because they deemed it over-complicated, perhaps because they knew that its tiny rear wheel was a sad technical blunder.

For a year or two no great initiative distinguished this country. We were licking our wounds after the humiliation of the Boer War, meditating on its cost in blood and treasure, and puzzling our heads over the discovery that we seemed to be so unpopular with other nations.

Nevertheless, under the surface, many vigilant eyes were taking stock of the transport situation in terms of two or three wheels, no less than of four. The spark which really touched off an explosion was the 1,000-Mile Trial of 1900. This was, of course, principally a boost for the infant motor car trade. But the entry included four motor tricycles, two motor quadricycles, and two motor bicycles. Of these eight machines, five were of British manufacture—two Ariel tricycles, one Ariel quad., one M.M.C. tricycle, and an Enfield quad. (Moreover, the Ariel tricycles were undeniably better than any French rival, their workmanship being superior, while the mounting of the heavy engine inside the wheelbase vastly improved stability and comfort.)

There were by this date quite a number of British machines on the road, mostly of rather an experimental character. Probably their sponsors did not feel ready to have their shortcomings exposed in a public trial.

The slogan which best describes this period is " underground activity ". Only a few people—and those almost exclusively men engaged in the trade—retain the least conception of the innumerable schemes and designs which stirred in the opening years of the 20th century. Perhaps the simplest method of driving this fact home is to catalogue the names of motor cycles built mostly during the years 1898–1903. I do not propose to be tedious and attach dates to each, for some quickly perished, while many others appeared in a swift succession of improved models. But their number and variety indicate that the Motor Car Act of 1896 had already begotten a new industry.

Here is a list of remembered and recorded names, which is probably far from complete:—

Accles	Enfield	Pennington
Allard	Eureka	Phelon & Moore
Anglian	Excelsior	Phoenix
Ashford	Garrard	Precision
Ariel	Gibson	Quadrant
Bat	Hillman	Raleigh
Beeston	Hobart	Rex
Bollée	Humber	Riley
Bradbury	Iris	Roc
Brown	James	Rover
Buchet	Kerry	R. & P.
Century Tandem	Kitto	Scott
Chase	Lawson	Shaw
Coventry Motette	Matchless	Singer
Coventry Eagle	Morris	Starley
Dennis	M.M.C.	Swift
Derby	New Hudson	Triumph
Eadie	Ormonde	Vindec
Eagle Tandem		

The reader, to whom a majority of these names may well be unknown, will wonder what became of them all. Their fates were varied. Perhaps a third of the machines were tricycles of one type or another which, owing to their cost, discomfort, inconvenience and storage problems, perished as soon as motor bicycles reached a practical phase. Some were tentative experiments launched by eminent cycle factories, whose directors, during a serious slump when the new century was a few years old, decided that motor cycles possessed no real future. Others were eagerly produced by small men, who spent their entire capital on developing one or two samples, and compulsorily retired from the struggle when nobody was prepared to finance them any further.

The Buchet is an example of types which were certainly rushed on to the market by energetic cycle retailers possessing no sizeable market and little capital. It consisted of a small French engine mounted inside the diamond frame of a good cycle built in a small cycle shop. As far as I know, only two were ever built. As they produced no profit, the agent wisely withdrew from the new business, The Century and Eagle tandems were far more ambitious vehicles, carrying 8 h.p. water-cooled engines and seating two people in fair comfort; they died when small cars challenged the tiny vogue which they had acquired—on baddish roads a three-wheeler is never very comfortable.

A great many of these machines were fitted with either imported engines or copies of foreign engines, sometimes unblushingly copied and sometimes manufactured under licence. I am afraid the list is a monument to many dreams which ultimately came to nought.

The vast majority of machines were either built or assembled in the Midlands within easy hail of the light engineering factories in the Birmingham-Coventry-Wolverhampton area. Two—the Bradbury and the Eagle tandem—hailed from Lancashire. Two more—the Phelon & Moore and the Scott—were sound Yorkshire constructions from Cleckheaton and Saltaire respectively; they survive to earn enduring fame. Many others were hasty assemblies in the London area. The Ormonde, for example, had a Belgian Kelecom engine, and was originally put together in a cellar off Oxford Street. The Morris was an early venture of Lord Nuffield, carried a De Dion engine—he knew the best, then as ever—and was retailed from a showroom near the Morris Garages, which later begot the famous M.G. cars. The Pennington was one of the less grotesque imaginations of that notorious invader, who used plain steel tubing devoid of radiating fins for his cylinder barrels and claimed that a patent " long mingling spark " endowed all his products with fantastic power.

As a personal opinion, the Quadrant and the Excelsior accomplished as much as any of the others in persuading the public that, if ownership of a pioneer motor bicycle was never unmixed fun, at least the idea was worth perpetuation.

Any machine of this date which emanated from a British cycle factory was always beautifully made so far as the components familiar to its sponsors were concerned. The " electrics " might be shoddy, the engine dubious, and the brakes satisfactory only on the far lighter pedal cycle, but the finish was always superb. The steel tubes were usually " lined " in gold and scarlet or purple by hand, the work of a craftsman who earned his £10 a week even in those far-off days when a pound was a pound. A later chapter will set out in vivid detail the tribulations which invariably beset any hopeful innocent who paid his £45 for a motor bicycle of this era or, maybe, his £120 for a tricycle with a detachable forecar.

Presently, the constructors lost something of their premature optimism. Cycle dealers ceased to spend their August holiday in crossing the Channel to ransack the workshops of France and Belgium in search of a foreign engine which might adorn their " Walthamstow Wonder ", or whatever they christened the new projectile. There were far too many makers. Production had been hasty, ill-prepared, and altogether premature. The public was— well, either too cautious or insufficiently enterprising?—to buy in any quantities. A lot of money went down the drain.

One achievement had, nevertheless, been fulfilled. Most cycle agents and a modest army of amateur enthusiasts were convinced that, with more knowledge and better design, the motor cycle would always be a worthy handmaiden of the motor car. It would ultimately offer cheap, safe, fast, healthy, personal transport at a cost necessarily far, far lower than that of any car which could ever be designed. Ideals were not so much jettisoned as post-dated. Research and invention continued. The soundness of the original idea was amply justified in due course. By 1949 there were 2,000,000 private cars licensed on the roads of Great Britain, flanked by more than 600,000 motor cycles. Simultaneously, the British motor cycle was destined to earn a very substantial sum annually to meet the cost of imports, for its prestige and quality were never again challenged long or seriously by any foreign rival.

This chapter would be incomplete without a glance at the state of the motor cycle industry on the other side of the Channel. First and foremost, Belgium, France and Germany were far ahead of us in both the engineering and electrical aspects of the new industry, although Germany as yet displayed no keen interest in motor cycles. British engineers, as recorded in the previous chapter, were familiar with stationary gas engines, but 1896 had caught them devoid of any experience with light mobile, petrol engines. For the moment they could only study imported engines, modify their knowledge of the principles of the gas engine to suit the new fuel and the new usages, and start more practical activities by copying foreign engines or purchasing a licence to build them under royalty.

Meanwhile, although motor cycles were not really booming across the Channel, some of the Continental products stimulated British design admirably. Eminent among them was the De Dion tricycle with a small water-cooled engine. This was first commercialized about 1902, when a model with a 120 c.c. engine scaled about 90 lb and cost £50. Before long the De Dion had a 2¾ h.p. water-cooled engine, and was adorned by a two-speed Bozier or Dupont epicyclic gear.

As stated earlier, Werner Frères, of Paris, were the first firm to produce a practical motor bicycle and sound the knell of the previously popular tricycle. Their first model was an atrocity, but the quick-witted Werner brothers swiftly grasped its main faults. It consisted of a standard " safety " pedal bicycle with a small engine mounted over the front wheel, which the engine drove through a twisted rawhide belt. This layout was essentially top-heavy, and the machine proved to be the champion skidder of all time. I still recall trying to keep it vertical along the Euston Road on a wet November day, when the roadway was smeared with a terrible greenish paste compounded of pulverized horse-dung, rainwater, and the assorted filth of an imperfectly scavenged city.

Worse still, its carburettor was of the " swish-box " type, a metal biscuit tin containing perhaps a pint of 0·680 sp. gr. petrol. To complete the list of perils, the ignition was by " tube ". A short platinum tube, closed at the outer end, was set in the cylinder head so that its open inner end protruded into the combustion chamber. The outer end was covered by a perforated box enclosing a petrol burner, which kept the platinum tube red or white hot. The incoming charge penetrated the open inner end of the incandescent tube, and was there ignited. When the Werner skidded, a conflagration was practically inevitable!

But the second model was the true ancestor of the motor bicycle as we know it today. It had a vertical engine, bolted to act as the link between the base of the front down tube of the cycle frame and the base of the saddle-pillar tube. The bottom bracket carrying the spindle of the pedal gear was mounted a few inches astern of the engine. This new Werner simultaneously attempted to improve on the tiresome twisted hide belt. The inner face of the engine pulley bore a ring of projecting steel rods. Over these were threaded a number of perforated leather washers, forming a flat leather facing perhaps 1 inch wide. They were easily and cheaply renewable as wear developed, and the flat belt led to a flat-based belt-rim on the rear wheel. The Werners considered that " leather on leather " would furnish a non-slip drive; they were misled by machine-shop practice, wherein long flat belts, immune from grit and moisture, operated machine tools so efficiently. They were very quick to realize their mistake and, after a year or so, adopted the V belt.

I always wonder what became of them, as all their designs evinced imagination and resource. When their first spray carburettors gave trouble, through dust choking the fine orifice of the jet, they placed the carburettor *inside the tank* to protect it from dust; it was unfortunate that the edges of the tank compartment were so sharp that my hands became badly scarred in the effort to adjust the carburettor's inaccessible parts. Nevertheless, with all their faults, the succession of Werner models taught our juvenile engineers many useful lessons.

Of complete foreign machines, only the De Dion tricycle and the Werner motor bicycle were genuinely stimulating examples. But several foreign engines, especially the Minerva, the Kelecom and the Peugeot, proved magnificent inspirations to us. At one time it became difficult to sell in Britain any motor cycle which did not carry a Minerva engine. Even the great Triumph Company meekly adopted it. The early 2 h.p. model was widely fitted in this country, and its successor, the $3\frac{1}{2}$ h.p. with side-by-side mechanically operated valves, created an immense sensation, and ended the popularity of the automatic (or " atmospheric ") inlet valve.

Once we had secured a reasonable layout for the machine as a whole, and had obtained a decent engine, British cycle experience, superior to that of any other manufacturing nation, ensured the production of a better motor cycle than could be obtained elsewhere.

It is fair to add that we remained out of touch with progress

in the more remote parts of Europe.   Presently, when international
motor cycle racing was introduced, we discovered to our great
discomfiture that, far away in Austria, unknown firms (for example,
Puch) were building machines capable of beating ours over distant
circuits where our men were played for suckers by adversaries who
evaded all the regulations while insisting that we observed them to the
very last hair.   But that is quite another story.

CHAPTER 3

FIRST IMPRESSIONS OF A NOVICE

AT THIS POINT THE SEMI-TECHNICAL STORY of invention and progress on the wide scale may be interrupted to describe the birth and graduation of a private owner. Such a genesis was quite a rare phenomenon at the dawn of the century. By 1950 the number of privately owned motor cycles in Great Britain was in the region of 700,000. In 1900 the total may have been as low as twenty—no statistics exist. I had my first ride on a motor tricycle about 1899—possibly 1898. The next year or two were mainly devoted to cycling. Finance was not responsible for this abstinence. The sight of a motor cycle in motion on the roads was extremely uncommon—indeed, I can count such occasions—nor was there anything about them to tempt one to take the plunge.

When I bought my first machine, I did not know of a single private owner of a motor cycle in the large county wherein I lived. The nearest approach to a private owner was a road surveyor who rode a motor tricycle by compulsion rather than from choice, since his large jurisdiction could not conveniently be covered in any other way, at any rate a horse was the sole alternative; moreover, he owned a large block of shares in the cycle company which built the machine. Within a radius of 50 miles, I knew three men who owned primitive cars. They were all well-to-do, and regarded their unusual purchases as extravagances and rather as scientific toys than as either pleasurable or utilitarian locomotion. Possibly they were moved partly by sheer ostentation.

Mentally, across the years, I compare both myself and them with certain later friends, who bought crude samples of the first television receivers. Be that as it may, my own transition from an enthusiastic pedal cyclist to a fanatical motor cyclist happened as shall now be described. It was a tardy and not a volitional progress.

In 1901 a cycle dealer in the centre of Oxford created a sensation by exhibiting a Singer motor tricycle in his shop window. Listed at £75, it was really a fortified pedal cycle plus the addition of a " motor wheel " in its front fork. This compact little clot of mechanism contained a tiny engine, a tank holding enough petrol for 60 miles, a " surface " carburettor, and a single-geared, spur drive. Ignition was by a Simms low-tension magneto. The rest of the machine, apart from the necessary controls, was literally identical with a pedal tricycle. The finish was wonderful. The machine was enamelled in black, picked out in green and gold. The motor wheel had eight wide spokes on each side, made of highly polished aluminium. The machine as a whole was more than handsome.

This exhibit inspired many an undergraduate to revise his notions of motoring, which until then was generally considered an absurd and perilous hobby, adopted only by lunatics with too much money. Hitherto we had regarded motorists with amused contempt. They threaded the town occasionally, in such small numbers that they attracted public notice. The men wore black leathers, huge gloves, enormous goggles, and, in winter, ridiculous coats of China goatskin. They were normally smothered in dust, which a shower of rain rapidly converted into mud. Their cars shook and rattled. The daily Press recorded how they caught fire, or got out of control down hill.

We watched them attempt to restart outside our principal hotels. First, the owner crouched down at the handle, which he wound interminably, sweating profusely. For a time silence alone rewarded his herculean efforts. Then he wrung a few feeble coughs from the mechanism. Next he took a breather and readjusted his levers. More winding—a rattle and a roar. He hastily ordered his veiled, dusty women-folk to take their seats, whereupon the engine stopped, and the ordeal recommenced. Eventually, the engine condescended to run until all were aboard. He then moved a pedal or a handle. The front wheels lifted a foot into the air, dropped with a heavy thud—and the engine once more stopped!

We were also accustomed to the spectacle of an occasional motor bicycle. One very wet day I watched a soaked and dirty figure attempt to ride past Carfax. He skidded, and fell heavily, as well he might, for the machine was very tall and carried all its mechanism on a small platform above the front wheel, while his tyres were practically bald. As soon as the machine lay flat, it caught fire and burnt furiously. Small wonder, since much of its petrol was spilt from the tin swish-box which formed its carburettor, while the ignition consisted of a platinum tube rendered incandescent by a petrol burner. This front-driven Werner pardonably impressed me as an unnecessarily complicated form of suicide.

Our convictions by no means prevented us from cadging short trips aboard any and every type of motor vehicle owned by other undergraduates or their rich friends. Such experiments were liable to be both costly and dangerous, facts which never deter irresponsible youth. I can recall quite a number. One acquaintance possessed a motor tricycle—probably an Ariel—of the one front wheel, two stern wheels type. The rear half of a lady's pedal cycle was bolted to the middle of its back axle, thus producing a two-seater with four wheels in diamond formation.

This ingenious combination provided a total of four leg power to assist the monstrosity up hills, and we felt we became benefactors whenever we accepted his invitations. But since he did not understand the mechanism in the very least, such parties were apt to get themselves benighted miles out of town, and the proctor fined us £5 a time if we failed to book into college by midnight.

Moreover, the brakes of all motor vehicles at this date were frankly ridiculous. The standard brake of the period consisted of a strip of spring steel formed in the shape of the letter C, and placed around a microscopic drum. Its lining must have been a compound of cheap leather and cardboard, for, as soon as it became hot, it began to stink abominably and, shortly afterwards, burst into flames. After which the crew's sole hope of survival was to abandon ship before the pace of the runaway vehicle became too ferocious.

But this Singer deflated such prejudices at sight. It was light, trim, workmanlike and beautiful. We clustered round the window, returned to the window daily, and discussed fantastic plans for raising £75 that we might own a duplicate. (My father allowed me £3 per annum pocket money. Oxford tradesmen of those days offered practically unlimited credit to every undergraduate, aware that they could put the screw on parents before the lad took his degree. It follows that many spirited undergraduates were heavily in debt after a couple of terms.) I could devise no method of raising £75, but I approached the cycle agent for a trial run.

Apparently no other applicant had gone quite so far. He seemed charmed, and arranged that I should cycle to a straight lonely road a few miles out, where he would meet me at 7 a.m., before traffic developed. Both he and I received a violent shock at my first essay. I had never ridden a tricycle, and could not resist the temptation to use its front wheel for balancing, as well as for steering. The immediate effect, of course, was that the tricycle veered powerfully for the ditch.

Somehow or other he contrived to stop the engine as he ran alongside. We returned to Oxford, and he gave me a short lesson on a pedal tricycle before our next dawn appointment in the suburbs. This second trial brought disillusion. In 1901 our roads were " water-bound ", that is, they were constructed of layers of 2-inch stones, pasted down with mud by a 10-ton roller. The iron tyres of carts, the iron shoes of horses, the disintegrating effects of rain and frost, the drip from overhanging trees, soon destroyed the binding, and the surface began to break up into every type of pothole.

The Singer tricycle had a rigid, spring-less front fork, further trussed into the stiffness of concrete by steel girders. The complete wheel probably weighed about one hundredweight. It bounced up over every tiny hump in the road as a Chubb safe would bounce down the steps of the Monument. It thudded into every pothole as a tank would land after falling over a low cliff. The effect was to loosen the teeth in one's gums, and make one's eyes feel about to quit their sockets.

I have since been told that if one opened the throttle boldly, these effects were less pronounced. But I still felt nervous about the ditches on either side, and the engine drove by a small naked cog-wheel meshing into a large naked cogwheel, a transmission which is at its worst when the speed is low. I handed the tricycle back to the discomfited agent after a couple of miles, jettisoned all my plans for winning £75 on the turf, and rode back to Oxford on my push-bike like a scalded cat!

My views on the sanity of motorists in general and of motor cyclists in particular were now deeply rooted, and might almost be described as invincible prejudice.

The next incident in my graduation consisted of an accidental meeting with J. van Hooydonk, who later was to become president of the Motor Cycling Club. He was a cycle agent in Hertfordshire, busy experimenting with clipping tiny foreign engines to the front down tubes of pedal cycles, and selling them under his own transfer as the Phœnix motor cycle. He had ridden up from Biggleswade, and his abdomen probably contained about a quart of road dust by that time. He had stopped outside an Oxford pub to irrigate his interior. Some of us accosted him in playful mood.

I was rather taken with his motor bicycle. It accorded with D. S. Heather's canons of beauty, because you couldn't spit through it anywhere. The whole of the frame was filled with metal containers of one sort and another, all beautifully shaped, enamelled, and gold-lined. (They included, of course, a battery case, a surface carburettor, a capacious tool box, the main petrol tank, and a reserve petrol tank between the seat-pillar tube and the back wheel. At that date petrol depots were few and far between except along main roads in the Home Counties.) The machine included a host of clever little gadgets, and certainly bore the stamp of a practical mind.

The phœnix, of course, was a mythical Arabian bird, which built its nest of aromatic spices, periodically set fire to its nest by friction resulting from violent wing-flapping, perished in the flames, and anon rose from the ashes lovelier than ever. So, remembering the sad fate of the front-driven Werner, we asked Hooydonk how frequently his Phœnix caught fire, whereupon he became extremely angry. A pint or two calmed him, and we parted good friends, with our anti-motor cycle prejudices slightly eroded.

I still seized every opportunity of talking to motorists and sponging on them for trial runs. Do you ask why? I cannot tell you. Maybe, the eternal engineer who slumbers in every juvenile male, and too often never comes to birth. Maybe, like the Athenians in the days of St. Paul, we loved to hear of some new thing. Freud ascribes most human actions to some sexual motive. It is true that during this period I was in the throes of calf love. My fair maiden dwelt some 18 miles out of Oxford. After a long morning of lectures on some such brain-splitting subject as philosophy, and an afternoon at the boats, or rugger, or soccer, or cricket, one was bound to dine in college at least five nights a week. The prospect of pedalling 36 miles nightly in all weathers was mildly deterrent.

Freud may be right. Perhaps my secret motive was to visit the beloved at a reduced expenditure of fat and sweat. Anyhow, the requisite cash was not forthcoming. I backed horses. I wrote articles for a myriad obscure journals. I secured a freelance post as cage-bird expert to some feathered paper—at 5s per 1,000 words. But my creditors were growing anxious as my degree examination approached. I left the University with several thousand motoring miles to my credit, but I was still without a motor of any kind.

Having, as yet, no definite ideas about a career, I promptly accepted a mark-time post as senior master to a preparatory school, which specialized in winning public-school scholarships and in passing boys into the Royal Navy via H.M.S. *Britannia*. My life now became that of a lotus eater. The work was easy and full of interest. We were comfortably housed and magnificently fed. We had plenty of games, both at the school and with neighbouring adult clubs—the headmaster considered it valuable publicity that his staff should make friends with parents in the county. We had every evening free, together with at least half a week-day and the whole of Sunday.

A misogynist friend of mine died a bachelor, because he hated small children. He always said he would have loved to have had a large family, provided one could draw them from store as adolescents, but that to share a house with small children was his notion of Hell. Without going so far as that, towards the end of every thirteen-week term, I found myself growing a little tired of the inane chatter of innumerable small boys. But the school was remote from public transport, and the surrounding country literally bristled with single-figure gradients, which made pedal cycling repugnant at the end of a working day.

It fell on a day that I cycled into the neighbouring town to inquire about a New Rapid pedal cycle. I had read a plausible leaflet about it, which averred that, if you used 8-inch cranks and an 84-inch gear, a pedal cycle practically propelled itself. Going into the back shed of the cycle dealer's shop, I encountered a familiar stench, accompanied by a familiar rattle and dense clouds of blue smoke. The agent was tuning up a Werner motor bicycle, perched precariously on one of the portable metal lattice stands of the period.

This Werner had developed out of recognition since the days of the ancestor which I had seen commit suttee in an Oxford street. It looked safe, for the standard cycle fork had been superseded by a most impressive reinforced design (two of my friends had been killed by snapped fork blades). The agent drew my attention to other perfections. Doubtless, I knew how the twisted, raw-hide belt of the period slipped? I certainly did. This machine used a flat leather belt according to the best engineering practice, which I had doubtless observed in all the famous engineering shops? I had so observed such flat belts. Yes, and, in addition, I was presumably familiar with the coefficients of friction? I nodded sagely; why should I expose my technical ignorances to a tradesman? Well, the new Werner pulley was faced with a series of leather discs, threaded over some dozen steel spindles, and thus easily replaceable when

29

worn; and, of course, leather on leather furnishes the best coefficient of friction in the universe. More nods.

Now he came to the price—a mere £45! I had so nearly been taken for a sucker by the Singer tricycle that I was not going to swallow hook, line and sinker so fast as that. I said I would think it over, and call again.

Never a prudent man, I nevertheless chanced to remember that there was another cycle dealer in the town. I strolled round there to inspect his wares. No, he had no motor cycle in stock—I was probably aware that the demand was immense, and deliveries rather behindhand. But he *was* county agent—exclusive, too—for the world's best motor cycle, the Ormonde! (I'd never heard of it.) I made careful inquiries, and discovered that neither agent had ever sold a single motor cycle, but that both were hoping to get the first start in the district, and skim the cream of the imminent market. I played one off against the other.

Eventually, the Ormonde agent secured my money, with what must surely have been the oddest agreement ever signed between dealer and client. He pledged himself to provide me with the latest model Ormonde at trade price. He further agreed that his mechanic should accompany me (on his racing pedal cycle) for a distance of not less than 50 miles weekly for the first three months. In return I was not to " crab " the Ormonde with my friends or acquaintances. I was also to return it to him on short loan on the eve of every market day, so that he could furbish it up and exhibit it in his front window. In that moment the seeds of motor cycle mania were rooted deep in my soul, where they have flourished ever since.

In a later chapter I enlarge on certain oddities in the engineering atmosphere of the pioneer motor epoch. For the moment I will only say that in some respects the Ormonde was a thoroughly bad motor cycle even for those early days. To cite actual examples:— It had a crude spray carburettor, apparently made of some forgotten metal closely allied to putty. The float needle habitually wore a shoulder on its point every 50 miles, with disastrous effects on the carburation. The belt drive was probably the worst ever conceived by the mind of man.

The engine was miraculously tucked into the exiguous space between the seat-pillar tube and the back mudguard. This reduced the distance between pulley centres to the absolute minimum. In fact, the belt probably contacted about one-third of the groove of the engine pulley, and no belt in history has ever slipped more readily and perseveringly. (Compare this with the original Enfield and Raleigh motor bicycles, which carried the engine on top of the front mudguard, and used a " crossed " belt, running in the form of a figure 8, so that it embraced at least two-thirds of the front pulley.) Incidentally, this engine location applied the tip of the sparking plug to the muscles of one's left thigh, which received innumerable shocks therefrom.

The electric wiring was not stranded, was insulated with a

substance resembling paper, and was threaded through various sharp-edged holes in the metal battery case. The contact-breaker was incredibly flimsy, and required adjustment two or three times a day, as its setting affected the engine timing. The rear brake was an ordinary Bowden-operated, pedal-cycle brake, perfectly incompetent of coping with the stresses involved by a 150 lb mount at 45 m.p.h. Worst of all, the gears and cams of the valve gear were secured to plain spindles by steel pins, which were prone to shear.

In spite of these glaring faults, which could so easily have been remedied by any competent engineer, I was not once seriously stranded with this rather naïve model. On Sundays I occasionally covered up to 200 miles in the day, including the ascent of some of the worse main-road hills in England, though a single gear of about $4\frac{1}{2}$ to 1 naturally compelled an owner to pedal on mild gradients, and either to run alongside or simply to push up the steeper climbs.

I never availed myself of the full scope of the agreement which put the mechanic at my disposal. He knew very little more than I did about internal-combustion engines, and was dead keen to learn. He was a magnificent cyclist, and on his light racing iron could keep up with the Ormonde provided I did not flog it on the level. His main usefulness to me was education in the caprices of a shocking electrical layout. There were a hundred ways in which this could fail on the Ormonde. Its sparking plug cost 1s 3d, and was the second commonest culprit, with the shoddy contact-breaker an easy first. In those days we carried a small box-wood case containing a 4-volt electric bulb and a couple of short leads. Having mastered the layout of the circuit, it was then a simple matter to find the particular section wherein the current had ceased to flow.

In the early days, of course, the fault was usually in the accumulator—a small, flimsy affair, with celluloid walls so weak that they frequently split and leaked acid. As this absurd component was housed inside the sheet-tin tank, and insulated therefrom merely with corrugated cardboard, the circuit was seldom in action. Fortunately, the cells were a very loose fit in the tank, and packings of thin wood backed by heavy sheet rubber enabled even this silly little battery to stand up to the job.

The weakness of the brakes was compensated by wearing stout, hobnail boots, and grinding them down on the road surface in emergencies. The tyres, of pedal-cycle tandem type, stood up remarkably well, and punctures were quite uncommon. A squawk-horn caused a ridiculous amount of trouble, as such reeds are extremely sensitive to dust, and at that date there was not a square inch of tarred road in the British Isles.

By day the belt and by night the lamp were the chief obstacles to progress. The belt was a ply leather type of $\frac{5}{8}$ inch V section, made by Dawson, of Lincoln. Owing to the faulty layout, it could never hope to escape slip; but the load on it was small. After every run it was removed, hung from a tall apple tree with a small anvil attached to its lower end to take up stretch. Its sides were rubbed free of grit, and then dressed with patent dubbins.

No special motor cycle lamps were as yet procurable. I used a de luxe pedal-cycle lamp made by Lucas under the trade name of " King of the Road ". Being attached by a spring hinge to an ordinary pedal-cycle bracket, it bobbed up and down phenomenally at motoring speeds. This first interfered with the action of the acetylene generator and, secondly, broke the hinge. It was so tiresome that at one period I motor cycled with a 1-inch wick *oil lamp*! Eventually I procured a German lamp, the Schmidt, affixed by two rigid prongs and altogether more substantially made.

In retrospect, the most amazing feature of this crude motor cycle is that, although I rode it many thousand miles, it never once caused me to miss a professional appointment. That fact is, possibly, rather a tribute to my own resource and the mechanic's training than to any inherent virtue of a thoroughly bad machine.

I eventually traded it off for a later Ormonde model with a slightly larger engine and, as that was equally tiresome, I traded the second machine for a Bayliss and Thomas Excelsior. This machine began to introduce me to the real pleasures of motor cycling. It was graced by a 2¾ h.p. engine, of M.M.C. make, possibly produced under De Dion licence, but certainly a remarkably close copy of the De Dion engine then being imported on French motor tricycles. It was slung under the front down tube of the frame, which furnished reasonable belt centres and certainly mini-mized belt slip. Memory credits it with being far more reliable than the Ormonde, but one factor in the contrast was that I had concluded my novitiate.

In two items it was certainly less troublesome than its predecessor. It had a surface carburettor, in which there were no wearing parts whatsoever, though the mixture was apt to vary over bumpy roads. It further boasted the rugged De Dion contact-breaker, which retained its adjustment for long periods. (I eventually substituted a " wipe " contact with a trembler coil, which proved 100 per cent reliable.) Its brakes were even weaker than the Ormonde types. The Ormonde had at least a dependable front brake, consisting of a large rubber shoe forcibly depressed upon the top of the front tyre by an enormous lever resembling a Turkish scimitar. (This gripped well on a dry tyre, but skidded helplessly over wet rubber.) The Excelsior had two Bowden brakes, with small shoes and many tiny parts which fell off much too frequently.

By modern standards the machine must have been grotesquely uncomfortable, for its saddle was small, its fork was springless, and the tyres were only of 2 inch section and were necessarily run practi-cally board-hard. These aspects did not trouble a rider who was young, tough, and had no experience of more luxurious travel.

Incidentally, it was tolerably free from a trouble which was chronic on the Ormonde—namely, a seized free wheel. On motor cycles the free wheel was, of course, in practically continuous action, whereas on the pedal cycles, for which the free wheel was designed, the clutch of the free wheel was only required when coasting. The speed of the motor cycle stirred up clouds of dust over untarred roads, so that grit soon penetrated into the free wheel and jammed it. Until the rider dismounted and either dismantled the free wheel or washed out the grit with liberal injections of paraffin, the pedals revolved continuously at high speed to his great discomfort. The Excelsior rejoiced in a specially designed and reinforced free wheel, which could be trusted for, say, 200 miles after every cleansing.

In fact, I was now the proud owner of a machine which was fast and reliable—quite incredibly so by comparison with the more complicated designs of the period. I very seldom got stopped on the road by it, apart from the impossibility of climbing any formidable hills under power.

Why, then, did I sell it? The answer is simple. Motor cycling is always a solitary sport by comparison with team games or driving a car. Nowadays one can find plenty of companions to share one's rides on their own solo machines. But at this date there were certainly not a score of motor cyclists in my county. In my immediate neighbourhood there were two private owners of small cars; two private owners of so-called " tandems "—heavy three-wheeled cars rated at 8 h.p.; and not even one motor cyclist, apart from some three cycle retailers. These retailers bought their machines as a speculation in the hope of building up small motor businesses. They regarded them as showroom stock, kept them in new condition, and barely used them except for purposes of demonstration to potential buyers.

Consequently, practically all my riding was entirely solitary, and I began to explore the possibilities of companionship. This experiment soon emptied my pockets and introduced me to a wholly novel chapter of suffering, trouble, and painful experience.

c

CHAPTER 4

A PIONEER PREPARES FOR A RIDE

N OWADAYS A MOTOR CYCLIST STARTS AWAY from home without any preparation beyond seeing that his tanks are full, unless a very long or specially arduous journey is in prospect. Fifty years ago each ride demanded forethought, and the work might start a day or two in advance. First, the route must be laid out to detour all severe hills. My 1901 machine, single-geared, and of $2\frac{1}{4}$ (nominal) h.p., would just about carry my weight up half a mile of 1 in 17 gradient without pedal assistance. That is no more than an athletic pedal cyclist would climb without dismounting. Head wind or heavy roads reduced this small ability.

I lived in a very hilly part of England. One could, of course, push up ascents like Porlock, or Sunrising, or Sutton Bank, but this entailed a delay of perhaps half an hour, and left one soaked with perspiration at the top. Riding on in damp clothing created a threat of fibrositis—the vocational disease of all cricketers, who so often " dry off " in the field without changing shirts after a long spell of bowling. So the route must be planned with a Gall & Inglis contour book.

After the previous trip the belt had been removed from the machine for reconditioning. If wet, it had been dried slowly out, and dressed with some patent leather preservative—possibly neats-foot oil. New belts always had a lot of stretch to lose. My apple tree served as an operating table, on which greasing, drying, and de-gritting could be carried out. The fastener and its holes were inspected. If the belt was of the twisted raw-hide type, it would be twisted up a little shorter. If it was the V, three-ply, Lincona type, there was little more that one could do, beyond vetting the fastener holes, and dressing the leather.

The battery was the next anxiety. The " service " battery in the tank, approached through a hinged trap-door, fastened by a steel skewer, was normally a light 20-ampere-hour type in a brittle celluloid casing. Its charge was verified with a 4-volt lamp bulb, mounted in a little wooden case, fitted with two short leads. The battery was possibly the real Achilles' heel of the primitive motor cycle. Its flimsy construction encouraged paste to fall off the grooved metal plates and cause short-circuits.

Moreover, the battery was stored in a metal compartment, and manufacturers used nothing more than a few squares of corrugated cardboard to pad it. Since the vents in the cell tops were devoid of any anti-spray gadget, and vibration was considerable with a rigid front fork of pedal-cycle type, acid soon destroyed the cardboard packing, or almost any other substitute which a careful owner could devise. On really long runs, some of us carried a reserve 8-ampere-hour battery in a leather case slung round our necks. These cases might disintegrate along the road as the result of leaking sulphuric acid.

The low-tension wiring was of disgracefully poor quality, and was threaded through unprotected holes cut in the sheet metal of the tank. One frayed spot and the battery ran down almost instantaneously. To reduce the strain on the cheap wire, the maker cut each length many inches too long, and wound the surplus inches in the semblance of a valve spring, so that the appearance was most untidy. Few of us knew even the simplest elements of electricity, but so long as there was any current in the cells, the circuits could easily be tested by using the glow lamp to bridge each section in turn.

Flimsy French contact-breakers were fitted, as no English maker supplied such articles in the early days. The adjustment of the two platinum points was always rickety, and affected the timing of the ignition very seriously. The platinum points were tiny and of inferior quality—sometimes the points were mere German silver. Oil leaked along the driving spindle and fouled them. It was therefore wise to vet the contact-breaker before any run, and also along the road if the power seemed to be evaporating.

Next the free wheel clamoured for skilled attention. Free wheels were still comparative novelties on pedal cycles. I saw my first about 1900 on a cycle ridden by Harcourt Gold, the Oxford stroke, who created a sensation in Oxford High Street by gliding along with his feet resting on stationary pedals.

Then came the brakes. Those numbered three, namely the front brake, the rear brake, and the rider's boot soles. On my 1901 machine the front brake, as I mentioned in the previous chapter, was quite good on dry days. A huge steel lever was pivoted near the left end of the handlebar with its grip near the right end. This operated a vertical shaft parallel to the steering head, terminating in a large rubber shoe poised above the top of the front tyre. When potently depressed, this shoe, on dry days, applied real friction to the tyre. On wet days it had comparatively little effect on the tyre, except that it served as a squeegee to remove all the road mud from the tyre and fling it back on the rider. (There was no mudguard extension in front of the forks, and machines were consequently very dirty indeed.)

The back brake consisted of a steel horseshoe just behind the rear fork. A small and flimsy fibre shoe was clipped to each tip of the horseshoe, and was supposed to be kept at its correct clearance from the wheel rim by a tiny pull-off spring, anchored to a flimsy clip bolted to the tubular fork. Provided this layout remained intact and held its adjustment, it generated modest stopping power but all its tiny items were apt to shake loose under vibration, when the horseshoe ceased to be central, developed a tilt, or shed its shoes.

Alternatively, the anchor clips of the pull-off springs slid up the tubes, or fell off. Vibration was naturally excessive, thanks to inferior road surfaces, small tyres, and springless front forks. If such a horseshoe brake lost its setting, the first pull on the control lever might cause a shoe to rip one or more spokes from the wheel. Fortunately, a good pair of hob-nail boots, firmly pressed against the road surface at a suitable angle, acted as quite tolerable stoppers in average emergencies.

These preliminaries took quite a deal of time, and there was not the slightest guarantee that each or any of them would avert trouble for very long.

Tyres gave extraordinarily little trouble, an item in which we were far better off than contemporary car owners. Our tyres were normally light 28×2 inch patterns, practically identical with similar tyres developed for tandem pedal cycles. They had clincher beads, not wired edges, and were quite easy to remove and repair, although the machine was delivered without any stand. The risk of petrol and acid leaks prevented us from laying the machine on its side or upside down after the manner of a pedal cyclist afflicted with a puncture. But we could hunt up a big stone and put it under the crankcase to act as an improvised stand during tyre repairs.

Finally, the preparation included coaxing the engine into an easy-start mood. Engine compression was never very tight on a brand-new machine and, after a very few hundred miles, became decidedly leaky, since no designer could obtain really suitable materials for piston rings and valves. The carburation was decidedly vague, for the carburettor consisted of a large steel box, to which petrol was admitted (via a screwdown valve) to a level indicated by a float from which a tell-tale wire protruded through a hole in the top of the tank. At the exit from this swish-box a lever-controlled valve admitted air to a small mixing chamber. The air and throttle levers were small wooden handles, resembling chess bishops, mounted on a short spindle across the top of the tank. If both levers were accurately set, an approximately correct mixture was not really difficult to obtain, especially as we were supplied with spirit of 0·680 specific gravity at 9d or 1s a gallon.

Here let me mention that some anxiety attached to petrol supplies at all times. Garages were few and far between along the road. Railway companies were very nervous about transporting such highly inflammable liquid. Once, for a short period, the railways reached a deadlock with the petrol companies on the wording of the consignment notes, and I had to order my own supplies from London, 200 miles away. To secure such supplies I had to sign a paper which practically committed me to rebuilding St. Pancras Station in the event of any serious conflagration.

Despite the weak and leaky compression, and the inefficiency of the carburettor, engine starting was never easy from cold. This was due to the appalling quality of the lubricating oils of the period. The piston might be on the loose side, but it could give a fair imitation of a welded joint when the engine was cold, for the vile lubricant gummed it up very firmly in the cylinder. However, compression was relieved for starting purposes by a gadget known as a " pet-cock " in the cylinder head. This was controlled by the third of the chess bishops on the tank top. (The fourth " bishop " controlled the ignition timing by altering the angle of the movable contact breaker.) If the engine was gummy, one injected a few drops of paraffin through the pet-cock. This was allowed to soak the piston rings for a minute or so. Then, with the pet-cock open, one moved the entire machine to and fro till the piston began to free itself.

There was neither kickstarter nor handle. For home use we kept a small stand constructed of light steel strip in the form of a miniature Eiffel tower. With this stand supporting the back wheel, one mounted the saddle, opened the pet-cock, pedalled hard for a few moments, and then shut the pet-cock. When the engine seemed to be running nicely, one switched off (by rotating the right-hand grip which covered and operated a concealed switch), and put the machine away, ready for tomorrow's ride. The last attention was to inject a little more paraffin through the pet-cock to guard against more gumming up during the night.

By a later refinement, the stand was secured in position by the large nuts on the rear spindle or by special clips. It was then moved up and round on to the top of the back mudguard, where it served as a luggage carrier, being secured by a short leather strap to the back of the saddle. We seldom used it as a stand along the road except in real emergencies, as all luggage had to be removed before it could serve as a stand.

But the job was not yet complete. The toolbag, strapped to the rear of the saddle, was one of the tiny pattern supplied with pedal cycles. The surplus gear had to be transferred to the pockets of a waterproof riding " reefer ". This kit would normally include—

1. A very large monkey wrench, for such jobs as straightening bent pedal cranks.
2. A paraffin squirt-can.
3. A complete set of spare nuts.
4. A complete set of spare Bowden brake parts.
5. A spare belt, with several fasteners.
6. A tyre repair outfit.
7. A tin of spare carbide for the gas lamp.
8. The electric test lamp.
9. Knife and gimlet for belt repairs.
10. Three spare sparking plugs (price 1s 3d each—French porcelain types).
11. Some copper wire and a strap or two.

It was advisable to line the coat pockets with leather for such heavy duties.

CHAPTER 5

A PIONEER TAKES A RIDE

AFTER THE COMPREHENSIVE PRELIMINARIES described in the previous chapter, a pioneer could essay a short run in tolerable confidence. I lived some three miles from the nearest town, and frequently visited it at the end of a day's work without any trouble at all. As I grew increasingly expert, at week-ends I would occasionally tackle cross-country runs up to 200 miles in really hilly country without encountering any serious compulsory stops of a technical character apart from the problem of surmounting long hills.

But it is impossible for any modern to realize the general atmosphere of such rides. It was, of course, quite a gamble whether one would regain home with the machine on the same day, or even within seven days. Engines were so lightly stressed that, despite their crude character, they seldom broke down hopelessly. Still, it was essential to plan a long trip for a time when it did not really matter whether one returned punctually or not—and the term " punctual " might be a matter of days rather than hours. In a large agricultural county, ill-served by railways, there might be no alternative method of completing a journey. You could not, of course, hire a taxi—there were no taxis nor hire cars. " Posting ", that is, chartering some horsed vehicle, was incredibly expensive and very limited as to distance.

One Sunday evening four of us had a serious breakdown with a car only 14 miles from home. The families of the two girls who figured in the party would probably have insisted on a couple of what the Americans call " shot-gun weddings " if we had failed to restore their darlings to the parental bosoms before midnight. We " posted " the 14 miles and the bill came to nearly £20, as, owing to the lateness of the hour, no publican would hire out horses to us for more than 5 miles, and we had to charter three separate vehicles to save the ladies' honour.

Apart from the mere question of punctuality, we were Ishmaels. Every man's hand was against us in a horsey county. Nor could public opinion be blamed. It was the Horse Age. The modern horse in 1950 has long since been completely " broken " to motors. It is his turn to be tolerated rather than welcomed on our roads. But in 1900 we were not even tolerated. Horses are suspicious and nervous in temperament. Even today a thoroughbred is prone to develop the weirdest imaginations at the sight of an old copy of the *Daily Mail* blowing across the tarmac. Our roads were full of horses from the sporting butcher's blood mare to thoroughbreds in training and skittish over-fed hunters.

In 1900 the parson's family travelled in a little tub drawn by an elderly and corpulent pony. Such ponies for the first time in their lazy lives smelt the odour of burnt hydrocarbons, heard the whistle of open compression taps, the staccato of exhausts, sighted small projectiles approaching at 30 miles an hour, ridden by dusty demons wearing enormous Paris-Madrid goggles. The pony instantly went stark, staring mad. It reared up like a stallion mustang, it spun round and bolted in the opposite direction. All horse owners without exception dreaded and hated us, and they had every conceivable reason for their hostility.

Towns and cities were even worse than country lanes. In London, street cleaners darted and dived incessantly amid the thick traffic armed with little dust-pans and brushes, with which to remove the incessant deposits of steaming horse dung. The driver of a three-horsed bus in the Old Kent Road loathed us just as violently as the country squireen with his portly Dobbin. We were a genuine menace. If a good horse is once let down on his knees, his cash value depreciates by pounds in ten seconds, even if he does not capsize his vehicle and injure the occupants.

Pedestrians found us equally obnoxious. No walker cares to be within kicking distance of a frightened horse. They questioned our control of our machines—they had no guarantee that we should not ram them. On roads where the speeds of other traffic seldom exceeded 10 miles an hour, the mere spectacle of our speeds—modest as they are in terms of 1950—were definitely alarming. Some religious folks literally ascribed our origin to Satan!

The dust nuisance mightily increased anti-motoring prejudice. We were mostly young, and had little leisure for riding except at week-ends. Most churches were fairly full on Sundays, and the racket which we created was a gross abomination to the quiet-Sabbath keepers. On Sundays practically everybody wore their best clothes, and their best clothes were dark. There was not one square yard of either tarmac or concrete on British roads in 1900. In the big cities the streets were swept and watered regularly. In the country the roads were of waterbound macadam or of mere " dirt ".

When a 40 h.p. Mercedes crossed Devon on a wind-less summer day, its transit was marked by beige dust clouds often a mile in length and 20 feet high. In sunken roads through deep combes, the dust cloud would hang long in the air, and might be perceptible an hour after the vehicle had passed. The lovely green, flower-spangled hedges were beige with dust to their summits, robbed of all natural beauty, stained and tawdry. Moreover, the dust was penetrating. It not only made eyes smart, and fouled ears or noses, but it went clean through clothing, and made bodies feel gritty. No ordinary brushing would remove such dust from a Sunday suit. Nor was the dust clean road matter. It was full of decaying organic filth—the pounded droppings of horse, cow and pig.

The horse owners, the farmers who bred the horses and grew feed for horses, the pedestrians whose nerves were startled, and whose clothing was fouled, the hunting and racing gentry, controlled the police. The police began to regard—and to treat—us as the modern cop regards smash-and-grab men. They were out to " get " us at the first opportunity. My local squire let his manor house to a rich American who owned one of the early 40 h.p. Mercedes cars. From the manor gates a single road led east and west. After one week's experience of the Mercedes' dust, the local watch committee stationed a cop at his gate, and another cop down the road one mile away in each direction. They pinched him practically every time he took the car out.

Another neighbour drove his 7 h.p. Panhard to the market town, and put up at the principal hotel for lunch with his wife and sister. In the hotel yard a farmer's horse took fright at the car. The farmer attacked my neighbour with his whip, using filthy language towards the ladies. The motorist summoned the farmer. The case against the farmer was promptly dismissed by the horsey magistrates, on whose instructions the police prosecuted the motorist for speeding, and he was fined £5.

So each of my rides began in the wariest possible spirit. I knew I was liable to be attacked by any horse owner whose steed was frightened by my machine. I knew I could expect neither mercy nor justice in any local police court. The roads round London and some provincial cities bristled with police traps, wherein police evidence of timing was accepted as gospel, and any motorist was pre-judged as an inveterate liar.

These conditions lasted until the foundation of the Automobile Association. Even the A.A. failed to furnish adequate protection until its specialist counsel, the late Staplee Firth, educated himself to become an expert in the use of stop-watches and exposed, in a long series of court actions, the inadequacy of the police evidence. By that time many people of moderate income had themselves become motorists, and the overbearing horsey folk were at long last themselves overborne.

As a humble motor cyclist I enjoyed two special advantages over the pioneer car owner in these hostile days. Apart from using all possible consideration and caution, my two small wheels created nothing like the degree of dust nuisance which wider, heavier and unstreamlined vehicles could not minimize. Furthermore, I enjoyed the inestimable benefit of having no free engine clutch. When I encountered a nervous horse, I perforce stopped my engine, drew into the extreme edge of the road or into a side-turning, and waited silent and immobile until the driver had safely coaxed his quivering steed past me.

By contrast, a pioneer car owner dared not stop his engine except under weighty pressure, because engine starting for him was an arduous and even a risky business—some pioneer drivers broke their wrists in using starting handles. Moreover, his bulky vehicle loomed much too large in the eyes of a palpitating thorough-bred, and could not be pressed into the hedge like a motor bicycle. I kept out of the courts and, by civility and consideration, avoided rough houses with angry farmers.

I had plenty of other troubles. The first was getting away from the home gate, as my house lay in a dip between two mild ascents. There were three possible methods of getting under way in the absence of a clutch. One was to run alongside the machine, dabbing with one hand at the pet-cock lever after attaining some impetus, and then vaulting into the saddle. The second consisted of hopping along behind the machine with one foot on the small iron step screwed to the rear wheel spindle in the fashion then common among pedal cyclists. The third was by pedalling away in the saddle.

All three methods were arduous enough to induce a heavy perspiration, especially as one usually wore fairly warm clothing. My 1901 machine could manage up to 45 m.p.h. under favourable conditions. Drying off sweat in a cool wind is calculated to cause a severe chill. So I normally pushed 30 yards or so up one side of the dip, and got a flying start at the opposite gradient. Similarly, all day long we timed our stops to secure a downhill restart whenever possible.

Once away, progress was usually easy and pleasant until one met a terrified horse or a hill. As already described, it was fairly simple to pass a horse by using a little common sense, provided always that one did not suddenly encounter the horse at a side-turning or a bad corner.

The hills were another matter. Grades of 1 in 17 were the non-pedalling limit for my engine. Much has been said and written of what was euphemistically called " light pedal assist-ance "—" l.p.a." for short. The engine began to fail at 20 m.p.h. up a gradient. Now 20 m.p.h. is about the pedalling limit of a strong athlete on a pedal cycle. The motor cycle pedal gear had much the same ratio as a standard roadster pedal cycle. It was literally impossible to help the engine much at 20 m.p.h.—one's legs just couldn't pedal fast enough. I tried using a higher gear ratio for the pedals, but that ratio was too high for other purposes, such as pedalling when starting off, or to start the engine on a stand.

So l.p.a. was really of very limited use. After a very few yards of l.p.a., the engine usually threatened to stall, when the rider jumped off and ran alongside with his heart thumping. When he was too blown to run any farther, he switched off, and dripped with perspiration as he waited to recover his breath. (Quite a percentage of the pioneer motor cyclists resembled university oarsmen, in that they died of heart trouble in middle age.)

On long hills I personally kept my eyes open for some path or road leading away on either side. After the first engine failure, I would preferably wait till my pulse had returned to normal, and then push up such a side track, turn the model round, and charge down for a fresh rush at the hill. But quite often one got baulked by a frightened horse or a flock of sheep low down on a long hill. On such occasions it paid to go back to the bottom, and hope for better luck on the next attempt.

Readers familiar with British hills will realize the time and the exhaustion involved in reaching their summits with the pioneer machines, and even in later years with any single-geared model of greater efficiency. I am familiar with most forms of athletic exhaustion—rowing, sprinting, and cross-country steeplechases—but I am quite sure that the determined ascent of a really severe hill with any early type of motor cycle produced as complete an exhaustion as the human anatomy can sustain.

Belt trouble was probably the chief hoodoo after horses and hills. Theoretically, the V belt is quite a good transmission, provided that the belt is mechanically flexible. The manufacturers of the early belts failed to produce an accurate cross-section when the belt was new. As the belt became deformed in wear, it departed farther from the ideal angle. The pulley grooves soon became worn to a false angle by abrasive grit. When wet, the belt always slipped under heavy load. Crude fastening methods, such as an ordinary steel hook of S or double C formation, inserted through holes drilled in the leather, produced tearing of the leather and weakened the belt structure. (The twisted rawhide belt, which had a roughly circular cross-section, afforded even less grip on the steel pulleys.)

Belt slip and fastener trouble were endemic. In theory, the best belt ever produced was the built-up Wata-Wata, which was really flexible and did not " hoop up " or compress itself over the small front pulley. But being made of leather, it could never hope to cope with grit, wet and dryness. The least troublesome belt ever produced was made of stout canvas plies, heavily impregnated with rubber; but even these were not proof against moisture in wet weather.

Fortunately, it was nearly always possible to tension a bad belt so that it gave some sort of a drive. The only occasion when I was practically stalled by belt drive occurred years later on a Douglas machine in a torrential Scottish Six Days' Trial. This machine had a primary chain drive, followed by a very short rubber belt secondary drive. The wet belt slipped so badly on dripping wet pulleys that it literally failed to propel the machine up severe grades.

Brake trouble was usually a main annoyance in genuinely hilly country. On narrow country roads fifty years ago, complete baulks were quite common. In those days there was far more cattle traffic than exists today. A frightened horse or a flock of sheep creating a complete baulk on a steep descent was really dangerous with dubious brakes, as boot soles, pressed hard against the surface of the road, could keep descending speeds within the limit of safety, but could not bring a total load of 200 lb or so to a dead stop down single-figure gradients.

Ignition was often tiresome, but was usually curable even by an ignoramus with rule-of-thumb use of a test lamp. Sparking plugs were a fertile source of annoyance. The cheap French porcelain plugs were very brittle, and quite capable of blowing most of the thin insulator into the air. Punctures were rare. Engine trouble was almost unknown. When it occurred, it was often curable. My most frequent sample of it was the shearing of a small steel pin which fixed a cam or a pinion on the half-time spindles. This could be temporarily fixed with a French nail. After two such experiences I began to carry spare pins made of tougher steel than the engine maker had considered necessary.

As already remarked, petrol could be a worry, since comparatively few cycle dealers troubled to store it, being deterred by the stringent regulations imposed by law. But the tank held a gallon, sufficient for about 90 miles.

I almost always returned home in the saddle, though on rare occasions I was much later than my pessimistic time estimate had suggested.

The free wheel usually caused one or two stops on a 200-mile trip, but always yielded to tinkering.

A tumble was a serious matter, as it normally bent a pedal crank—easily straightened at the next smithy—or even snapped off a pedal spindle close up to the eye of the crank.

Sideslips were fairly frequent, as the machine was top-heavy, while even a new tyre was practically smooth, the ribbing of the treads being merely nominal. In some areas, especially limestone districts, waterbound roads could be extremely slippery in certain conditions of moisture. Cobble stones, tramlines and stone setts always suggested caution.

The fact that I never for a moment lost my gusto in the new hobby proves that the tribulations were not excessive, and usually had their funny side.

CHAPTER 6

THE DAWN OF DESIGN

W HENEVER WE LOOK BACK across a gulf of years at man's earliest efforts in some sphere where he is now almost omniscient, we are apt to despise the pioneers. Today the inventors of the first aircraft, the primitive radio sets and the " penny-farthing " bicycle, seem to have been fumbling and clumsy. Our condescensions are never justified. There are two stages in the development of any novel engineering project. A certain degree of sound theory is essential for a start. Real progress is even then impossible until sound theory has been supplemented by considerable practical experience.

At the birth of the British motor cycle industry its founders lacked both theory and experience. They knew more about the design and construction of the pedal cycle than any of their foreign rivals. But they were abysmally ignorant of the small petrol engine, and their ideas of the modifications which a pedal cycle of A.D. 1900 must undergo before it could develop into a first-class motor cycle were merely vague compounds of deduction and inference.

Hence a patronizing attitude towards their prentice ideas is utterly unjustified. Like any other invader of untrodden territory, they had much to learn before they could travel with a sure step. As already hinted, they were severely handicapped in competition with their opposite numbers on the Continent, who stole a long start thanks to the far more liberal road laws of Germany, Belgium and France.

By and large, Continental design of the period was as ludicrous as our own early experiments. It is true that in the motor car field the $3\frac{1}{2}$ h.p. De Dion voiturette of 1900 was astonishingly advanced for its time. Its designer possessed several years' experience, and was a genius. Consequently, his little car could thus early boast a reliable ignition (based on a good induction coil, a substantial contact-breaker, and dry cells of considerable capacity); a workable two-speed gear; and a rear-axle layout so efficient that it has lately been revived on certain excellent modern chassis.

But his notions were so little understood that a forgotten British designer failed to profit by them in the general confusion. This engineer was a Ford in embryo, born before his time. He yearned to supply the world with a cheap car, and schemed to produce £100 vehicles in quantity. His frame was made of light steel slats, as springy as a cheap bedstead, designed to absorb vibration. Its engine was mounted across this wobbly frame. The long crankshaft

44

was hardly thicker than my thumb. It was mounted in two phosphor-bronze brackets bolted to the side slats. Oil cups mounted on top of these brackets supplied a constant drip of oil to the tips of the shaft, and were replenished by hand from a spouted oil can every ten miles!

Contemporary with the sound little De Dion car was France's first motor bicycle. Since even on the Continent motor bicycles lagged several years behind the four-wheelers, this front-driven Werner, as I recorded in Chapter 2, was, in fact, an atrocity. Werner's second design was comparatively faultless in all its major features, though it still suffered from inadequate brakes and rather a tiresome transmission. Better than this, Werner could not do, even though he enjoyed about five years' start of British motor cycle engineers.

British engineers displayed in full measure the chief quality incumbent on intelligent men trapped in such an awkward position. They remained *modest*. For the moment they reined in their natural instinct to *design*. With admirable self-restraint, they decided to study and to imitate. They purchased their components abroad—engines, ignition and carburettors. Only in respect of the actual cycle frame could they rely on personal experience. For the rest, they bought, they tested, they criticized, they took out licences. They assumed the humble role of " rider-manufacturer ", and lived on the roads to accumulate the maximum of practical experience as swiftly as possible.

The natural result was that within a very few years they were building motor cycles of good quality for the period, in which every single item was British made and British designed. The components which they developed from Continental prototypes were always superior to the original patterns.

Yet another obstacle hampered all the larger firms. These were not new-born mushroom concerns, but bicycle factories of great reputation and without peer on earth at their own job. Their directors were responsible to their shareholders to the tune of very large capital assets. We must remember that as yet nobody *knew* whether the new locomotion had come to stay, or was merely a sensational novelty due to fade as rapidly as it had flashed on a suspicious, contemptuous and hostile world. In this dilemma the boards showed great wisdom. They allotted reasonable sums for experiment, and proceeded with considerable caution. Even if the motor car was founding a new major industry, it did not necessarily follow that either the motor tricycle or the motor bicycle could count on a great future.

If our first products appear slightly ludicrous in retrospect, as viewed across half a century of progress, the pioneer manufacturers unquestionably earn our unqualified admiration for their sound sense, intrinsic modesty and remarkable self-restraint. Compared with the eccentricities of men like Pennington and Lawson, they were great men.

The established cycle manufacturers were by no means the only or the best of the pioneer builders. It was not possible for an isolated individual like myself to try or even to inspect all the early experimental machines. I consider that three cycle manufacturers' models were among the first to deserve or achieve any reputation or success. In the tricycle field the Ariel was not only much better made than any of the Continental tricycles, but was the first to possess a balanced chassis. The typical foreign tricycle mounted its engine, tanks and gear behind the back axle. This concentration of considerable weight at the tail end of a stumpy wheelbase caused the light front wheel to bob clear of the road over every tiny bump.

The Ariel designer used a longer wheelbase, and placed his heavy engine in front of the back axle.

Similarly, the $2\frac{3}{4}$ h.p. Excelsior and the 2 h.p. and 3 h.p. " single-lever " Quadrant motor bicycles were all beautifully made, carried their engines in the best position available, short of scrapping the standard cycle frame layout, had good road performances, and attained a surprising degree of reliability considering how crude some details still remained. All these were produced by famous cycle factories. Eight motor cycles were entered for the famous Thousand Miles Trial of 1900 which celebrated the repeal of the 4 m.p.h. red-flag regulations. Five of them were British, and four of the five came from cycle factories (Ariel and Enfield).

But there were already many other Hotspurs in the field.

A few completely new companies, exclusively devoted to motor cycles, appeared, though few of them survived for very long. The Ormonde Co. were typical. As already recorded, they bought Kelecom engines in Belgium, ordered most other components (except ignition) in England, and assembled the parts in a basement off Oxford Street.

A weird assortment of assembled machines sprang up like mushrooms all over the country, most of them sponsored by keen cycle retailers. The cycle dealer of those days was often far more than a mere salesman on commission. He derived most of his income by selling famous pedal cycles—the Beeston Humber *de luxe* was listed at £25 at the dawn of the century. But a commission dealer had plenty of leisure. Many of them had learnt their trade in a first-class cycle factory. They could build wheels and braze frames as good as any factory product. Many of them sold a pedal cycle under their own transfer at less than the price of factory models.

Some of these men got bitten with the motor cycling bug, and a few of them made machines superior to any factory product of the period. They usually fitted foreign engines, with the Minerva as a ruling favourite. But lacking capital, and failing to secure many sales, they usually abandoned their enterprise after a year or so. One of the very best motor tricycles which I ever encountered was made by a retailer at Ashford in Kent, and I doubt if he ever built a second. One of the very best pioneer motor bicycles, long since

46

forgotten, was constructed by a retailer at Southsea, and fitted with an Aster engine of higher than normal horse power. I believe that he sold two or three locally, but he, too, quitted the business in disgust.

For two or three years such pioneers ransacked France and Belgium till they found a small works making more engines than were ordered. They bought one, two or even three engines, possibly persuading the builder to cast their name on the crankcase. They purchased ignition items—coils and contact-breakers in Paris. They procured the other materials and components in Birmingham or Coventry—and lo!—a new make was born.

Patriotism, pride and commercial enterprise soon reacted on this procedure. British electrical firms began to make and advertise coils, batteries, cables, accumulators, and switches. The Motor Manufacturing Co., of Coventry, took out a De Dion licence, and began to market an air-cooled copy of that famous unit in the $2\frac{3}{4}$ h.p. size. The De Dion engine had one serious fault known as the automatic inlet valve. This was opened by the depression created in the cylinder by the downward stroke of the piston and closed by the spring when the piston began to ascend. Obviously, this crude intake could not charge a cylinder with gas very fully, nor supply high engine revolutions. I believe the Belgian Minerva Co. were the first to realize the fault in terms of motor cycle engines, and they brought out, first, a 2 h.p. and, later, a $3\frac{1}{2}$ h.p. engine equipped with mechanical operation of both valves.

Incidentally, the immediate effect of such large engines as the $2\frac{3}{4}$ h.p. M.M.C., the 3 h.p. Quadrant, and the $3\frac{1}{2}$ h.p. Minerva was to kill the industry's pristine ideal of a " motor-assisted pedal cycle ". Such large power units inspired dreams of miniature projectiles, contemptuous of pedal gear, demanding far stronger frames bearing little resemblance to push-bike conventions.

At some speed trials in Phœnix Park, Dublin, the Ormonde Co., petty though its resources were, registered 60 m.p.h. with a new Paris-Madrid model. This had a quite special frame, housing a really enormous engine packed into the space between the seat-pillar tube and the rear wheel, and screened by a stiff wire grid to protect the jockey's clothes from the hot cylinder and the high-tension current of the sparking plug.

By this time any engineer whose notions of petrol had been largely cluttered up with mere gas-engine practice, was beginning to see visions and dream dreams. He could dismantle, inspect and measure any or all of the imported power units, which had translated several years of petrol-engine experience into steel and pistons and valves and rings and timing gears. He was no longer confined to fumbling plagiarisms. He could test a sample foreign engine on the brake and on the road. He could probably spot flaws in its design, invent valuable improvements, calculate stresses, and estimate the required strengths and clearances for a rather different engine.

I still remember congratulating a pioneer manufacturer on his first 5 h.p. twin-cylinder, and asking him who designed it. It was a great shock to me to learn that he had asked the head of an engineering college to send him two of his brightest young graduates as soon as they received their diplomas, and that these two lads had developed his new engine. He did not tell me how much trouble or expense the job had incurred, but it was still very young, already very good, and with minor modifications it engined his most powerful machine over a term of years. Our dependence on the small engineering shops of the Continent had ended.

Parallel energy was seething in all the associated spheres by the end of 1904. Chapter 10 describes how and why the development of variable gears tarried so long. (After all, that delay is comparable to the introduction of variable-pitch propellers for aircraft, which registered an even greater dilatoriness many years later! " Hindsight " is often more critical than the human make-up actually justifies.) Quite soon the other components of the motor cycle began to advance by leaps and bounds.

Tyres remained comparatively stagnant for a decade or two. The push-bike tyre in a " tandem " size served our needs at first. It was easy enough to expand that into a 2-inch motor cycle tyre, which certainly gave us far less trouble than our wealthy neighbours were simultaneously experiencing with motor car tyres, which still punctured or burst with considerable frequency. Sound British ignition coils arrived quite soon and a little later the Simms-Bosch high-tension magneto rendered ignition almost foolproof. Our wiring soon surpassed the terribly shoddy stuff which satisfied France. The flimsy Continental contact-breakers rapidly yielded to substantial British designs, producing a definite leap in reliability, and also better maintained engine power, since power depended so much on accurate timing of the spark. Carburettors remained somewhat crude, as the patent laws relating to spray carburettors were hotly contested in the courts.

Numerous innovations in control of the machine were recorded. Believe it or not, the twistgrip is as old as the motor bicycle. In those far-off days, the right-hand grip handle formed the ignition switch, and you protected the model against theft by pocketing the grip bodily when you parked your machine. Other designers used a compound twistgrip, which operated both switch and exhaust-valve lifter. This latter control was pure British. On the Continent, compression was eased for engine-starting purposes by a " compression tap ", located in the cylinder head. We retained these " pet-cocks " (as they were sometimes termed) in order to inject paraffin prior to starting up, as the crude lubricants of the period usually gummed the pistons as the engine cooled. But we continued to use the valve lifter for easing compression before starting the engine.

Already a movement to liberate the novice from multiple controls was afoot. A genuine pioneer machine would have six

The Butler tricycle built in 1884 and probably the first genuine motor cycle. The engine was a twin-cylinder type with one cylinder on each side of the driving wheel

Gottlieb Daimler's single-cylinder motor cycle appeared in 1885. Noteworthy features are the vertical engine with belt-cum-gear drive to the rear wheel, and tiller steering

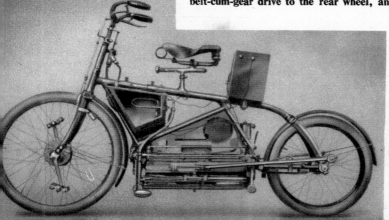

A machine built by Colonel Holden about 1895 and possibly the first four-cylinder motor vehicle of any kind

An early experimental spring frame
model produced in 1903. The Belgian
engine is a 2 h.p. Minerva and the
first with a mechanically-operated
inlet valve

A Singer tricycle of 1901 fitted with
the Perks and Birch motor wheel
embodying the whole power unit

A neat Singer of
1905. It had a spray
carburettor with hot-
air supply and a
high-tension magneto

A 3½ h.p. J.A.P.
engine of 1904.
The inlet and
exhaust valves
are both mechani-
cally operated by
a single rod from
timing gear to
rocker

One of the first
Triumphs. This 2¼
h.p. model was rid-
den by L. B. Tucker
in the 1903 Glasgow
to London non-stop
trial

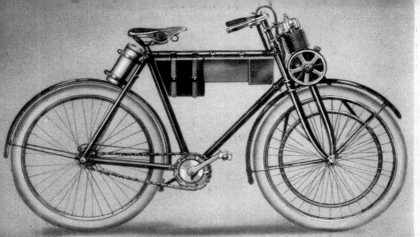

The front-drive Werner, introduced
in this country in 1900, was one of
the first practical, light motor
cycles ever made

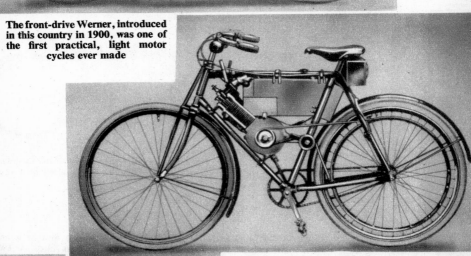

Forerunner of the A.J.S. built by the brothers
Stevens in 1897

The first P. & M. (1902), using
the sloping engine as an integral
part of the front down tube

Popular in 1903, the 2¾ h.p.
Ormonde was fitted with petrol
gauge and sight-feed lubricator

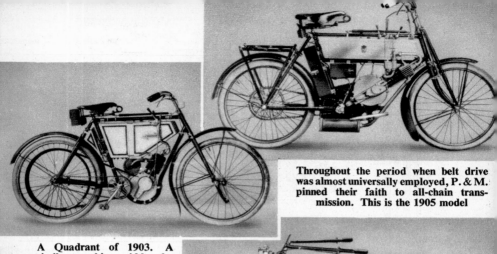

Throughout the period when belt drive was almost universally employed, P. & M. pinned their faith to all-chain transmission. This is the 1905 model

A Quadrant of 1903. A similar machine, ridden by Tom Silver, was the only motor cycle to make an absolute non-stop performance in the Glasgow-London run of 1903

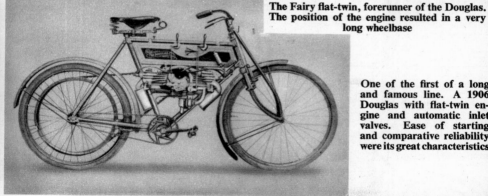

The Fairy flat-twin, forerunner of the Douglas. The position of the engine resulted in a very long wheelbase

One of the first of a long and famous line. A 1906 Douglas with flat-twin engine and automatic inlet valves. Ease of starting and comparative reliability were its great characteristics

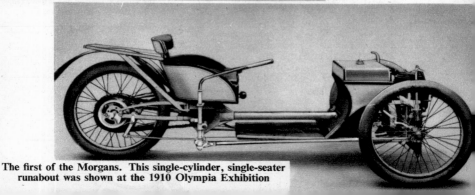

The first of the Morgans. This single-cylinder, single-seater runabout was shown at the 1910 Olympia Exhibition

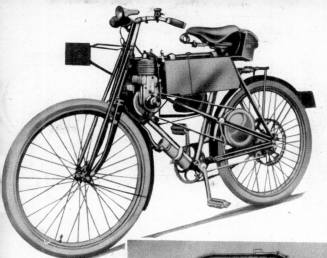

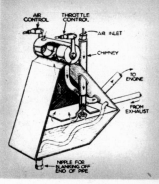

A surface carburettor of 1903. Vaporization was assisted by running an extension of the exhaust pipe right through the petrol

The first Scott (1903) motor cycle with twin-cylinder engine built high in the frame and fitted with belt and chain

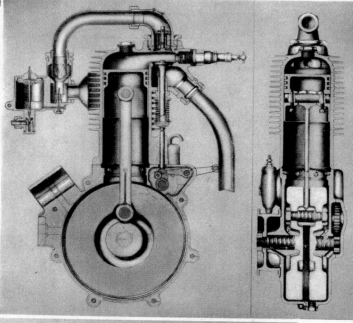

A typical single-cylinder engine of 1903 in section. An automatic inlet valve and a mechanically-operated exhaust valve are shown

(Below) The 3 h.p. Clarendon of 1903-4, one of the most symmetrical machines of its day

Superb finish was always a marked feature of Sunbeams. Symmetry of design plus the enclosed transmission characterizes this 1913 250 c.c. model

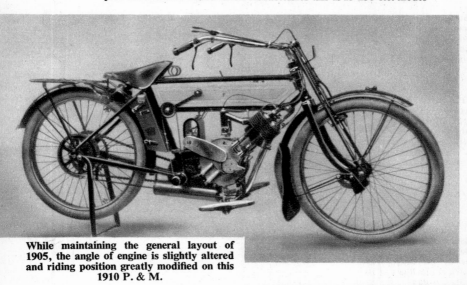

While maintaining the general layout of 1905, the angle of engine is slightly altered and riding position greatly modified on this 1910 P. & M.

D.R.s of 1914 will remember this Triumph—the famous 499 c.c., with three-speed gear in the hub

First of the famous 3½ h.p. single-geared Triumphs with the 82 by 86mm engine. This model achieved great popularity

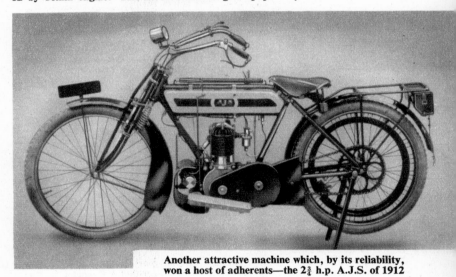

Another attractive machine which, by its reliability, won a host of adherents—the 2¾ h.p. A.J.S. of 1912

The 1913 Rudge Multi. The variable pulley was an immense asset to its popularity among sportsmen of that day

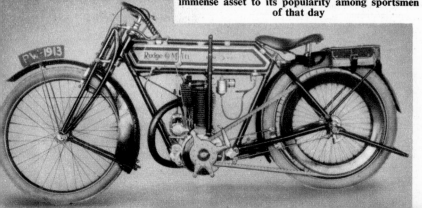

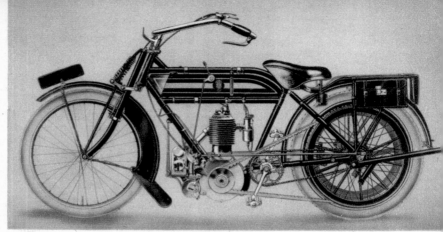

The 1912 3½ h.p. B.S.A. with three-speed gear in the rear hub. It cost £60 in 1912

Another variable-gear model—the 1911 Zenith Gradua, with J.A.P. engine

The 1911 Bat, with front wheel springing. Saddle and footboards were sprung in unison on their own special frame

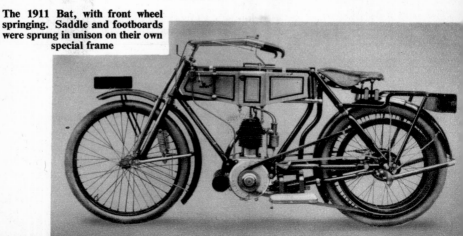

controls on the tank top. They were the four wooden handles resembling chess bishops which controlled the gas, the air, the spark and the compression tap. A knob would transfer petrol from the tank to the " swish-box " (surface carburettor). Another knob would seal the air chimney when the model was parked. Maybe, the tank top would also carry an electric junction box, with a tiny interrupter plug to prevent current leakage if the engine stopped with the contacts touching, or the owner forgot to switch off. The Quadrant Co. introduced their famous " single lever ", a super " chess bishop ", which operated the throttle, the spark advance and the valve lifter in due sequence! (Within a few years the air and throttle controls were transferred to the handlebar by means of twin Bowden levers working on a joint spindle.)

As soon as the patent situation cleared up, spray carburettors rapidly became standard, with the French Longuemare leading, only to be supplanted by the Brown and Barlow. In actual fact, primitive engines claimed so little mechanical flexibility that, for some years, almost any simple device capable of coupling a jet chamber to a float chamber was adequate.

Sideslips, of course, were far more numerous than now. The machines were built high to facilitate pedal assistance. I remember one maker listed frames measuring 22, 24, 26 and 28 inches to suit riders of different stature. I bought a 28-inch frame, and it took me some time to realize why the machine skidded so violently!

Design languished most in terms of brakes. Our first brakes consisted of a standard Bowden rim brake on the rear wheel and, on the front wheel, an enormous steel lever which depressed a solid rubber shoe on the top run of the front tyre. This arrangement was soon superseded by rim brakes on the front wheel, though these were seldom made of the requisite strength. In due course, pedal rear brakes operating shoes on the belt rim furnished some improvement. The pattern which worked inside the groove of the belt rim could jamb most perilously on occasions. The pattern which applied a shoe to the outside of the belt rim was less potent, but at least it could not jamb.

A few of us were supplied with band brakes, which were standard fittings on the front wheels of forecars. These were generally known as " bobby dodgers ", and served no purpose beyond complying with the law. Most of them were either " on " or " off ", and rattled continuously. If, by dint of much toil, you persuaded them to grip their drums, the linings burnt away on the first long descent. For decent brakes we had to wait till Mr. Ferodo perfected his metal-asbestos compounds for internal shoes inside drums.

Lamps had been one of our worst headaches in the opening epoch. We were then limited to cycle brackets supporting small cycle gas lamps. The brackets broke under vibration. The needle valve controlling the water drip was also liable to shake to pieces. Eventually we switched to a bracket composed of two rigid prongs, bolted to the handlebar. This eliminated broken hinges, but increased the vibration, which, in turn, convulsed the water drip more than ever. (In the U.S.A. our cousins were wiser. They quickly turned to cylinders of dissolved acetylene which does not foul burners.)

So nightfall implied (*a*) dismounting, (*b*) possibly unstrapping the carrier, and turning it down to serve as a stand, (*c*) turning on the water, (*d*) " waiting for the smell ". When the smell arrived, it usually came in a fierce rush, and proved that one or both of the microscopic gas holes in the burner was choked. If only one hole was fouled, a spurt of flame either burst the glass or blackened the reflector. If both were fouled, the entire lamp burst into flame.

Fortunately, the electric firms kept motor cycling representatives busily testing their brainwaves on the road. One of these rode an electrically equipped Ormonde in the first London-Edinburgh run of the M.C.C. He started with *four* 20 a.h. accumulators in a special metal container on his carrier. As they were of the feather-weight type now familiar in portable radio sets, they evinced no great enthusiasm for motor cycling (but he reached Edinburgh on time).

These visible and external advances in design were trivial compared to the invisible improvements. Year by year, our timing gears became more dependable, and presented our engines with a wider range of r.p.m. and with increased h.p. Year by year, our exhaust valves became tougher, and ceased to expect a re-grind every 500 miles. Year by year, our piston rings hardened up, and ceased to retire coyly to the bottom of their grooves after a few hundred miles. The cooling of cylinders was bettered, pistons were strengthened and lightened. Sparking plugs ceased to oil up, to soot up, to pre-ignite, to shed half their insulators into the cylinder, to explode half their insulators into neighbouring ditches. A whole new science of metallurgy was coming to the aid of our strange locomotion.

One component defied the most thoughtful engineering brains. In these pages there is much spasmodic allusion to vibration. Remember that we rode with rigid forks, small tyres, and cycle-type saddles on rather poor roads. Many an inventor grappled with these associated problems. Better saddles came first. Next, our tyres were enlarged. Then a weird variety of spring forks appeared. One may guess their intrinsic poverty by affectionately recalling the clash fork which adorned the otherwise excellent Triumph machines for a long term of years from about 1911. This was pivoted at its central crown. It bucked ceaselessly to and fro, its jerks being restrained by a powerful coil spring. The wheelbase, consequently, was eternally lengthening and shortening.

In my personal opinion the two best forks to appear in the early days were the French Truffault and the original telescopic fork fitted to the Scott two-stroke, which achieved a degree of good steering, fine road-holding and tolerable comfort previously un-

50

attained. It was, in fact, the direct ancestor of the very fine fork fitted to the German B.M.W. before World War II, and of the still finer " Teledraulic " fork introduced on the Matchless machines a little later. From this trio stem most of the best spring forks on the road today.

If this chapter sounds hypercritical, let us realize that it is retrospection, which is usually critical, whether in art, music, politics or engineering. If our faults were legion, at least we can boast that in this sphere we were never excelled by any other engineering nation. Right away from the start, our designers have led the world in this sphere.

CHAPTER 7

THE OUTSIDER BECOMES AN INSIDER

THE STORY NOW JUMPS AHEAD some six years from 1901 to 1907, during which period I rode at every conceivable opportunity, owned some fifteen machines of various makes, made touch with the industry, enjoyed my first experiences of club life, and took my chance in the simple competitions of the sport with occasional success. (My profession left no leisure for serious and sustained competition work.) Incidentally, as described in Chapter 11, I wrestled with various methods of taking a companion on my runs, most of which were decidedly expensive and grotesquely unsatisfactory.

These were climacteric days for the motor cycle. The daily Press, which as a whole was mainly anti-motor with the distinguished exception of the *Daily Mail*, bluntly opined that motor cycles had no possible future, and promulgated that doctrine by many pens. It was not a case of frequent road accidents. Most of us occasionally took a toss, probably thanks to smooth tyres over greasy roads. But I recall extremely few fatalities, most of them due to fatigue of the metal of the front-fork blades, which for a time were unsprung and barely heavier than pedal-cycle patterns. Such disasters ended when the girder spring fork was introduced, with the Druid as a notable example.

The pessimism and prejudice of the daily Press was largely ascribable to the knowledge that motor cycles were expensive and unreliable in the minor sense of those words. We usually concluded our journeys punctually by this date, but we certainly suffered plenty of petty stops along the road. Lay journalists quite failed to realize that we rather enjoyed pitting our wits against the whimsies of a primitive ignition, while a belt stoppage annoyed us neither more or less than a puncture irritates a pedal cyclist. The arrival of the Simms-Bosch high-tension magneto eliminated all the commoner ignition troubles, except an oily or sooted plug, and so registered a major advance in reliability.

During this period I owned three re-designed Ormondes, a Dennis quad, a Dennis tricycle, two V twin-cylinder Vindec Specials with 5 h.p. Peugeot engines and an excellent French spring fork (the Truffault), $4\frac{1}{2}$ h.p. and 9 h.p. Riley tricars, two Triumphs, and several second-hand machines of lesser interest. The list of serious stoppages with these machines, spread over a quinquennium, included gear trouble with the Dennis machines (owing to the gear-changing fork dropping off in the road and remaining unmissed till the next gear change); "dead" ignition coils on the Riley (until I removed the coil box from the back of the radiator, where the hot water melted its insulation); and certain timing-gear disasters with the Ormondes (due to strong valve springs inducing the heels of the tappets to grind through the case-hardening of their actuating cams).

Apart from these troubles, which were not repairable by the roadside, I invariably completed my journeys, even if I was occasionally a little late when belt or tyre trouble had delayed me. The Press diatribes were, however, partly justified if the new locomotion was viewed from the standpoint of a complete novice, to whom a simple short-circuit might prove hopelessly mysterious.

The Motor Cycle, founded in 1903 and published weekly, was regularly studied by thousands of would-be riders, and accomplished a great work in educating novices to face what lay before them when at last they graduated into ownership.

I should personally identify two factors which saved the sport and hobby from collapse or anæmia. The first was the invention of the Simms-Bosch high-tension magneto which was standardized about 1906. The second was the energetic intervention of M. J. Schulte, managing director of the Triumph Cycle Company. Schulte, by birth a German, was a man of great vigour, of cool and balanced judgment, and of considerable prudence. He was the first cycle-trade magnate to realize that a good motor cycle was likely to develop into the big brother of the pedal cycle, if it did not actually supersede the lighter machine.

As far back as 1895 he had ridden the crude Hildebrand-Wolfmuller motor cycle on the Coventry track, and from that date onward he never failed to study and to sample every motor cycle which came his way. A conservative by instinct, he never allowed himself to be hustled by impulse into precipitate action. Thus he was slower than some of the big shots in the cycle trade to build experimental motor cycles.

His initial experiment, about 1904, was to construct a good motor cycle with all the Triumph soundness of workmanship, and to power it with the best existing engine, the 1¾ h.p. Minerva from Belgium. There was nothing in the least shoddy about this machine, for even at this date there were considerable varieties of quality in British pedal cycles.

In 1906 he went a step further, and produced a Triumph engine rated at 3 h.p.—a simple, solid, side-valve type. He was so sure of its merits that he asked me to suggest some stunt which might convince the public of its merits. Together we decided that if it could be ridden 200 miles daily for six consecutive days, it would obviously be a good buy for any citizen who desired cheap personal transport.

It was, of course, single geared with a V belt drive and no clutch; therefore, it could not hope to carry my 12 stone up formidable hills. In actual fact, machines at this date were habitually geared

53

too high. Buyers desired speed, and the standard delivery ratio was 4½ to 1, which made 45–50 m.p.h. a possible maximum, and provided quiet, smooth running at ordinary touring speeds of 25–35 m.p.h. So six routes radiating from Oxford were plotted, all of them avoiding formidable hills. D. K. Hall, a famous Roads Record Association timekeeper, was engaged to verify the facts, and off I started.

Shocks were in store for both Schulte and myself. Late on the fifth day the machine suddenly began to feel as if it were floating on jelly. A hasty dismount showed that the duplex down tubes of the diamond frame had fractured. Moreover, the engine power had been steadily fading throughout the 1,000 miles already covered, and hasty examinations proved that the piston rings and cylinder bore had both worn unconscionably fast, while the exhaust valves were pitting almost to the scaling point. I do not know why Schulte had varied the standard frame, but within a few hours he had readied a second machine with the normal frame layout. Nothing could be done about the piston rings or valves.

When I started off again on the following Monday I was well aware that, day by day, the vigour of the light pedalling assistance required on hills would increase in quite a sharp ratio. I inserted a new exhaust valve every evening, grinding it into the seat as well as conditions permitted. This time everything went well, and the 1,200 miles were reeled out with consummate ease, except so far as my calf muscles were concerned!

In 1911 a subsequent Triumph model was ridden 400 miles on each of six consecutive days by A. E. Catt, of Northampton. He had no mechanical trouble, but, owing to punctures and bad weather, finished in parlous physical condition, his hands and feet being terribly swollen, while he could not get the sound of the engine out of his ears and had to be heavily doped before he could sleep.

Schulte was considerably disturbed by the behaviour of my valves and rings, but promptly set a metallurgist to devise better materials for these vital components. In 1907 he produced the 3½ h.p. Triumph, which was—belt apart—as reliable as Big Ben. Later, in the hands of Ivan B. Hart-Davies, it secured the John o' Groats-Land's End record, covering the 880 miles first in 1909 in 33 hr 22 min on a machine weighing 196 lb including a monster fuel tank and, finally (1911), in 29 hr 12 min.

A sister machine, ridden by Jack Marshall, won the 1908 T.T. This 3½ h.p. Triumph did yeoman military service in the First World War, and was probably the first completely satisfactory machine of its type in the world. Its success was principally ascribed to two factors—an unusually good side-valve engine and the superb, conscientious workmanship of its makers. Later, it was equipped with a disc, free-engine clutch in the rear wheel and, eventually, with a variable gear.

I do not pretend for one moment that it was the only satisfactory machine on the market in 1907 and onwards. Closely as some of its rivals pressed it (especially, at one period, the $3\frac{1}{2}$ h.p. Quadrant), it was unquestionably the best seller, and enjoyed public confidence to an unprecedented degree. One of my employees rode it quite fantastic mileages every year. He decarbonized it regularly once a month, its design enabling him to whip the cylinder off and to have it back again within forty minutes after attending to the piston, rings and the valves. On these journeys he carried no tools except the minimum, which—including tyre and belt repair kit—were packed into a military hair-brush case lashed to the front fork.

This model governed British design right up to the moment when variable gears were slowly standardized. It created a national ideal —that of a simple design, on rugged lines, executed in first-class materials by first-class craftsmen, with simplicity as the guiding principle. In outline, it was widely imitated, but I doubt if any rival quite succeeded in duplicating its staunch simplicity. Its leading rivals were probably the $3\frac{1}{2}$ h.p. Quadrant and the $3\frac{1}{2}$ h.p. Rex. As both these firms eventually disappeared from the field, it may be assumed that they were slightly inferior, or less wisely handled.

The Matchless was also excellent value over the same period, but being produced at that time in a comparatively small factory it did not attain quite a similar eminence.

To retrace for a moment, during the years 1903–1905 I served both on the Committee of the Motor Cycling Club and of the Auto Cycle Club in London. These two bodies were to some extent aspirants to the government of national motor cycling affairs. The latter was in effect a sub-committee of the Automobile Club of Great Britain and Ireland, as the R.A.C. was then called. Its members were nominated, and most of them were rather amateurish. The M.C.C., by contrast, was a small coterie of hard-riding enthusiasts, several of whom were in the trade. Unlike the A.C.C., the M.C.C. was extremely democratic and enterprising. It had a full programme, comprising many week-end social runs (with ladies) to pleasant places within 50 miles of town and numerous competitions.

Indeed, one enormous cup, presented by the famous S. F. Edge, its chairman, proved something of an incubus in 1905. It was to be awarded to the member who survived longest in an interminable non-stop. So low was the committee's opinion of motor cycle reliability that a short lap of some 20 miles was selected in Hertfordshire, and the cup was expected to be won in three or four circuits of this small loop on a single Saturday afternoon. Most of us fell out for some trivial cause before very long, but two men—Leonard Jones on a bitza motor tricycle and Milligan on a 3 h.p. Bradbury— went on and on and on, till we grew quite tired of providing observers to survey their eternal peregrinations. Eventually Jones survived Milligan.

This astonishing revelation of perpetual motion in terms of a motor cycle so impressed us that in 1906 we promptly began to organize a 400-mile reliability trial between London and Edinburgh, starting in the late evening. The warier members resisted this innovation, afraid that very few machines might finish, and that the weak and erratic acetylene gas lamps of the period might lead to nocturnal crashes. But the doubters were scoffed out of court, for 34 motor bicycles, out of 52, finished punctually within 24 hours, as did four tricars out of 15.

The fixture soon assumed national importance. Before long, special cups were offered for completing the double journey of 800 miles within 48 hours. The original route along the mild undulations of the Great North Road had to be stiffened by detours in search of formidable hills, and a far more exacting time schedule was adopted, embodying plenty of intermediate checks, together with " secret " checks by travelling marshals to ensure that people rode at a regular speed.

Thus early, a reasonable degree of road reliability had been achieved. This went hand in hand with durability. Engines were not yet designed for really high performances, and specifications were still comparatively simple. No motor cycle could yet be described as everlasting, but only the extravagant few dreamt of buying a new model every year. The average machine remained in service for a period of years. The simpler the specification, the less the expenditure on repairs and replacements.

Apart from the hill-climbing weakness of the single-gear belt drive, there was small cause for complaint. We had not yet been educated to expect conveniences which later and more luxurious generations were one day to take for granted. We tolerated gas lamps. We made no angry complaints about the discomfort imposed by small tyres and indifferent spring forks. We accepted with docility the lack of a free-engine clutch, which compelled us to stop the engine at any traffic halt, and to return to the bottom of any modestly steep hill if we were baulked by traffic half-way up.

A few of us were slowly realizing that such defects stood between the machines of the day and a really large market. But the majority of riders had grown case-hardened to existing shortcomings. Whatever might be said in criticism of current patterns, the motor cycle claimed enormous advantages by contrast with the pedal cycle. Whatever time was available for pleasure travelling, the motor cycle multiplied the radius of a pedal cycle by some such factor as four. A touring pedaller averages perhaps 8 m.p.h. But, as early as 1904, G. P. Mills had ridden his Raleigh motor cycle 900 miles in just under 51 hours between Land's End and John o' Groats— an average speed of nearly 20 m.p.h. in foul weather and largely over very bad roads. In short runs over good roads, averages of 30 m.p.h. and over were often recorded by private owners.

Already many a dreamer had begun to picture his ideal machine, and shrewd engineers were scheming to translate such dreams into reality. There might be no real remedy except better clothing for the problem of exposure to weather. But all the other defects should surely surrender to intelligent design?

CHAPTER 8

DESIGN AT A GALLOP

F ROM 1898 TO 1911 the story of the motor cycle falls naturally
into two distinct chapters. The pioneers—De Dion, Werner,
and some of the firms whose honourable names are listed in
Chapter 2 of this book—gradually satisfied each other, and a small,
but annually increasing public, that a motor cycle was a technical
possibility and a practical vehicle. In the teeth of prejudice, ridicule
and even mild persecution, they stuck to their guns. By approximately 1905 their initial task was complete. Designers and manufacturers now settled down to the spade work of the second period.
Their next task was to work out the best specification possible from
the knowledge, experience and materials at their disposal.

Progress was not particularly rapid. The impact of the petrol
engine upon the light engineering industries had been as sudden as
it was violent. It had caught them completely unprepared. Nor
were technical problems their sole headache. The switch from slow,
horse-drawn vehicles, with wooden wheels and either steel or solid
rubber tyres, to fast, power-propelled cars and cycles, was a positive
revolution. The single factor of speed was troublesome enough.
Public opinion resented and dreaded it. Only a few years previously
pedal cyclists had been harried by the police for speeding. The
powerful horsed interests were up in arms. The dust nuisance
provoked fierce antagonism from even the meeker citizens.

Meanwhile, manufacturers were necessarily animated by financial motives. Successful firms were answerable to doubting share-
holders, and responsible for the livelihood of their employees.
In such a situation they were bound to ca' canny, as the Scots put it,
to " make haste " slowly, as the ancient Romans would have said.

A few sanguine financiers, like H. J. Lawson, had emulated
Kipling's fool " who tried to hustle the East ". Thousands of
pounds—perhaps, even millions—had been poured down the drain
by wild-cat company promoters. If, by 1905, the entire cycle
trade, plus a few new and eager companies, had settled on the
rough outlines of the contemporary motor cycle, nobody could
afford to risk vast sums upon its development. The sagest method
of procedure was to secure enthusiastic recruits by supplying the
small circle of customers with satisfactory mounts.

In this atmosphere, the 1905 motor cycle set out to beget a
worthier offspring. It was, as we have seen, a machine weighing
somewhere between 150 and 200 lb on the average; single-geared
with—almost universally—a V belt drive; clutchless; simple;

sturdy; and moderately reliable. No major improvements as yet loomed up on the distant horizons. For the moment manufacturers must struggle to improve its design and workmanship in detail, while racking their brains over every criticism which the factory riders and their amateur customers were able to identify.

By 1911 this comparatively simple task was just about complete. In that year the $3\frac{1}{2}$ h.p. Triumph and, in rather lesser degree, the $3\frac{1}{2}$ h.p. Rudge and the Matchless, were more than sound. The high-tension magneto and simple, spray carburettors (developed from the French Longuemare with its easily choked " rose " jet) had satisfied the primary needs of any engine which the factories could design. Efficient lubricating oils had been developed by the oil companies. Tyres were still on the small side (about $26 \times 2\frac{1}{4}$ inches) and, proportionately, failed to furnish the comfort bestowed in a later age by tyres of double that size; but, even thus, they were immensely more reliable than the average car tyre of the period. Reliable free wheels had superseded the gimcrack toys of five years back. Sparking plugs had risen in price, but were improved out of recognition. Fuel consumption was low—seldom much under a hundred miles per gallon.

Performance in terms of engine starting and road speed was adequate to the normal demand, though hill-climbing was a grievous blot. The rider was liable to be baulked in a climb, through the lack of a clutch and a variable gear, while a heavy rider could not hope to climb really steep gradients, though a light man with a clear run, and perhaps some pedal assistance, could surmount nearly all main-road hills.

Brakes had improved out of recognition, thanks to the adoption of a main brake on the rear belt rim and front rim brakes of much sturdier construction than the old pedal-cycle types. The belt drive had been transformed by the adoption of very stiff canvas V belts impregnated with rubber. Unlike the obsolete leather belt, these required no dressing and did not glaze under friction nor squeeze hopelessly out of shape over the pulleys, though they were too stiff to flex readily round an engine pulley of small circumference, and were prone to excessive slip on hills in pouring rain.

Special and suitable steels and cast irons had been found for valves and piston rings respectively, so that an engine maintained its power quite creditably in prolonged use.

If a 1950 rider were to examine a 1911 Triumph, Rudge or Matchless, he would find very little indeed that suggested possible trouble. Punctures, belt stretch, pulley wear, torn-out belt-fastener screws—these were obvious weaknesses, but neither very frequent nor serious. The Triumph T.T. model, a favourite with hard, sporting riders, had discarded its pedalling gear. Its rear wheel could be dropped out by unscrewing its pair of spindle nuts, and the beaded edges of the tyre cover permitted the tyre to be ripped off in a few seconds.

What next?

Some optimists had actually begun to assume that any radical progress might already be impossible.

Had that facile optimism been justified, the motor bicycle would never have enlisted the 700,000 enthusiasts living in Great Britain in 1950. Alike in things small and great, every intelligent rider was conscious of much discontent. The lesser criticisms may be considered first.

One source of dissatisfaction, for instance, was the lamp. The pioneers had begun with colza-oil cycle lamps burning wicks an inch wide. Mine was a beautifully made Lucas " King of the Road ", attached by sprung hinges to the standard pedal-cycle bracket. Its hinges did not last a month, and its light was grossly inadequate for the modest motor cycling speeds of 1901. I replaced it by a large pedal-cycle acetylene gas lamp with far stronger hinges. Such lamps consisted of an upper water reservoir, which dripped water through an adjustable screw valve on carbide in a lower chamber.

Provided these lamps were kept spotlessly clean, they burned quite well, assuming always that the road vibration (accentuated by a possibly rigid fork or a crude spring fork, plus the spring hinge action) did not jerk carbide dust up into the valve, and upset the precision of the water feed. After an hour or two, the carbide charge was either exhausted, or so sodden that its gas producing efficiency was wrecked. Then one dismounted, thanking heaven if a bright moon was shining, cleaned out all the mess, and inserted fresh carbide.

Traffic was the next hoodoo. In the absence of a free-engine clutch, any enforced traffic stop compelled one to dismount till the road ahead cleared. This was a disaster half-way up a hill like Birdlip. (In the 1909 A.C.U. Six Days' Trial, a bonus of 25 marks was offered for a clean ascent of three test hills—Dinas Mawddwy, Birdlip and the easy Cat and Fiddle. Despite pedal assistance and the free use of adjustable engine pulleys, only one rider in ten qualified for 75 climbing marks!)

Normally, we did not grumble overmuch when traffic halted us on the level. But, on the standard gear ratio of about $4\frac{1}{2}$ to 1 for a 500 c.c. machine, almost any hill in a town or city might produce a baulk. When a tired man, wearing heavy clothing, possibly dripping with rain, is compelled to halt on a hill, the run-and-jump start throws him into a heavy sweat. His clothes must be left to dry on him. Lumbago, chills and fibrositis were common results. A number of firms—notably Triumph and Roc—began to insert disc free-engine clutches between the rear hub and a separate belt rim. These were better than nothing, but a clutch start from rest on a $4\frac{1}{2}$ to 1 gear ratio required dainty handling even on the level and, frankly, such a layout was practically useless when we were baulked on a perceptible gradient. Free-engine clutches and a variable gear were obviously essential to the future of our sport and hobby.

59

In a later chapter (pages 65 *et seq.*), the evolution of variable gears is discussed in detail and at length. One obvious excuse may be offered in defence of designers who hesitated to face this great experiment. At this date all air-cooled engines were prone to reach high temperatures under continuous running on the road. Many of them, when they grew hot, would " knock " audibly and perceptibly by feel. The phenomenon was known as " overheating ". If an engine of the then current design " overheated " at a good speed on a high gear ratio, what would happen if the machine were equipped with a low emergency gear of, say, 10 to 1, and then flogged up steep hills by ignorant customers on wide throttle openings? Designers feared that the metals so painstakingly evolved for valves and rings and pistons and cylinders would start to make serious protests.

Not until research on aircraft engines was scientifically tackled in World War I, did engineers fully realize that the term " overheating " was largely a misnomer. The pre-1914 side-valve engine was ludicrously asymmetrical. The valve chest was a huge metal excrescence on one side of the engine. True, the exhaust valve was placed in front to benefit from the maximum cooling draught, and the cooler inlet valve was located at the rear in a simple attempt to maintain an even temperature throughout the cylinder walls. But the valve-chest excrescence always provided a very hot spot on the valve side of the engine by contrast with the symmetrical hemisphere on the opposite side. This tended to " pull out of round " every circular component in the engine—cylinder, piston, piston rings, and both valves.

" Overheating " was practically eliminated after World War I, sometimes by using a symmetrical engine with the valves centrally mounted in the cylinder head, but even more by using fins with thick roots which enabled the heat to flow through the broad path of metal and helped to balance the temperature all round the cylinder. Thus the possible evils of hard work on a low gear ratio were largely eliminated.

Hooters were a third annoyance. The squawk-horn with a compressible rubber bulb was the stand-by of 1911. It utilized a " reed ", composed of a thin tongue of spring brass. This was instantly silenced by a minute speck of dust on its blade. Nowadays road users are better trained to rely on their eyes for road safety, and to observe complete caution at blind corners which—incidentally—were far more numerous and severe thirty years ago; thousands of them have been pared away in the interim, while much heavier traffic teaches us all increased caution.

When an accident occurred in 1911, the magistrates' first question was whether either participant had blown his horn. If he confessed that he had not blown it, the admission was tantamount to pleading guilty. Quite often the victim had pressed the bulb, but a speck of dust on the reed prevented a squawk. Car owners were beginning to use mechanical or electric klaxons, but these were too bulky and heavy for motor cycling use.

Fourthly, motor cycling was obsessed by vibration, emanating in its two main forms from the engine and from the road. No single-cylinder engine is ideally smooth. The engines of 1911 were definitely very rough compared with those of 1950. Moreover, their intrinsic lack of balance was enhanced by frames inclined to whippiness. On the earlier Scotts with chain drive, it was quite absurdly easy to jerk the driving chain off its sprockets while starting from rest on the clutch of the two-speed gear, simply because the frame whipped under the load and threw the sprockets out of alignment.

But road vibration was a graver handicap than engine vibration. The modern motor cyclist has no experience of 45 m.p.h. on 2-inch tyres, with a rigid or feebly sprung fork. Despite the modern luxury of big tyres, a well-balanced engine rigidly mounted in a stiff frame, a large, well-padded saddle, and a hydraulically damped telescopic fork, he buys a rear-sprung frame if he can afford the extra cost. I have no wish to exaggerate the element of discomfort on 1911 machines. It did not deter athletic youngsters such as I then was, nor did we make a song about it. Nevertheless, it was present. On occasions when I rode 200 or 300 miles in a day, I might finish the run as stiff as a poker, and hobble like a rheumatic septuagenarian for some time after dismounting. The thigh muscles would ache, and the fingers would feel cramped.

When A. E. Catt rode his 1911 Triumph 2,400 miles in six days, he had padded both footrests and handlebar grips with heavy bandages of soft fabric. But by the end of the week his wrists and ankles were very seriously swollen. Better forks were appearing as early as 1911. But the Triumph spring fork, until the end of the 1914–1918 war, joggled to and fro on a pivot at its crown against a compression spring (or springs) fitted at its upper end. This design, of course, varied the length of the wheelbase continuously, and clashed over rough going. Compared to 1950, comfort in all its forms was at a discount in 1911.

Tolerant as we all were of belt drive in those far-off days, it was, in fact, quite a nuisance in a minor way. It frequently enforced a road stop, though it never ended a journey. In 1950, riders may often be heard clamouring for a shaft drive, and denouncing the petty infrequent nuisance of their rear chains, which may require adjustment for length perhaps once in each thousand miles, coupled with occasional cleansings and dressings. In 1911 I carried a couple of spare belt fasteners and a miniature vice with an opening to fit the V of the belt, through which a drill could be forced by a spanner. The compressed and rubbered fabric of the belt was not easy to perforate, and at regular intervals its end would tear off across the screw hole. In a six days' trial we all carried spare belts, and made many stops to alter the gear ratio given by our tool-adjusted pulleys. Imagine how critical car owners would have been, if, in like manner, every gear change had compelled a stop and the use of the tool kit!

Thus our dreams of an integral change-speed gear, such as every car and most tricars already enjoyed, carried with it a desire to bid our belts an eternal farewell, even if they were cheaper, quieter and smoother than we imagined any more rigid drive could hope to become.

At this stage the yearning for variable gears automatically became articulate. Their absence was the worst blot on the standard motor cycles of the period preceding World War I. Until their advent only sturdy and athletic youngsters were likely to remain enthusiasts for the defective machines of the period.

CHAPTER 9

A CRISIS !

A N INCREDIBLE PERIL assailed the further progress of the motor cycle around the year 1911. It was quite widely believed that the motor cycle had at last reached its zenith. We riders were mostly young and athletic. We could buy a light, speedy, durable, and utterly reliable machine from any of a dozen firms for about £50. Most of us lazily thought it would be very pleasant if we could emulate the motor car by starting from rest on a clutch and climbing the steepest main-road hills by changing gear once or twice, as the gradient might demand.

But such aspirations were neither constant nor vigorous. A majority of riders were more content with such a model as the $3\frac{1}{2}$ h.p. Triumph. Discontent and dreams characterized a mere minority, accustomed to set their machines to sterner tests, especially in mountainous country or under the added load of a sidecar and its passenger. In such usage a current motor cycle fell far short of all practical ideals.

It was not only the more sedate type of rider who suffered from such complacency. It had filtered into many factories. Earlier in the movement, almost every manufacturer had also been a rider. His road experiences rendered him more acutely conscious of any shortcomings in his mount, and his engineering brain was quicker to imagine new developments. Moreover, his bread and butter depended on his sales.

But by 1910 most motor cycles were produced in sizeable factories, the majority of which were public companies. Their directors were often stout, and even rather elderly, men, whose motoring was enjoyed on four wheels. They naturally received reports from their technical staff. But their main preoccupation possibly concerned finance. They desired their company (which included their share-holders and themselves) to register steady or increasing sales with concomitant profits. They rejoiced that their motor cycle branch, which had been definitely shaky in the past, now seemed comparatively stable and established. They hesitated to meddle with a specification which sold well and performed with reasonable credit in public tests.

Every man who has served on the board of a public company manufacturing products of which he possesses no special technical knowledge, is familiar with such a situation, and its dual threats of conservatism and complacency. There were, of course, innumerable exceptions to any such generalisation, especially among men with technical training. Nevertheless, the danger was real.

63

The counter-irritant was provided from four distinct sources, apart from any gnat-like personalities in the employ of particular companies. It is difficult to range these sources in order of value. There were many eager inventive brains among the younger engineers. On several occasions I was invited to certain board meetings in the capacity of a practical rider, to listen while some passionate inventor tried to " sell " his innovational patent to the directors.

A minority of motor cyclists steadily bombarded the factories with their ideas for improving the next season model. The motor cycle Press, in particular, educated the riding public to the still unrealized possibilities of the motor cycle.

But perhaps the most insistent of all the forms of pressure brought to bear on complacent directorates was the massed effect of a continuous series of public trials. All over the country, local clubs carried out full summer programmes of competitions in great variety. In every trial the majority of the entry naturally failed to register a perfect performance, even if the standards of the day were actually set rather low.

Of the sporting programme, three events ranked as national— the Auto Cycle Union Six Days' Trial, the Isle of Man T.T., and the Scottish Six Days' Trial. The A.C.U. Six Days' depended for its mere survival on trade support and was, therefore, unable to wield the big stick. But as far as circumstances permitted, it courageously pilloried the unsatisfactory climbing powers of current machines. The Scottish Six Days' was run by an amateur club, largely as an almighty lark. Its promoters suffered from no commercial motives or scruples, and they relentlessly exposed the weakness of existing motor cycles on the Scottish hills.

But the shrewdest blow of all was struck without any timid manufacturer having a chance to realize its inevitable result, when during the 1910–1911 winter the T.T. Races were switched from the short, comparatively flat Peel-Kirkmichael circuit to the present " long " or "mountain" course, embodying the twisty ascent of the northern shoulder of Snaefell. From that moment two alternatives were available—either the T.T. Races must be scrapped or competitors must resort to variable gears.

The mere fact that this assortment of sly methods for exposing any faults of design received hearty support from many members of factory staffs was not sufficient. Any united trade opposition could have held the motor cycle pegged down to 1910 specifications for a term of years. But this inside support reinforced the outside dissatisfaction and revolutionized the entire layout of the roadster motor cycle within ten years. Ten years seems a long time, until we recall that the ten years included four years of a desperate war for mere survival, followed by two years of equally disturbing reconstruction. The real figure, therefore, is more like four years than ten.

Revolution, when at last it came, was a co-operate effort, to which trade, Press, clubs, riders and independent engineers, all made substantial contributions.

CHAPTER 10

VARIABLE GEARS

CHAPTER 9 SUMMARIZED A MOST INTERESTING CRISIS in the history of the motor cycle which ultimately led to the installation of variable gears on all motor cycles, except those which are better described as " motor-assisted bicycles ". This revolution was delayed until about 1912 by two main facts, the desire to retain the cheap, light and smooth transmission by belt, and doubt whether air-cooled engines would wear well and keep cool if thrashed by ignorant users on low emergency gears. The transfiguration wrought by this innovation in terms of road pleasure is hard to describe in words. Let the reader ask himself how he would relish driving a car confined to a single gear ratio of about $4\frac{1}{2}$ to 1.

If twelve years had been spent in reaching a conclusion that gears were indispensable, we riders had to wait a further period before the new transmission crystallized into the dominant form of all-chain drive, including a countershaft gear box, usually with three or four ratios. (There were sub-forms on smaller machines.) But the period of delay, as I have stated, was extended by the interruption due to World War I and the industrial reconstruction which followed it.

Not until 1920 did—for example—the Triumph Company market such a drive, although several leading firms produced three-speed gears with chain-cum-belt transmission just before the war. From then onward any motor cyclist enjoyed precisely the same transmission conveniences as had long been at the disposal of any motor car owner. He could start from rest under power on his clutch, and his gear ratios provided a similar range of power and speed and climb.

The delay in developing suitable gears is the less explicable, when we recall that one or two firms, notably the Royal Enfield and Messrs. Phelon & Moore, of Cleckheaton, Yorks., developed a two-speed gear during the earliest days of the industry. By modern standards the P. & M. gear was not of any great excellence. But it was—within limits—cheap, light, simple and moderately efficient. Two short primary chains ran from twin sprockets on the engine to a countershaft located where the bottom bracket is found on a pedal cycle. This countershaft was mounted in an eccentric, by which the two primary chains could be adjusted for length. (As the wear on the two chains could never be equal, they could not both remain in perfect adjustment; but at least they never flapped enough to risk being thrown off.)

E

65

The countershaft sprockets were mounted on clutches controlled by wedge-bars, so that either could be coupled up at will. A third chain drove the rear wheel. This layout disposed of all belt troubles, and afforded excellent hill climbing. It had no serious drawbacks, though the machine was heavy, and lack of proper cushioning produced more vibration and a rougher drive than the unreliable, but smooth, belt. Why did not this shining example inspire rival makers to launch research work upon alternative forms of gearing?

The explanation is extremely complex. First and foremost, very few designers desired to switch to chain drive, which would put up weights and prices, and threatened to create vibration and to feel harsh. Secondly, the motor cycle market was incredibly precarious. At one date, perhaps 150 firms were competing for the custom of no more than 50,000 motor cyclists, if in the 150 we include small retailers who bought engines and assembled machines under their own transfers and titles. The larger firms were mostly successful builders of pedal cycles, who still regarded the motor cycle as a slightly dubious offshoot of their main business. If such a factory had built up a steady, though limited, demand for its motor cycles, it was terrified of switching to a new design which might not appeal to the public. A firm which had evolved a fairly good seller, clung obstinately to its general outline, and only ventured to make petty modifications unlikely to affect its popularity.

Also, the private owner had no experience of any more efficient motor cycle, and was inclined to regard the current model as the tops. Finally, the firms were so small that they failed to attract brilliant and imaginative engineers, who found more promising careers in the motor car sphere. This inertia was probably the main factor in the general stupor.

The Auto Cycle Union organized speed hill-climbs, as did many of the smaller clubs. These had no great effect on the gear-box question, as competitors used super-tuned engines and ultra low gear ratios. In the annual Six Days' A.C.U. trials, the selected route included gradients which no standard machine in private hands was likely to climb, even with a burly ex-cyclist hard at work on the pedals. But the time penalties were so liberal that the riders lost no marks.

I do not exaggerate when I say that in such trials we all scrapped as fast as possible from each control to the next formidable hill on the map. At its foot, we screwed down our adjustable engine pulleys to supply a gear of $6\frac{1}{2}$ to 1, packing away the belt on the carrier and substituting a spare belt ready cut to the precise length for the low ratio. At the summit of the hill, we screwed up the pulley to a touring ratio and replaced the longer belt. (If the A.C.U. had tightened the time checks to eliminate such chicanery they would have got few or no entries.) Even at that, when Summer Lodge Hill was first included in such a trial, not a single machine in the entry achieved a non-stop climb.

We of *The Motor Cycle*, together with many other idealists, tried every conceivable method of educating public opinion. Without immodesty, it may fairly be said that we played a leading part in the slow revolution which ultimately standardized change-speed gears on all roadster machines.

One glance made it clear that there were three possible locations for a gear on a motor bicycle, namely: (1) on the engine shaft; (2) on a countershaft amidships; (3) inside the rear wheel.

In the pioneer period there were serious objections to all three locations. At that time Britain possessed no engine designers. We bought our engines abroad—mostly in France or Belgium, or we copied foreign engines under licence. The crankshaft protruded from the crankcase on the drive side in the shape of a very stumpy taper, just large enough to mount a pulley. Later, the Neckarsulmer Co. of Germany (" N.S.U. ") produced a beautifully made epicyclic gear combined with an engine pulley, but it did not wear long and failed to furnish a real emergency ratio. Belt problems ultimately proved fatal to several adjustable pulley designs, e.g., the Zenith, the Rudge, and the Philipson.

For a time the rear wheel struck many inventors as the best position. This fallacy died hard, and was not wholly abandoned until after World War I. It was largely kept alive by the success of hub gears on pedal cycles. A hub gear was quite attractive so long as its weight was light. But as engine power increased, a hub gear became continuously heavier. The result was an excessively heavy rear wheel, producing appalling discomfort. I rode one such model which felt as if its back tyre was stuffed with lead.

A time came when a $3\frac{1}{2}$ h.p. (500 c.c.) roadster engine developed 15 b.h.p. or more, and such an engine demanded a substantial gear box. Gear boxes were particularly desirable on sidecars, which used engines up to a nominal 8 h.p.—possibly over 20 b.h.p. No matter what design or material was employed for such hub gears, they rapidly became impracticable, and at long last—by about 1920—the countershaft was finally identified as the only possible location for the variable gear.

It is easy to excuse the industry for dilatoriness in reaching a conclusion which now appears so obvious. The motor bicycle was the child of the pedal cycle. It was at first regarded only as a " motor-assisted " bicycle. The ideal was to retain the known and proved merits of the pedal cycle, including its light weight and low price, while relieving the driver of as much muscular effort as possible, enlarging the radius of his rides, and endowing him with a little more speed—after all, any speed over 20 m.p.h. was not only illegal, but was daily penalized in the courts.

That ideal explains the tendency to retain the mechanical outlines of the pedal cycle. There were several immensely practical factors. The centre of the bicycle frame was occupied by the " bottom bracket ", a short horizontal tubular cylinder, in which the spindle and bearings of the pedalling gear were mounted. For several years, nobody, except the Bat Company, dreamt of abolishing the pedals—they were considered essential for starting and for helping the wee engine up hills. If the centre of the lower frame was consecrated to the pedal spindle, there was little room for a a gear box. Moreover, a countershaft gear box would impose a two-step transmission. Nobody was foolish enough to think of using two short belts. True, Phelon & Moore, the Humber Co. and one or two other people, preferred an all-chain drive to the belt, but their productions were not convincing. They were deemed too heavy, and insufficiently smooth.

Manufacturers temporized by allotting a small dribble of their surplus funds to building a few motor cycles. Their expensive machine shops were laid out to manufacture pedal cycles, and their operatives were trained to build pedal cycles. They shrank from the costly and radical alterations of plant and of training their hands which must accompany any slashing departure from pedal-cycle outlines. It is not in the least surprising that they viewed variable gears with doubtful and jaundiced eyes.

In particular, the deep-rooted prejudice in favour of the cheap and silent belt drive was a powerful factor in the resistance movement. At first, we accomplished absolutely nothing, beyond inspiring the industry to produce a weird assortment of adjustable pulleys, coupled either with adjustable belt-fasteners or with some mechanical method of varying belt tension without requiring the rider to dismount and fiddle with spare belts or quaint fasteners.

Three of these devices caused a lengthy pause in the movement towards better things. One was the Zenith Gradua, which coupled a lever-controlled engine pulley adjustment with a sliding back wheel, operated by the same lever. This furnished a gear range of approximately $3\frac{1}{2}$–6 to 1. The upper ratios were quite useless except with a big twin-cylinder on flat roads. The lower ratios were certainly helpful on grades, but encouraged belt slip. (Obviously, no engine pulley could be reduced in diameter below a $6\frac{1}{2}$ to 1 ratio, at which belt-slip was chronic.) Incidentally, the Zenith engineers never developed a rear brake which could retain full efficiency in all the available settings of the rear wheel. The Rudge Multi incorporated a roughly similar notion, improved by retaining a fixed rear wheel with a sound brake and taking up the belt slack on low ratios by closing the belt groove of the rear wheel belt rim.

The Zenith acquired great renown, as its riders contrived to win nearly all the speed hill-climbs, since they could set their gear to suit the varying gradient of hills with " landings ", whereas their rivals were compelled to use one ratio all the way up. The Zenith was officially " barred " from the single-gear classes of sprint climbs, which created a false and inflated idea of the Zenith transmission. In this *impasse* my Editor encouraged me to write weekly about the urgent need of better gears, and to test every experimental gear on the world market.

I could fill every page of this book with narratives of my sufferings. My first naïve experiment was to buy a couple of the Phelon & Moore

68

three-chain gears previously described and to fit them to popular modern belt-drivers. For this purpose I selected two very fine belt-drivers. One—converted to P. & M. gear about 1905—was a Vindec Special, a composite machine produced by W. H. (" Billy ") Wells, later famous as the English agent for the American Hendee company's " Indian " machines. The Vindec embodied a common illusion of the day—that hill climbing was merely a question of engine power, whereas, in fact, climb depends on ratio rather than on h.p. The illusion was almost universal at that date. (A certain D. M. Weigel imported it into the motor-car sphere, by designing an enormous chassis equipped with a single-geared engine of umpteen cylinders and 100 h.p.)

The Vindec boasted a 5–7 h.p. vee-twin Peugeot engine, while a pair of French Truffault spring forks endowed it with a comfort unknown elsewhere at that date. With some trouble I grafted a P. & M. gear on to this machine. Thus mounted, I defeated all the professionals in two eminent hill-climbs, organized respectively by the A.C.C. and the M.C.C. As a matter of hindsight, I believe that this Vindec struck the first serious public blow at the single-geared belt-drive complex.

For two excellent reasons I perceived that this conversion had been something of a blunder. First and foremost, the riding public largely ascribed my successes to the size of my engine. " Who could help getting up with such a walloping engine? " was the pardonable reaction. Secondly, although the staunchly made Vindec withstood the stresses and vibrations of an almost rigid chain drive superbly enough, the light chains disliked the big engine more than somewhat, and critics too often caught me fiddling with the eccentric chain adjuster, not to mention inserting half-links, and so forth. Certainly, I stormed up the hills in fine style, but at the cost of incessant chain trouble. (A heavier set of chains was not obtainable.)

My second experiment was even more lugubrious. I pitched on the most popular machine of the day—the 3 h.p. Triumph, which preceded the far more famous 3½ h.p. model of that ilk, probably the first really excellent motor cycle ever built. The 3 h.p. model was not good. The king of the Triumph factory was the late M. J. Schulte, a great character, who had been passionately interested in our movement from those dreadful days when E. J. Pennington dazzled our engineers by using un-finned steel tubes for air-cooled cylinders, and got away with it by giving brief demonstrations in small fields and on short tracks, thus concealing the fact that his pistons would seize after a run of more than five minutes.

Schulte had all the cynical conservatism of a Scots engineer, joined to a sound scientific mind. He liked to make sure that every detail was right. He never changed except upon adequate cause being shown. His pedal-cycle business was remunerative and he handled motor cycles as a tentative offshoot with distant possibilities.

But he and his staff, like many engineers of the period, were

69

tolerably ignorant of metallurgy as it affected light engineering and small internal-combustion engines. His 3 h.p. belt-driver looked trim, dainty, staunch and, very definitely, " right ". But—there was always a " but " in 1906—the metals selected for its exhaust valves and piston rings were grossly unsuitable. The exhaust valve would scale within 100 miles. The piston rings required renewal after a week's hard riding. Usually in too big a hurry, I bought a 3 h.p. Triumph on its looks, and converted it to all-chain drive and P. & M. gear immediately before an A.C.U. Six Days' Trial from Land's End to John o' Groats.

No pen could describe that Odyssey. The machine was far too light and weak to stand up to the pitiless hammering of a chain drive embodying no shock absorber except a large spring washer behind one of the engine sprockets. Almost everything on the model, except the frame, surrendered during that terrible week, either falling off at short intervals or shivering into pieces. In addition, we struck some perfectly abominable engine oil—possibly salad oil tinned up by some cheap-jack. The Triumph engine, being of the side-valve type, protested vigorously by overheating on low gear in the most shameless fashion.

If engines possessed consciousness, that 3 h.p. unit must have had a terrible trip to Groats. Remember that by the end of the first 100 miles, its exhaust valve had scaled till its surface resembled a telephoto of the mountains of the moon. That simultaneously its piston rings had been chafed down to the likeness of thin wire circlips. That it was glowing like a hot coal, partly owing to the lubricant, partly to the low P. & M. climbing ratio, and partly to general anæmia. That I had no time to attend to anything, because my spokes, mudguard stays, brake rods—indeed, almost everything —were giving every imaginable kind of trouble. Even the lamp fell off, and the hooter disintegrated!

The cruellest blow of all was when the dual P. & M. engine sprocket shook itself loose, and dived into a deep, nettlesome ditch on one of the few occasions on which I was making up lost time at 45 m.p.h. (This dual sprocket was quite a corpulent morsel, and I soon retrieved it. Not so the nut which attached it to the tip of the crankshaft, nor the key which prevented it from rotating idly thereon. I ultimately found the nut. I promised a gang of roadmen a golden half sovereign if they should find the key. They failed, and I hacked a new key from the hard wood of one of their broom handles.)

All the devils in Hell must have giggled sardonically when I eventually dashed into Groats with about 20 seconds to spare, and secured a gold medal for covering the 1,000 miles without loss of marks. But no competition rider ever got such a ribbing as I did. The Triumph team included three riders on standard, belt-driven models. All three had completed the distance with ease, since the route included no really stiff climbs—Berriedale is the worst. They had enjoyed ample time to tighten nuts, clean away oil stains, dust off road films, and so forth.

My worst tormentor was Joe van Hooydonk, who had secured a gold medal on his Phœnix quad, fitted with an epicyclic hub which occasionally gave him plenty of trouble, but had been most adroitly jollied through the trial by some miracle. However, I got my own back on him, for, at the end of the trial, we were riding back to Wick for the night, when I saw his two rear wheels gradually start to fold outwards from the bottom. I laughed so much that I fell off at the spectacle of Joe seated on the road with a rear wheel lying flat on each side of him. Meanwhile, the Six Days' had done our variable-gear campaign no sort of good. But I could always chip Joe when he advertised weekly for months afterwards that his quad had come through without loss of marks!

I happened to be living at a wonderful place for trying out variable gears. My house was situated at the top of a mile-long packhorse track which included landings and plenty of 1 in 4 grade. From the base of the hill there was no rideable way back to civilization, except up the hill, which was deemed far too stiff for trial use, even by my hardy north-country neighbours. So now began a quiet campaign, based on making touch with all inventors of variable gears. I invariably invited them up for a weekend and, when they had essayed a demonstration on my private hill, they resembled the Queen of Sheba . . . there was no more spirit left in them.

I particularly remember an engineer whose name eludes my memory. He had a logical mind. He led off with, " You know, Ixion, there is no *space* aboard the standard motor cycle for an efficient gear box ". As he thought in terms of cars, this was true enough. " The belt is as dead as the dodo! " he continued. I could not agree more, even if the maxim was a trifle premature. " So . . ." and he drew my attention to the originality of his own machine.

In most respects it followed the normal layout. But amidships, at footrest height, it embodied a broad tubular platform. Across this was an immense three-speed gear box on car lines, about the size of those cylindrical cushions which at one time decorated Chesterfield settees. At its centre was a colossal leather-faced cone clutch. The primary drive from engine to countershaft was by chain. A second chain conducted the final drive to the rear wheel. It was clear at a glance that the ground clearance under the lower arc of his clutch housing did not exceed 2 inches. His rear brake was a Bowden horseshoe of pedal-cycle type.

He invited me to descend the hill on his 5 cwt monster, and guaranteed that I could make a hundred consecutive re-ascents without a qualm. Knowing the hill, and having inspected his brakes, I modestly refused. " You go down! We'll wait here and watch you. I should hate to bend anything while you are so far from home." (I think he came from Hampshire, 300 miles away.)

He slid away gaily in neutral, and I soon gathered from his agonized movements that the heavy bus had taken complete charge. Halfway down he fell over sideways. With my family I scampered down the 1 in 4 to his assistance. The clutch casing was cracked. The tubular platform had assumed a somewhat crumpled rhomboidal form. In the end I fetched a tarpaulin to cover the wreckage for the night, and in the morning a cart and two horses retrieved another idle dream.

But by this time somebody else had struck a blow for gear boxes. The Bristol firm successively known as Barter, Fairy and, finally, Douglas, had evolved a lightweight $2\frac{3}{4}$ h.p. model with a flat-twin engine, a combined chain-cum-belt drive, and a lovely little two-speed gear, based on the back gear of a lathe. It was true that the first public appearance of this historic design was an anti-climax. It created a veritable sensation, but, in its first big trial, all three machines had serious front-fork trouble. But at least it had informed the world that the design of a variably geared motor cycle was basically quite a simple affair. From that date the battle of variable gears was won, though the full fruits were not to be reaped until after the end of World War I.

This Douglas was good, but in no sense an ideal machine. The distribution of the gas charge between two widely separated inlet ports was faulty, especially when the pipe froze in bitter weather. Its metallurgy displayed faults parallel to those which handicapped the 3 h.p. Triumph. The chain-cum-belt drive was admittedly an attractive compromise to designers who funked the radical switch to all-chain drive, but it was almost as prone to trouble as the plain belt drive. In an exceptionally wet Scottish Six Days' Trial, a Douglas belt slipped far more perseveringly than any alternative belt drive in my experience, while the plug of the front cylinder was not easily protected against wet flung up from the road.

The city of Bristol, where the Douglas was made, did not at that date boast a " pool " of competent mechanics such as had long been available in Coventry, Birmingham or Wolverhampton, nor was skilled labour mobile in those days. But the infant machine contained the germs of a magnificent motor cycle and, though it has repeatedly enjoyed spells of popularity, it still remained for some vigorous directorate to make the utmost of its possibilities. Its golden moment arrived at a later Show, where the board staged a most attractive layout. They secured far more orders than the works were able to fulfil punctually.

Another shrewd blow was struck almost simultaneously by a north-country engineer. Each spring the Coventry Club was accustomed to hold a hill-climb at Newnham, outside Daventry. The hill was not especially formidable or interesting. But just as Ascot races are the great day of London dress designers, so the Newnham climb used to tempt our motor cycle designers to unveil their novelties. Everybody in the trade crowded to watch. Alfred Scott of Saltaire chose the 1908 climb for the début of his open-framed two-stroke twin-cylinder, and won three classes on the efficiency formula.

In envious company it is seldom that spite and criticism auto-

72

matically surrender to worship. Scott, in ten minutes, conquered the motor cycle world. The mere look of his epoch-making machine was sufficient. Gleaming with silver-plate and purple enamel, its sheer beauty immediately vanquished the onlookers. It made three ascents of the hill. We all felt that a new era had dawned on our world. He started the machine by a gentle depression of a short pedal—none of that ungainly run-and-jump business. He had haughtily scorned to fit pedals. The smooth, cat-like purr of the two-stroke engine put to undying shame the staccato chatter of the super-tuned four-strokes which had mustered to steal all the day's glory. Amidships, the trim little projectile housed a two-speed gear, complete with clutch, daintily operated by a single rocking pedal. Finally, the entire drive was by very light chains.

We must all eternally regret that, although this brilliant design established a genuine cult of an almost religious character and, prior to World War I, proved itself as formidable in the T.T. as it was eminent in all the softer amenities of the hobby, restricted finance has hampered Scott's successors from launching the research work which might have enabled this wonderful model to hold its own with the famous " Big Six " of today.

Just before World War II, I revelled in a most halcyon day astride a three-cylinder Scott, which purred like a Rolls, evinced the torque of a six-cylinder engine, and developed a most lofty performance. That experimental model languished whilst the factory busied itself with Admiralty work.

Would that Scott had lived! Would that some worthy successor may yet evolve all the latent possibilities of this fascinating and unique projectile!

But back to our muttons. In spite of these clear and definite leads, the industry in its wisdom elected to indulge in yet another wasteful interim. Today, as all living motor cyclists know, the industry annually produces an immense assortment of gear boxes. providing two, three or four ratios to suit every type of mount from the tiny 98 c.c. Villiers two-stroke to the Vincent 120-miler. None of them ever gives any trouble. None of them requires any frequent or arduous attention. They are sturdy, silent, reliable, easy to change—in a word, just as near perfect as any commodity designed and constructed by mortal can hope to be.

There was a period when we had a spot of bother with their clutches, which occasionally betrayed the foul habit of " dragging ", so that it was difficult to engage a gear with the machine at rest. That flaw has now been trounced, and we can dismiss this prolonged controversy on gears with real pride in its happy conclusion, even if those who passed through all its aggravating stages sometimes wonder how trained engineers could ever have committed all these recorded stupidities.

These assorted reminiscences illuminate the extremely confused notions on transmission which marked the years from 1900 to 1920. The climax, as I recorded in the last chapter, arrived secretly and almost unnoticed in 1910. Few folk guessed that a revolution had broken out when a somewhat stormy meeting decided to abandon the " short " T.T. course—a mildly undulating 15-mile lap east of Kirkmichael—in favour of the so-called " Mountain " course of 37-odd miles, involving a climb over the shoulder of Snaefell to a height of 1,400 feet. It was clear to almost everybody that a single-geared machine stood precious little chance over the new course, and there was a tremendous flurry in the factories to develop some sort of gearing before June, 1911.

The Manx week of 1911 brought a thunderclap. Various British gears, mostly of the improvised type, performed with slight credit in the Junior event, won by a new 2¾ h.p. Humber with a light multi-speed hub. But intense humiliation marked the Senior race. First second and third places fell to Indian machines, produced by the Hendee Manufacturing Co., of Springfield, Ohio. The fact that they were ridden by three Englishmen—Godfrey, Franklin and Moorhouse—was no great consolation. But their victory was a blessing in disguise. They were fitted with countershaft gear boxes, and their transmission was all-chain—with only two chains at that!

What America had done, Britain could surely do? Even then we learnt our lesson slowly.

Before war broke out in 1914, several leading firms had produced excellent three-speed countershaft gear boxes. In 1920 some of the leading factories boldly came out with three-speed countershaft gear boxes and a properly cushioned all-chain drive. Everybody wondered why so simple a design had not appeared ten years earlier.

Perhaps one strand in the answer was that earlier engines might have run red hot in private ownership, if flogged up steep hills on gear ratios as low as 12 or 15 to 1. But aircraft-engine experience during the war soon taught us how to minimize heat distortion in air-cooled engines, and a manufacturer could now trust his stupider customers with the combination of an air-cooled engine and a low gear ratio equal to climbing anything short of a vertical precipice.

The battle of variable gears was now won! It had been a long battle, with plenty of sound argument on both sides.

Its sequels are unimportant by comparison. Long before 1950, every machine larger than an autocycle included a gear box with from two to four ratios according to price, size, and power. The operative control has mostly been changed from a lever in a quadrant on the tank-side to a pedal. This enables a rider to change gear without taking either his eyes off the road ahead or a hand off the steering bar.

Trouble with gear boxes is now unknown in the roadster field. It may still crop up in racing. A T.T. Norton develops 50 b.h.p. from 500 c.c. Round the Ramsey hairpin it becomes almost station-ary, and the rider flings in the whole of his horse power in the flick of an eyelash to accelerate in bottom gear up the mountain climb. His gear box does not complain. But as late as 1949 a rival firm found that one of their gear boxes wilted under that terrible impact, the communicated heat being fierce enough to fuse the housing of a shaft bearing. Within a matter of days they had modified the gear box to face that stress comfortably.

At the moment there is no plausible talk of any radical revision of motor cycle transmissions, except that the shaft is being substituted with increasing success for the secondary chain. Casing of the rear chain has never been either easy from a mechanical standpoint, nor handsome to the eye.

The primary chain is quite a different proposition. It can readily be encased and continuously lubricated. If the shaft eventually becomes universal on roadster machines, we shall be rid of rather a finicky and dirty component. There is a similar tendency to construct the gear box in one unit with the engine, on which opinion has not yet crystallized. However these two controversial items go in years to come, we are in the happy position that we have no complaints to make of the transmissions of 1950.

CHAPTER 11

A SEAT FOR THE GIRL FRIEND?

A MOTOR BICYCLE, IN MOTION, FURNISHES RATHER SOLITARY TRAVEL. The cheapest modern remedy is a pillion seat. In the early days we had no pillion seats. Our machines had no carriers on which a seat could be mounted. Some of us bought, as accessory equipment, a stand composed of light, strip metal. It was hinged to the rear spindle, lowered to act as a stand, raised and strapped to the saddle to serve as a carrier; but it was far too weak to take even a 7-stone fairy. Moreover, the earliest motor bicycles were no sturdier than the autocycles of 1950, and wholly unfit to bear extra weight, much less to propel it. Since men are gregarious, and young men are amative, this compulsory solitude was recognized as a blot upon the new sport, and steps were soon taken to cope with it.

Believe it or not, I have owned or ridden at least fourteen distinct types of passenger-carrying motor cycle, of which only three survive today. Each deserves some separate description.

THREE-WHEEL TANDEMS

As far back as 1902, two firms, located respectively at Willesden and Altrincham, turned out a few two-seated three-wheelers, technically rated as motor cycles, though they closely approached car standards except for the lack of a fourth wheel. Known as the Century and Eagle tandems, they were imposing and costly vehicles, priced at about £150. Oddly enough, both have passed into complete oblivion, and I have not heard them mentioned for many years past; apparently not one rusty example has survived.

The weight probably approached half a ton. A huge, comfortably upholstered armchair was suspended on plated cee springs between the two front wheels. A low floor amidships carried an 8 h.p. water-cooled engine and a small fauteuil for the driver. The Century steered by wheel, the Eagle by a vertical tiller on the right-hand side which moved radially fore and aft, according as one desired to turn right or left. There were two speeds, probably attained by two separate rear chains with individual clutches. Starting was by a detachable handle, located amidships low down on the left side. The tyres were large, and the comfort was considerable for those days.

Indeed, I have often wondered why the type expired so quickly. Certainly, conversation was not too easy, as the front occupant was some distance in front of the driver and faced forward. Women disliked the vulnerability of the front seat, especially when horses reared, or droves of frightened cattle had to be faced. The three tracks produced buffeting on rough roads. These three defects proved fatal to the tricar in later years. However, when a young friend of mine bought a Century, I enjoyed many happy miles aboard it and, if my purse had been deeper, I should certainly have bought a sample of the type. They were extremely reliable for the date, hardly any trouble being experienced except with the tyres of the period and with brake linings, which apparently consisted of some leather composition, and had to be rested down any long hill to prevent the heat charring them.

TRAILERS

The first generation of motor cyclists solved their passenger problems with trailers of various types. The gear-driven motor tricycles with water-cooled engines were at first burdened with absurdly ambitious trailers. One of my friends hauled a two-seated coachbuilt trailer behind his Ariel tricycle, until he tardily realized that this total load was far too cumbrous for an engine optimistically rated at no more than 2 h.p.!

He then hurriedly switched to a " Whippet " trailer. This curiosity could best be described as a lady's pedal cycle minus its front fork and wheel. A pillar resembling the steering head of a pedal cycle was then mounted vertically above the rear axle of the motor tricycle, and the rear half of the lady's pedal bicycle mounted thereon, plus a fixed dummy handlebar.

This quaint fixture had two real merits. It provided the lightest imaginable accommodation for a girl friend—total dead weight, about 12 lb—plus an additional pair of pedals with which the lady, if muscular and kindhearted, could assist the engine uphill. But it possessed one devastating fault. Having four wheels arranged diamond fashion, having no form of springing whatsoever, and being shod with very small, hard tyres, its vibration over bad roads was reminiscent of a pneumatic drill. I do not know how many were made, but their few purchasers swiftly tried to resell at a generous discount.

The third type of trailer had already been marketed for use with pedal cycles. It consisted of a cane or wicker armchair with water-proof knee apron, slung between a pair of cycle wheels and attached by a long drawbar to the saddle pillar of the towing cycle or motor cycle. Such trailers were cheap and light. In fact, they were far too light for the comparatively high speed of a motor cycle. When the metal of the drawbar developed fatigue, it might snap without warning, as mine did.

When that happened, the trailing chair turned a back somersault with quite surprising vigour, catapulting the lady backwards on to the road. Whether she landed on her skull or on her *derrière* depended on the speed of the motor cycle at the moment of detachment. If the accident did not fracture her spine or her skull, it usually fractured the romance. Quite apart from such disasters, of which I myself was cast as the villain on two lamentable occasions, the lady seldom enjoyed her trip.

Conversation with the beloved was practically impossible. If she was decanted astern, as just described, her Prince Charming might be unaware of her predicament and ride happily on till the next hill, when the unusual vivacity of the engine under its reduced load might arouse his suspicions. During the entire ride she inhaled the partially diluted exhaust of the engine, which its prudent owner often lubricated to the smoking point. She also became smothered with dust from the back wheel in dry weather, and with mire from it in wet weather. Only a completely infatuated damsel was likely to accept a second invitation.

TANDEM MOTOR BICYCLES

The first decade of our era was inevitably a period of experiment. As we grew sensitive to the defects of other passenger devices, several firms sustained brainwaves and built astoundingly elongated motor bicycles roughly corresponding to tandem pedal cycles. On paper these looked uncommonly good. Neither the weight nor the cost was appreciably increased by the extra saddle and the slightly longer frame. Meanwhile, a second pair of legs was available for helping the model to start or to climb a steep hill. Both the Phœnix and Ormonde designers, whose tandems I rode, were confident that they had hit on something very good.

At this period, racing cyclists were using pedal cycles mounting three, four and even five heroes for pacing purposes on tracks—or was it merely from publicity motives? Anyhow, nobody could deny that the two-seated pedal cycle tandem was sound enough. I remember riding one from Oxford to London and back in a day, and playing a ferocious football match in London at the half distance. Nowadays we see young couples on holiday astride such pedal cycle tandems with a baby seated over the front wheel, and all the family luggage on a rear carrier. So I am not quite sure why the tandem motor cycle was such a flop.

I lost all my enthusiasm for it in a millionth of a second, while riding it on Westminster wood paving in November grease. Its 2-inch Clincher tyres were practically bald when brand new, possessing no more than faintly perceptible ribs resembling a single strand of knitting wool. The rear tyre suddenly surrendered all adhesion, and forty-three years later I still shudder as I recall the immense leverage of that skid. The wheelbase was, of course, longer than that of any standard pedal-cycle tandem. On reflection, we must all admit that the modern pillion-motor-bicycle is simply a close-coupled tandem. The detail design, rather than the principle, must have been at fault.

PEDAL-CYCLE COUPLERS

The next atrocity was known as " couplers ". They consisted of short rods of plated steel, embodying clips and hinges, wherewith a pedal cycle was attached, at about 12 inches distance, to either the off or near side of the motor bicycle, converting it into a four-wheeled combination for two persons. Here again we see the fetish of doubling the available leg power at a minimum cost and at a minimum weight increase. I say " fetish ", because we usually desired to take a girl with us, and one seldom dates the type of girl blessed with the sort of leg which is capable of a high b.h.p. output up a mile of single-figure gradient.

I made three tentative essays with these abominable couplers. One could never be quite certain how the four-wheel contraption would behave when its crew disembarked. It might capsize on a camber. It might collapse after the fashion of a deck chair. Occasionally it behaved oddly even when in motion. Perhaps the joints permitted too much motion, but sometimes the two cycles would lean in when the pedallers rolled from exhaustion up a hill, or they leant out for unknown reasons, and the relative actions of the two machines were quite unpredictable in any skid.

I still regard it as the most dangerous form of transport which I have ever sampled, with just two exceptions—an experimental monowheel and a crude form of primitive aircraft.

DETACHABLE QUADS

Several firms during the " tricycle " era of motor cycling (*i.e.*, its very first chapter) marketed " quadrycles ", which were, in fact, cycles, though under existing law they would rank as light cars. They were simple conversions of the tricycle, effected by removing the front wheel of the tricycle and substituting a forecarriage by means of long tubular side members running back to the rear-hub spindle, plus a couple of inclined struts from these side members to the steering head. The steering of the two front wheels, thus attached might be direct or claim a small Ackermann flavour; the link arm was bolted to the slots in the tips of the tricycle fork.

A few such quads, as, for example, the French Peugeot, were built as four-wheelers; but customers preferred the " convertible " type which facilitated bachelor rides on the tricycle whenever a small tiff was shadowing conjugal relationships.

I had plenty of fun with a Speed King detachable quad built by Dennis, of Guildford. It had the most marvellous mudguards of polished aluminium, and cost me £120! My enthusiasm for it wilted when I realized the limits of the performance to be obtained from a vehicle of this size and weight with an engine of nominally 2 h.p. (The c.c. was probably well under 350.) It had a French Dupont two-speed epicyclic gear.

Friends used to gibe at my " ten-speeded " motor cycle. Its speeds were:—

1. Top: High Dupont ratio. Crew immobile.
2. 9th speed: High Dupont ratio. Driver pedalling.
3. 8th speed: High Dupont ratio. Both pedalling.
4. 7th speed: Low Dupont ratio. Crew immobile.

5. 6th speed: Low Dupont ratio. Driver pedalling.
6. 5th speed: Low Dupont ratio. Both pedalling.
7. 4th speed: Low Dupont ratio. Driver running alongside.
8. 3rd speed: Low Dupont ratio. Both running alongside.
9. 2nd speed: Low Dupont ratio. Driver pushing; passenger walking.
10. 1st speed: Low Dupont ratio. Both pushing.

In actual fact, within about 20 miles of a start only the uppermost three speeds were normally available. The fork operating the low gear usually dropped off unostentatiously on the road, after which only the high gear remained.

In tricycle form, the machine betrayed affinities with a hydroplane. Since all the weight lay far astern, the front wheel was mostly airborne over the wavy roads of the period. Owing to the actual driving gears being naked, and sustaining rapid wear under the intrusion of road grit, it emitted a noise like a farmyard chaff-cutter and rendered conversation almost impossible. I sold it for £45, and was grateful to the poor sucker who bought it from me.

DETACHABLE FORECARS

When the tricycle perished unwept, unhonoured and unsung, its successor was the detachable forecar, fixed to any motor bicycle precisely as the forecar had been attached to the motor tricycle to form a quad. I expected that I should be swamped by damsels eager for dates as soon as my little world beheld this purchase. I was, in fact, conscious of many inviting glances as I first rode it along a west-country sea front.

Pride received its first fall that very afternoon, when, clad in a new dove-grey pin-stripe suiting, I steered it with one hand. Suddenly I became aware that men as well as girls were gesticulating and shouting. My perplexity vanished as a pungent smell assailed my nostrils, and I realized that a dottel from my pipe had dropped into my front jacket pocket, and that the flames were being fanned by the breeze into a blaze.

The second trip was equally disastrous. This particular forecar had no such long side-members as the Dennis quad. A single clamp attached the forecar to the front down tube of the diamond cycle frame. A sudden swerve to avoid an irritated dog caused this clamp to rotate on the down tube, with the result that the forecar now pointed almost at right angles towards the left, instead of right ahead. I capsized with an awesome clatter.

Nothing daunted, I made a new double clamp extending rearward to grip the saddle pillar tube as well as the front down tube. For the Easter holidays I imported my sister, carefully avoiding all mention of previous calamities. We stayed at Dawlish, of all places, in the heart of the South Devon hills. The engine was roughly comparable to a 98 c.c. Villiers two-stroke in b.h.p. output. The single-gear belt drive had a ratio of about $4\frac{1}{2}$ to 1. The outfit weighed 2 cwt, and our joint live weight was 21 stone.

Incredibly enough, we enjoyed our three weeks enormously, and what with pedalling and pushing we practically covered the county, though we had sense enough to avoid Porlock. I used to rush all hills. When I could pedal no farther, I hopped off and ran alongside. When I could run no farther, I stopped, sent Miranda ahead on foot, descended, made a fresh rush, and overtook Miranda higher up, after which we jointly pushed up the remainder of the grade. We went to Lynton, Parracombe and Clovelly.

TRICARS

By about 1903 the industry had digested all these experiments, and concluded that there was a real future for what they then described as a " tricar ". (Something which " tries " to be a car was the cynic's gibe!) In other words, a substantially built non-detachable forecar, with two or three speeds and perhaps a water-cooled engine, it was thought, might solve our passenger dreams. The notion was not new. As far back as 1898 the Humber Co. had exhibited at the Agricultural Hall Show their " Olympia " tandem, which was simply a close-coupled tricar with the engine peculiarly mounted on *an outrigger platform of steel tubes behind the back wheel.* Perhaps a modernized version of the Olympia would make good?

Nobody knows how many of these tricars were born between 1902 and 1910, for the majority were stillborn, and many were mere " one-offs ", assembled by dreamers minus the capital required for survival. The first to secure a fair market was J. van Hooydonk's Phœnix Trimo, with an epicyclic gear in the rear hub. Presently a kind of tricar rash afflicted the motor cycle industry.

One of the most interesting though short-lived tricars was the Arielette, a modernized version of the ancient French Leon Bollée of 1895. Old Bollées still appear annually in the run to Brighton. The chassis was tricar style. A single-cylinder engine lay horizontally alongside the rear wheel on the left side. The transmission was by a wide flat belt, furnishing three forward gear ratios on the fast-and-loose pulley system. Practically all the controls were conjoined in the form of a vertical column, terminating in a spade handle. The column utilized a radial motion to serve as a steering tiller, and provided a clutch action by varying the belt tension, while rotation of the spade handle at its upper end changed the gears. Unless memory deceives me, the company ultimately decided that production costs were too high to ensure commercial success.

My best experiment was a water-cooled $4\frac{1}{2}$ h.p. Riley, with a countershaft two-speed gear and chain drive. Even in those far-off days, Riley workmanship was superb. My first trip was unforgettable. The water header tank and radiators formed a tall vertical bulkhead on each side of the steering head. Dapper little mahogany boxes were bolted to a panel of this bulkhead. One box held tools, the other contained the ignition coil.

Some 40 miles out of Coventry the new engine ran rather hot, and the heat from the water tank melted the insulation of the coil. The works were closed on Saturday afternoon, but frantic 'phone calls located one of the Riley brothers, who came out on a motor bike with a new coil. Somewhere on the top of Dashwood Hill, this second coil similarly collapsed, and we slept in a ditch. On reaching home I moved the coil to a cooler position, and the tricar behaved really well for many years afterwards.

My next venture was a superb 9 h.p. Riley, with V-twin, water-cooled engine and three-speed countershaft gear box, capable of quite high speed, and a fast climber of almost any hill, including Sutton Bank. Not a little of its popularity was due to its colour scheme, copied from the Gladiator cars of the period—scarlet leather upholstery and sage-green panelling, picked out in thin black and white lines. Fully sprung at both ends, it rode most comfortably.

It was disfigured by one minor annoyance and one grievous threat; the latter only developed with mileage. The annoyance was a detachable starting handle, which was necessarily rather a tight fit on the shaft. When the engine started, the handle was prone to jamb on the shaft and revolved with it at high speed in an almost invisible blur. Too modest to criticize a famous engineer, I accepted this as part of the discipline of life.

At first, I chocked the whirling handle with the sole of my boot till it fell off. As painful weals developed on my foot, I began to use a seat cushion as a chock. It walloped the stuffing out of the cushion. I then carried a billet of wood with which to bat it off the shaft. One day in Daventry I batted it at the wrong angle. Flying through the air it struck an errand boy on the leg, and his yells rapidly assembled a large and menacing crowd. So I had to design and make an outrigger bearing and a push-off spring.

I had yet to discover the concealed threat. One day, months later, I was cruising at 45 m.p.h. when the steering suddenly seemed to go all haywire. Fight as I might, the machine asserted a deter-mination to quit the road on the right-hand side. Deterred by the sight of a deep ditch full of murky water, I fought it with all my strength, whereon it attempted to capsize on the road centre. By this time the ditch had been replaced by a bank. I surrendered and let her ram the bank. Dismounting I ruefully inspected the damage to the car and front wings, and began to seek for a reason.

This was fairly obvious, The rear tyre had burst. There was nothing to hold the rear wheel vertical under such conditions. So the fat tyre lay out of one side of the rim, forced one spring wide open, and closed up the other spring. The wheel then leant over at a sharp angle, and ruined the geometry of the steering. (If I had only known it, the Lagonda Co. were manufacturing a very similar machine, on which precautions were taken against this emergency.)

What was I to do? I had invested all my cash and credit in this homicidal monster. At this precise moment some ardent chemist invented an emerald-tinted sausage meat, which he was marketing for the filling of inner tubes. He claimed that it made punctures impossible, was more resilient than compressed air, and lasted for 50,000 miles, whilst its cost was negligible. Samples were even then undergoing an R.A.C. test of 10,000 miles on a Siddeley car. In despair I volunteered to act as official observer for a 400-mile run.

The car felt rather as if its tyres were filled with lead, but at least they remained rotund. So I had the Riley tyres charged with the green sausage meat. This proved more costly than expected, as the wheel had to be sent to the inventor's works, since only a gang of Samsons armed with 10-foot levers could coax the almost solid tube into the rim. All went well for the next 5,000 miles, except that the now rather solid suspension was apt to generate corns on my *derrière*.

One day we stopped to admire scenery and light a cigarette. " What," cooed Mabel, " is that funny green stuff on the road behind the Riley? " Icy chills rippled along my spine. Yes! the rear tyre had developed a short split, and was oozing green sausage meat along the road at a cost of about 2s 6d per furlong. So goodbye to the Riley!

When these super tricars had been on the market for three or four years, their popularity began to fade, partly for reasons suggested earlier in connection with the Century and Eagle tandems, and partly because the sidecar was now on the up and up. By 1914 they were further confronted by the embryo challenge of cheap baby cars which expanded so rapidly after the Armistice of 1918. A third factor was also involved in their decease, namely, the more sociable seating arrangement and lower prices of the sidecar outfits. The pure tricars all perished during this contest, the sole survivor being the Morgan, which, in addition to marked mechanical merit, possessed side-by-side seating, plus a hood and screen (if desired), and was also definitely cheaper than the de luxe tricars.

SIDECARS

Originally inspired by a humorous cartoon from the pencil of the late Percy Kemp, the sidecar tickled the fancy of several engineers interested in the passenger aspects of our hobby. The idea was susceptible of several diverse layouts, and some years were to pass before unanimity was reached about their respective merits. The leading types were known as the rigid, the flexible, the castor wheel, and the duplex steering. (In addition, " folding " sidecars have been sold for easy storage, whilst " banking " sidecars have attracted some followers for racing purposes.)

The rigid type ultimately came to dominate the market. At first it lay under a cloud, as the addition of an extra track and much increased weight provoked plenty of trouble with the imperfect motor cycles of the period. The resultant fractures were ascribed to the brutalities of an unsprung rear frame, and to fierce cornering. These impressions temporarily boosted the sales of the Montgomery " flexible " sidecar. Maybe I handled my Montgomery chairs rather too roughly, but sooner or later they always shifted their attachments on the bicycle frame, with lamentable effects on the steering. Moreover, they could behave oddly on steep cambers, when the chair might lean in against the bicycle, and nip my corpulent thighs most painfully.

So I next tried the Mills and Fulford castor-wheel sidecar, on which the side wheel trailed freely from a vertical pivot mounted towards the front of the sidecar chassis. I am still uncertain why this design died so young. Possibly because the rigid type proved so satisfactory, provided that its design and manufacture were sound. Certainly, the castor wheel was capable of odd manners in car parks, when the side wheel might splay itself out at a huge angle with the bicycle if the park attendant pushed the combination backwards without caution.

The fourth type of sidecar was known as " duplex steering ", the side-wheel being connected up by suitable rods to the front fork of the bicycle and moving with the front wheel. This functioned beautifully when the makers gave me a demonstration of their test model, but was a failure as applied to my own machine.

The most original version of the sidecar layout was the famous Scott " crab ". At a casual glance, this quaint vehicle looked exactly like a small car which had shed its left-hand front wheel, for its rear half displayed a cockpit, with hood and screen, worthy of any smart light car. The design was in fact brilliant. It embodied the sweet manners and potent torque of the twin-cylinder two-stroke engine. The chassis was built up from a bundle of standardized steel tubes in a few sizes which any amateur could assemble with a spanner. Thus a user in darkest Africa could carry one spare of each tube, and repair his chassis in emergency a thousand miles from civilization. Technically, the machine was just a highly specialized rigid sidecar. Unfortunately, its eccentric appearance was fatal to commercial success.

The sidecar could not, of course, hope to achieve its full stature until the standard motor bicycle of the day was genuinely competent to haul a double load up all main-road hills. Hence, its popularity was restricted until the days of all-chain drive and countershaft gear boxes with three or four speeds. Such transmissions, as already recorded, were not standardized until after the second World War.

By that date passenger motor cycles had to face stern competition from light cars. A new 7–10 h.p. two-seated car cost £175 in 1914, was priced higher during the 1919 boom, and ultimately sank far lower, a Morris 8 h.p. being at one period catalogued at £100. A sidecar outfit could, of course, be purchased for much less than £100 in the lower horse powers, while even an 8 h.p. sidecar machine was definitely cheaper than a light car. But the cars were durable,

84

and used samples in fair condition at £50 or so soon competed directly with new sidecars.

It must further be confessed that the reliability of a sidecar outfit was necessarily inferior by comparison with the same motor bicycle used for solo work, while sidecar maintenance costs were on the high side. A two-track vehicle with a heavy load and no form of rear suspension must face rough usage. All these demerits were eliminated in due course, but in the earlier days a sidecar might prove quite a tiresome and expensive possession.

Moreover, as the motor bicycle continued its development towards its 1950 perfection, the pillion seat grew annually more and more attractive. Its cost is almost negligible. It makes a minimum addition to the load. It retains the comfort of the single track. Its running costs are almost identical with those of a solo bicycle. Its sole defects are that the occupant must be ready to face weather exposure. Cheapness, comfort and simplicity are high merits. Small wonder that in 1950 it shares with the perfected sidecar and the Morgan runabout an almost exclusive mastery of the passenger world.

The sidecar has gone very far since designers squabbled about the relative merits of its four leading types. In the most searching Six Days' trials it achieves a reliability almost equalling that of the best solo machines. It has been freely raced at home and abroad. Aided by the manœuvres of acrobatic passengers, it wins races at about 80 m.p.h. Sidecar races figured in the Isle of Man T.T. programmes of 1923, 1924 and 1925. In 1925, L. Parker, on a 596 c.c. Douglas sidecar, averaged 55·22 m.p.h. for four laps.

The Sidecar T.T. was abandoned for a variety of reasons. Entries were not numerous, and the daily Press played up the acrobatic cornering in a fashion which falsely suggested that side-cars were not suited to the average citizen. Today sidecars are common sights in the holiday season conveying entire families to the seaside, maybe with two toddlers sharing the chair with mother, while a larger offspring adorns the carrier.

As a purely personal opinion, I hazard a suggestion that the sidecar will not reach its zenith until it is the rule for both the side wheel and the rear frame of the motor bicycle to be fully sprung. At this date it seems a little crude to rely solely on tyres, saddle, and sidecar-body springing and upholstery for comfort in a two-track vehicle, which may scale up to 6 cwt and carry a live load exceeding 20 stone. Nevertheless, with large modern tyres the riding is not harsh.

The decease of the tricar did not sweep into immediate oblivion certain types of three-wheeler which seat two people side by side. Many such enjoyed a brief vogue round about 1906–1910. The Morgan runabout has retained its considerable popularity through all the changes and chances of the years. If anybody wonders why, let them visit the next Earls Court Show and carefully examine a naked Morgan chassis. Scarcely will they find anywhere in the whole engineering world an article which could form so superb a text for a lecture on first principles to a class of budding engineers. It reduces the needs of its objective to the smallest possible number of essential components, perfectly marshalled and knit into a cheap, simple and utterly convincing unity.

Incidentally, it has used from its far distant birth that principle of individual front springing which the motor car world has only recently accepted as the ideal. In its long history it has fought and defeated many competitors built to more or less similar specifications. Of that long list, only the B.S.A. three-wheeler has ever sold freely in competition with it.

At the moment, the sidecar, the pillion, and the Morgan defy all challenges, and—as hinted—we may yet see even better sidecar layouts. This chapter is written in an atmosphere of currency inflation and of national insolvency. It is a great misfortune that at the present time motor bicycle prices, still further swollen by a high purchase tax, have reached unparalleled heights, and that few motor cyclists can afford the inflated price of a 1950 sidecar, plus purchase tax, on the top of their other commitments.

CHAPTER 12

THE THIRD PHASE—1907 to 1914

IN THE FIRST PHASE a few of us lost our hearts to the primitive motor cycle. In the second phase, tiffs occurred, and many of us began to wonder if what we had taken for love was only a foolish infatuation. That was the period of the first great slump in motor cycling, a slump created by the crudity of current design, and the tardiness with which the industry tackled the motor cycle's shortcomings. (The second great slump was dictated by world-wide financial depressions after the 1918 boom, and the industry could in no sense be blamed for it.) The third phase might be called reconciliation. As early as 1907 there were faint signs that the motor cycle was about to emerge from its growing pains; among these signs the new $3\frac{1}{2}$ h.p. Triumph was dominant.

I should select 1911 as the golden year. Vigorous enterprise on the part of our engineers evoked enthusiastic response from a growing public. There was tremendous activity among the clubs, which grew in number, membership and initiative. Mutterings of war darkened the background—my 1911 Christmas story in *The Motor Cycle* most unseasonably was woven around a German spy! But just recall some high spots in the year's fixture list! Eight motor cycle meets at Brooklands! Four A.C.U. " quarterly " trials to furnish a debut for new models! Two hundred and seventy-five distinct models at the autumn Olympia Show, of which four-fifths boasted some type of variable gear (even if most of these novel designs were doomed to a brief life).

Gold medals for riding from London to Edinburgh and back (800 miles) within 24 hours! American machines (Indians) 1st, 2nd and 3rd in the Senior T.T.—a straw showing which way the wind must eventually blow, for they had all-chain drive and two-speed countershaft gears! Photographs of *women* astride motor bicycles in the Press, some of them middle-aged women and most of them on open-frame machines! Glance at the Motor Cycling Club's programme for the year: April 1, opening run to Brighton; April 14–17, Easter run, a 24-hour trial—London-Land's End-London; May 13, Members' hill-climb; June 2, London-Edinburgh-London run; June 17, Inter-Club Team Trial; July 1, Hundred-mile non-stop; July 8, Members' Brooklands meeting; July 15, Fuel-consumption trial; August 5, Hill-climb and brake tests in North Devon; September 2, Members' hill-climb; September 30, Speed-judging trials; October 29, Closing run; December 26, 24-hour winter run—London to Exeter and back.

(This ambitious programme also included numerous indoor and social fixtures.)

This boom must be ascribed to a vast improvement in quality, which of course brought reliability in its train. The tricar was already on its way out, though few experts expected its immediate demise. The sidecar was on its way in.

The market was already convulsed by symptoms of the coming cyclecar boom, though the word " cyclecar " was hardly yet born, and such quaint vehicles as the G.N. and the Bedelia were usually termed " spider quads ". These flimsy machines were destined to enjoy a brief and largely artificial popularity. They survived the 1914–1918 war, when their expiring kick produced the Carden and the A.V. The G.N. contested speed climbs as late as 1928, but the arrival of cheap baby cars—the Singer, Austin, Morris, Hillman and others—sounded their ultimate doom.

Thus the period between 1907 and 1914 was certainly a time of vigour. Nevertheless, there was no unmitigated joy, either among private owners or manufacturers. One deep dissatisfaction brooded over us all . . . the lack of variable gears for conquering Britain's innumerable hills, closely coupled to the need for some form of clutch or " free engine " device to facilitate starts and to simplify traffic stops.

This period evolved many " free engine " devices. One sample caused the flanges of the engine pulley to separate sufficiently for the belt to ride on a loose ring, running on ball bearings. More effective was a separate spoking of the rear belt rim, coupled at will to the rear wheel via a multiple-disc clutch. But just imagine effecting a start from rest with such crude clutches on a single gear ratio of $4\frac{1}{2}$ to 1! A dainty hand or foot could effect a start on the level, but the belt fastener rebelled and tore away far sooner than it would have done with the " fixed " engine plus " run-and-jump " start. Already every car in the world boasted a comparatively efficient clutch (probably a large leather-faced cone) and a gear box (furnishing from two to four ratios) for starting and hill-climbing.

These seven years were the incubation period of variable gears for motor cycles. There were already plenty of them on sale. Not a single one of them was destined to survive. Such as were belt driven carried within themselves the seeds of their own dissolution, since any clumsy amateur would multiply his inevitable belt troubles through rough handling of his clutch in starts from rest and rough handling of his gear change up hills.

It is not, however, possible to blame the manufacturers for the tardiness of their conversion. Their doubts and troubles were mirrored in miniature in my personal afflictions. Prior to 1907 I, as already recorded, had taken the bull by the horns and converted, first, a 5 h.p. Vindec and, later, a 3 h.p. Triumph to the Phelon & Moore two-speed gear (a three-chain type, in which the two primary chains shared a common adjustment). The additional vibration bred by the rigid drive literally shook both machines to pieces. Every minor component either broke or fell off!

It ultimately became clear even to my innocent mind that (a) the chain drive *must* come; (b) the chain drive would impose much sturdier construction of every single component, including such items as control levers and mudguards; (c) lower gears provoked heat distortion in all existing engines, since the engine speed rose sharply just when the cooling draughts weakened—an expert might cope with this threat, but a duffer would strike serious trouble; (d) new brakes must be designed, when the belt-rim type would cease to be applicable. Therefore, for this middle period of our evolution I scrapped the chain drive. The Indian T.T. victory had, so to speak, rubbed the industry's collective nose in the mud, and chains would come as soon as the factories felt that they could guarantee all that went with a smooth, reliable chain drive, that is, shock absorbers and cushioning devices, plus a wholesale reinforcement of every item in their specifications.

Meanwhile, I wanted to keep on riding. My growing weight reduced the grades I could climb. I was sick to death of pedalling my heart out up steep hills. I was still more fed up with traffic stops. Consider any urban hill, such as Exeter High Street. This is quite a mild grade; it was paved with setts in 1907 and usually greasy with rain. The bulk of the traffic was still horse-drawn. The street was not wide. Perhaps half my innumerable ascents of that street ended in baulks. Clearly, two carts or waggons, moving in opposite directions, were liable to baulk one as often as not. It might just be possible to effect a run-and-jump restart, followed by hefty pedalling to get the engine going properly.

So I experimented energetically with every available variable gear. A majority of the existing designs were bad, though I might fail to realize this until I tried them at length. Worse still from the money angle, very few of them were suited to " conversion " jobs, that is, it was necessary to buy the machine on which they figured, possibly one of the less popular types, which I could only re-sell at a loss beyond my pocket.

The easiest conversion job was a beautifully made engine-shaft epicyclic gear, from the German N.S.U. factory. You substituted it for your standard fixed pulley, clipped a " coffee-grinder " control handle to the top tube of the frame, and, for about £5, the job was complete. I was a passionate Triumph enthusiast, but the Triumph managing director was as busy as a bee with numerous designs of his own and I was loath to blow up a valued friendship.

At that time—about 1910—the new Rudge burst upon the market, a most charming machine, of superb workmanship, at least as potent as the $3\frac{1}{2}$ h.p. Triumph, beautiful to handle, fast, light, reliable. Its managing director, the late Victor Holroyd, was purring heavily over his own variable gear, which had been built and designed within ten days for the 1911 T.T. It was a definite engineering advance on the famous Zenith Gradua, speciously and inaccurately described as an " infinitely " variable belt drive. The Rudge version had a cam-operated variable engine pulley, with a side lever control which simultaneously adjusted the belt length by means of a sliding flange to the rear belt rim. The abuse of the term " infinitely " is clear when I state that the total range of gear ratios lay between $3\frac{1}{2}$ and 7 to 1; the upper ratios of this range were obviously of little use except downhill!

Holroyd grew quite testy when, after a brief trial of my Rudge Multi, I told him that, though his Multi gear was quite useful in a T.T., it was worthless for either the English or Scottish Six Days', which would bristle with real hills. Owing to the diameter of the Rudge crankshaft, the lowest ratio possible with an engine pulley was 7 to 1, on which belt grip was always precarious, doubly so in rain. With the N.S.U. gear, a lower bottom ratio was available. I converted Holroyd, and several of his trials machines that year were fitted with it.

Preliminary tests proved delightful. Provided that the weather was fine, and the belt accurately adjusted, a Rudge-N.S.U. could climb splendidly. It was not wise to use the low ratio as a starting clutch, but the feat was possible on the flat to dainty fingers.

Little did I guess what tortures awaited me in the Scottish Six Days'! First and foremost, Holroyd insisted at the last minute on substituting his latest brain-wave—a Bowden handlebar ratchet—for the German coffee-grinder control. On the first long hill this weak fitment broke up, and for the rest of the day I held the gear in with my fingers, a contortion which rendered steering on Scottish hairpins quite a problem. Luckily, the Scots officials were great sportsmen, and mainly eager that all the lads should finish; so they let me borrow a coffee-grinder from the local Rudge agent that evening!

More agony lay in store. The casing of the N.S.U. gear displayed a tiny oil plug. I was instructed that this was intended purely for grave emergencies. Nobody told me that all the factory-converted Rudges had a special oil leak from a hollow crankshaft, which had not been drilled on my engine! So the gear seized up solid on the second day, and I reverted to a single gear and grim work with my pedals. Once more, the Scots officials were benign, and that night—together with at least one other competitor—I fitted a new gear, and bought myself a large squirt packed with superfine lubricant. Thus I scraped through for a gold medal.

For the English Six Days' my crankshaft was converted to keep the gear juicily swimming in oil, and I hoped for a clean run. Not a bit of it! The hills were numerous and frequent. My engine had hitherto submitted so meekly to lots of throttle on low gear that I remained ignorant of a factor which was giving the entire industry headaches (of which they did not complain in public). The burden of this headache was, " How will my engine keep cool on an 8 to 1 ratio? " So on the very first day, after some joyous high-speed ascents with the engine near peak revs on the 8 to 1 ratio, my piston seized up solid, as if it had been welded. I freed it by the, at that time, familiar method of pouring paraffin into the combustion chamber, and then rocking the engine gently to and fro, draining off the paraffin, and re-oiling. Another gold medal, and that cruelly maltreated engine touched 60 on the long ride home after the finish!

Most makers were now frantically experimenting with every imaginable type of gear. Coventry was always a city of spies in a pre-Show period, and more than once I was invited to arrange a visit so that I could take away some new design under cover of dark. M. J. Schulte, of the Triumph company, was thinking particularly hard. His multi-disc, free-engine clutch had been a sad disappointment. Ham-handed Triumph riders, endeavouring to start on the clutch with a single 4½ to 1 ratio, simply ripped out the belt fastener, and got stranded because the shortened belt finally refused to cover its required distance over the pulleys.

Schulte deduced that either he must scrap the cheap, quiet, silent, smooth belt (which heaven forbid!) or inject a low gear to ease the starting shock. He could not find a gear which it would be safe to entrust to his clumsier clients. For a time he was tickled pink with a two-speed epicyclic hub, operated by a slick little handlebar control. It gave no trouble, and he summoned me to make one of my nocturnal loans, remarking that perhaps he'd got something. Its defect was that it had no free-engine clutch, but it weighed next to nothing, it was cheap to make, and his testers couldn't break it up. Maybe, the free-engine clutch could be shifted to the engine shaft, and then, with a low gear giving a 50 per cent ratio drop from the 4½ to 1 pulley, the belt fastener would stay put?

It would, and it did. The gear was charming—but for one snag. "Treat it rough!" were Schulte's orders. That meant making vile changes. If handled daintily, choosing the correct speed, using throttle or even valve lifter deftly, a 50 per cent gear drop spells some kind of a jerk. If one changed gear with mild clumsiness, it felt as if something very big and heavy had hit you very hard, and, as the main blow was administered by the saddle, the sensation was not lovable.

If one went a step further, and changed from high to low at 30 m.p.h., or from low to high at 5 m.p.h., worse things happened. Any idiotic downward change might send a rider flying over the handlebar. An idiotic upward change was liable to have the reverse effect. Delightful as the gear seemed after years of gear-less miles, it was definitely unmarketable. (How I missed it, after a month's ability to paddle off effortlessly at three or four miles an hour, or to shoot up Sutton Bank with the engine screaming!)

These are just samples of the industry's tribulations during this third phase. Any new design must be absolutely foolproof, since every factory's customers included a percentage of duffers. Nobody wanted to scrap the belt. Everybody was afraid that existing engines would give serious trouble if owners revved them merrily on double-figure gears. Nobody was anxious to raise price levels, and the simplest hub gear would add at least a fiver to the cost. Headaches were numerous and constant.

Few designers were at all quick to identify the first genuine compromise on the road to the right transmission. This was, of course, the countershaft gear with a primary chain and a final belt drive. It is hard to say why engineers hesitated so long over this switch. Personally, I give them real credit for trying their hardest to retain the belt drive, on which so many attractive qualities depended —silence, smoothness, low weight, and cheap prices.

A gasp of relief was almost audible when, first, Armstrong and, a little later, Sturmey-Archer offered three-speed epicyclic hub gears, combined with multiple-disc clutches. The provision of a very low ratio for starting reduced the stress on the belt fastener— and some of the newest rubbered canvas belts were pretty tough. The hubs retained a slow-running clutch of a type already approved in the car world.

Here surely was the solution of all our troubles. No doubt, engines could gradually be modified to keep cool on lower gear ratios, and the intermediate gear of, say, 6 or 7 to 1 would not threaten such sky-high temperatures as a bottom ratio of 10, 12 or 14 to 1. Stupid owners would dislike the noisy crawl in bottom ratio, and refrain from using it except for brief spells in serious climbing emergencies. (Fond hope—they began to use it on steep hills with heavily laden sidecars, scaled their valves, seized their pistons, and what not!)

But the intrinsic troubles bothered even a skilled user. The hubs required too frequent lubrication, and the sole method was a squirt. On a 250-mile run the hub must be oiled at lunch. Further, the controls for clutch and gears were spidery, plated rods, leading to a lever and quadrant on the tank top. There was only tiny clearance inside the hub and, since the fragile control couplings shook and waggled, adjustment was swiftly lost. On a hill the rider suddenly found that his lever provided three neutrals and only one gear. Recovering the correct setting was quite a business, and that setting was usually short-lived. No sane salesman could regard so delicate and vulnerable a device as a sound marketing proposition, even though the major internal components of the hub—its gear trains and its clutch discs—proved quite durable.

So the three-speed hub disappointed everybody. The atmosphere went all dismal again. I imagine that the next temporary compromise was in fact suggested by the Douglas example. There were brains in Bristol. The Douglas had already adopted a small, light, amidships gear box as a countershaft. Mechanically, it resembled the back gear of a lathe, and was not very different from the box on which the Indians had smothered us in the 1911 T.T. It meant extra weight and higher costs, but what matter if it worked? Best of all, it made the best of both worlds, if one used a primary chain and a final belt drive. (Few people paused to reflect that these secondary belt drives were technically vile, since they involved a minimum distance between belt centres and the belt contacted a minimum arc of the countershaft pulley.)

There was quite a stampede to fit the new transmission, and a large majority thought it was pluperfect and would hold the fort till the crack of doom. I rather thought so myself, cynical though experiments with a hundred different gear designs had made me. I learnt better one drenching day in the Scottish Highlands. The universe was adrip with water that day, the grades were continuous and fierce. A sodden rubber belt on a sodden countershaft pulley (perhaps with rather a worn groove) . . . The belt just slid through the groove without rotating the back wheel at all! I knew then— what we were all slowly and reluctantly learning—that we should have to accept chains with their weight, their dirt, their noise, and their cost. I did not yet know how utterly reliable a good chain transmission could be.

Odd, you murmur, that nobody thought of the shaft, which had already practically hunted chains off every motor car. Perhaps it was odd. But it is necessary to remember that a few rash spirits had tried the shaft—Kelecom had put it on a four-cylinder F.N. long before this. Horrible tales went abroad about some shaft experiments. The shaft had seized or broken up. The machine had stopped dead. The tester had gone over the handlebar. Coroner's verdict—a fractured skull!

No, we mustn't toy with the shaft. The conclusion was pusillanimous and untrue, but as far back as 1910–1914, when frames were still very light and whippy, it was a wise temporization. Before shaft drive could succeed, frame design and construction must undergo radical revisions.

For the rest, there is not much to complain of during the 1907–1914 period, which I labelled earlier in this chapter as the " incubation " time for variable gears. Our carburation was good. Our ignition was fine (except that magnetos were mounted low, and mud jammed their cam rings, converting variable timing into fixed timing, often to a rider's grave perplexity). Tyres were far too small for real comfort, but the extra weight to be imposed by the advent of chain drive changed all that.

In six-day trials we all carried at least one spare cover, plus spare tubes—usually of the butt-ended variety. Being small, tyres were insufficiently corrugated to minimize skids on greasy roads. Brakes were only fair. The front rim-shoe type had been fortified, but since the shoes were pivoted, and the parts were small, petty trouble with nuts and pull-off springs could still be tiresome. The rear brake—a shoe working inside or outside the rear belt rim, and pedal operated—was fairly powerful, though the " inside " type was apt to jam occasionally, when it naturally provoked a gigantic skid. The metal-asbestos shoe for internal-expanding brakes was still in the womb of the future.

These defects did not worry us so much as a reader might imagine.

After the first flush of excitement induced by the birth of the motor cycle in the 1900–1903 period had cooled off, many of us fell victims to qualms about its future. The 1907–1914 period had opened in a spirit of hope. We might be compared to children at the approach of Christmas, or to brides opening great piles of wedding presents. What we had, was better than anything we had previously sampled, and we always knew that design was alert and vigorous—tomorrow was going to be far, far better. The revolution which a usable free-engine clutch or a promising variable gear wrought in our whole outlook was incredible.

Lest the reader should assume from such recollections that these frequent changes and new purchases cost a fortune, I had better explain that aspect. Motor cycles were still cheap. On an expanding market, depreciations at resale were quite small—one could generally sell the model for a figure very near its original list cost, and the probable buyer was some eager lad up the next street.

Journalists were treated by manufacturers as " in the trade ", and were able to buy their new machines at a discount; indeed, it was sometimes difficult to prevent a maker from presenting a machine, or at least lending it to one for a whole season. Such offers had to be courteously refused, lest they should affect one's honest judgment, and make it difficult to be frank in print about the failings of an inferior design.

CHAPTER 13

THE FOURTH PHASE—1918 to 1920

WAR IS AT BEST A LUNATIC BUSINESS. Its immediate aftermath is even crazier than the battle-grip. Civilization has to be rebuilt not at the slow pace of its original creation, the slow march of millennia by patient peoples, but at a hard gallop by men whose natural impatience is sharpened by the interminable frustrations of war. The tumult and the shouting die. The captains and the kings depart. Men and women, embittered by years of deprivation, clamour angrily—no longer for those bygone amenities which war destroyed, but for a brave, new world by tomorrow about this time.

Nobody knows the new value of money. A greedy world demands supplies of raw materials, of which the stockpiles were long since exhausted. Pleasure is the general objective after the years of fear and pain. Chaos, inflation and disillusion are the natural outcome. There are two certainties. Anybody with desirable commodities for sale can ask his own price. As soon as some pale shadow of production can be launched, a boom must follow. As soon as eager pockets are empty, anxiety about security will be born, and all the world will want to work. Dreading the flooding of markets by alien imports and the slow draining away of diminished national wealth, a barbed-wire entanglement of tariffs and currency restrictions will spring up. A slump will follow.

Such was the atmosphere in January, 1919, when the motor cycle industry girt up its loins to resume the pursuit of those ideals which had shone just outside its reach in 1914.

The purely technical outlook was mightily encouraging. For all its grim horrors, modern war can claim certain meagre assets in the field of science. In our own sphere the mechanical aspects of twentieth century war had focused agonized attention upon the petrol engine. It was fortunate for the motor cycle that a special emphasis concerned the air-cooled engine, since aircraft required engines of a maximum power-to-weight ratio, coupled with invulnerability to bullets—water-jackets are both heavy and vulnerable.

For the first time in our history overheating, which is actually " heat distortion ", had become a primal study. The 250 h.p. Bentley rotary engine was air-cooled. The 400 h.p. A.B.C. Dragonfly radial engine was air-cooled. . . . 40,000 of the latter were scheduled for the fighter 'planes of 1919. Motor cycle manufacturers would only have themselves to blame if their post-war motor cycles resented plenty of throttle on low gears—gears as low as 15 to 1. Huge plants stood empty and idle, whilst their frantic directors hunted for peaceful operations. The national supply of competent mechanics and fitters had been enormously swollen. Idle capital was chasing new investments. All this was encouraging.

But other aspects were sinister. Customers might wave cheque books, but the demilitarization of an enormous industry proceeds at a snail's pace. The brains of the designers had been busy elsewhere for four exhausting years. The development of a new model is a slow business. When America entered the war, she had no aircraft engine. After a series of blunders, she commandeered the best brains of her entire motor industry, locked them in committee and bade them organize the immediate production of a single 350 h.p. aircraft engine against the clock. They evolved the famous Liberty engine in record time, and paid heavily for their prideful haste, since in its original form it was just a bag of trouble.

Similarly, a new motor cycle engine should be slept upon for weeks. At long last, drawings are completed, castings ordered, and two or three experimental samples are hand-made at fantastic cost. (All the time the factory is waiting, and the income remains steady at nil.) These tool-room samples are tested against the brake, on the road, amid the mountains. The teething troubles are identified and cured.

Only then can the material be ordered, the working drawings manifolded, the jigs designed, the machine tools readied. A year is never too long. In the interim the costly factory must be kept going somehow, the hands must be collected from the Services as released, paid, kept contented . . . it is all a costly, irritable, nerve-wracking business. Moreover, nobody can even dimly guess what the price of the product will ultimately be—price is an affair of narrow margins in the design of a motor cycle, and is determinative in its sales.

This frantic ordeal, inevitably conducted in slow tempo, was to result in the loss of many millions of pounds. A huge firm like Sopwith, with all its experience, with its immense and superb staff, resolved to devote one group of its quondam aircraft factories to the production of a popular motor bicycle—the 400 c.c. A.B.C. They accepted orders by the thousand. The motor cycle world raved about the design. The delays inseparable alike from design and production dragged on and on. The costs mounted. Finally, the figure for the machine was set at £160. In the meantime many applicants had grown sick of waiting, and bought elsewhere—perhaps, some semi-decrepit pre-war wreck. Others shied at the price, and cancelled their orders. The allotted capital had all been spent. The evolved model was not yet wholly roadworthy. The directors decided to cut their losses and cease production.

This was not the only type of tragedy, paralleled in almost every industrial field. Certain other firms rushed the job, staged their new design quickly with a fanfare of trumpets, sold a few, and perished because the few were bad. More commonly the industry, by and large, began to pay the penalty of its pre-war organization.

96

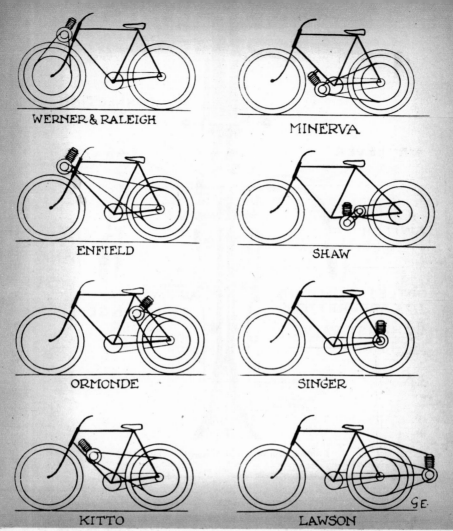

WERNER & RALEIGH

MINERVA

ENFIELD

SHAW

ORMONDE

SINGER

KITTO

LAWSON

G.E.

Where should the engine be placed? These diagrams show how unsettled were manufacturers'
ideas regarding engine position in 1900 to 1901

A 1¾ h.p. Beeston motor cycle manufactured in 1897. It was fitted with electric ignition
and tried out against other Beestons with hot-tube ignition in order to test the comparative merits of the two systems

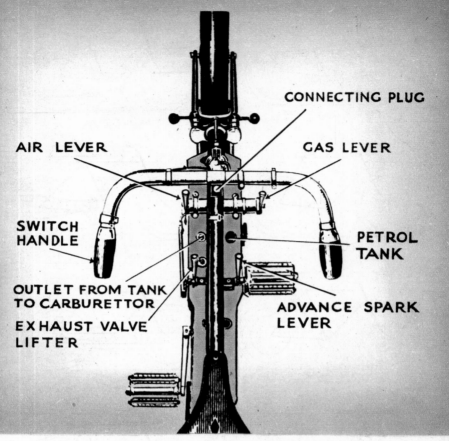

AIR LEVER

CONNECTING PLUG

GAS LEVER

SWITCH
HANDLE

PETROL
TANK

OUTLET FROM TANK
TO CARBURETTOR

ADVANCE SPARK
LEVER

EXHAUST VALVE
LIFTER

Control plan of a typical motor cycle of 1902

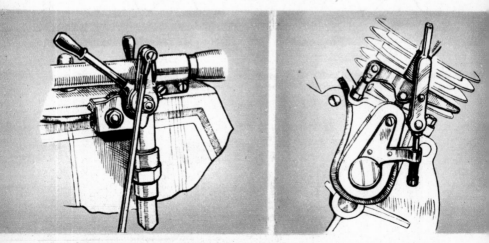

The Quadrant single-lever control of 1902 showing how the throttle lever was
inter-connected with the exhaust valve lifter and contact breaker

The 398 c.c. flat-twin A.B.C. of 1920 with leaf rear-springing, internal expanding brakes and unit-construction of engine and gear box. This advanced design probably provoked more discussion than any other motor cycle ever built

A neat Douglas of 1921 fitted with a 348 c.c. side-valve flat-twin engine

Although brimful of original ideas, especially regarding the triangulated chassis, the Scott Sociable never became popular. Its passenger comfort was exceptional for the size of the vehicle

Matchless "Silver Hawk" introduced for 1931. The narrow-angle vee four-cylinder engine was of 593 c.c. capacity, with overhead camshaft driven by shaft and bevel gearing

Wooler of 1922 equipped with a 345 c.c. flat-twin engine and plunger-type front and rear springing. It was nicknamed the "flying banana"

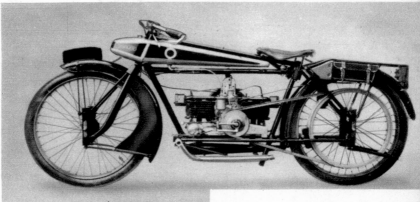

No sidecar machine ever had a greater reputation than the A.J.S. twin. This 1920 model had an 800 c.c. side-valve engine and interchangeable wheels

The classic two-speed Scott Squirrel compared with the 1930 Flying Squirrel T.T. replica which is fitted with a tank of more orthodox pattern

(Below) Remarkable steering qualities and efficient weather guarding were the outstanding features of the Ner-a-Car. This 1923 model is fitted with a 285 c.c. two-stroke engine

(Below) An engine that created great interest in 1920—the 309 c.c., three-cylinder Redrup radial. A machine fitted with this engine was tested by a member of "The Motor Cycle" staff in that year

During the first world war, petrol became as scarce as it was after the 1939-45 conflict and coal gas was to a small extent used in its place for both cars and motor cycles. The photograph shows the cumbersome gas bag towed by a Scott sidecar in 1917

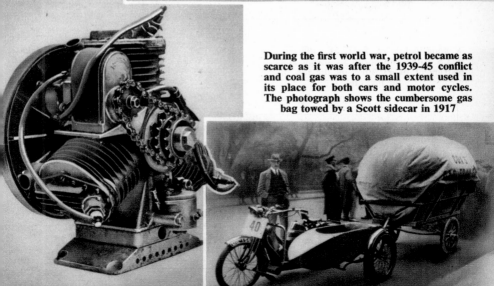

Straightforward in design, the 8 h.p. twin
Matchless was in its day a first favourite
among sidecar motor cycles. The machine
shown is a 1922 model

A newcomer in 1929, the narrow-angle (26
degrees) vee-twin side-valve "Silver Arrow"
Matchless of 400 c.c. capacity. Both cylinders were cast together in one rigid block
with cooling fins common to both barrels

A good-looker of 1931, the 498 c.c.
A.J.S. with a two-port o.h.v. engine and
instrument panel fitted on the top of
the fuel tank

A popular fast touring machine of 1924, the 499 c.c. four-valve Ricardo model Triumph

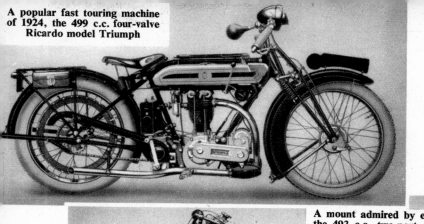

A mount admired by enthusiasts, the 493 c.c. two-port 1931 Sunbeam. Primary chain was enclosed in the famous "Little Oil Bath"

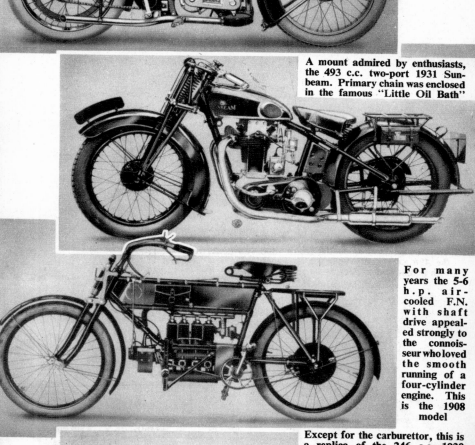

For many years the 5-6 h.p. air-cooled F.N. with shaft drive appealed strongly to the connoisseur who loved the smooth running of a four-cylinder engine. This is the 1908 model

Except for the carburettor, this is a replica of the 246 c.c. 1930 Excelsior on which the late S. A. Crabtree won the Grand Prix of Europe

One of the attractions of the 1928 Show at Olympia—the 985 c.c.,
all-enclosed A.J.W. The water-cooled engine and gear unit was
carried in a steel "chassis" with tubular cross-members; an
unorthodox method of steering was employed

Another all-enclosed model which made its début in 1928,
the 496 c.c. Ascot Pullin. Unit construction was adopted
with double-helical gearing for the primary drive. The brakes
were operated hydraulically

Two characteristic mounts of 1931. (Left) Norton with 490 cc. o.h.v. two-port
engine. (Right) The 348 c.c. two-port KTP Velocette with coil ignition

The 1912 Olympia Show had staged no fewer than 275 different models. That was the swansong of a conception of industry in which every workman was a craftsman. In simpler trades each operative had perhaps single-handed produced complete commodities—a shoe, a teapot, a jacket. On that basis, individualism was universal, and—as far as it went—efficient.

But long before the war, Henry Ford had preached the new gospel of mass production. No workman under that creed performed more than a single operation on a commodity. Repeating it a myriad times per day, he learnt to perform it at extreme speed and perfectly. It had been the boast of the Studebaker Co. before the war that not one of their fitters possessed more than a single spanner. The fitter who assembled a Studebaker front wheel to the chassis never touched a back wheel, and so forth. The war had extended this system with modifications through many British engineering works. So when the industry at last got into its stride again, the small firms found themselves unable to compete with the larger concerns, who had reorganized on flow-production lines.

For the small firms produced a tiny output by comparison, and a high percentage of the overhead charges—rent, light, heat, interest on capital, advertising and the rest—was debited against each machine in the slow, small output. Their costs were too high. Some of them switched to other industries while a little of their money still remained. Others were taken over by the big factories. Some just went bankrupt. The days when men were to speak of the motor cycle industry in terms of the " Big Six " were approaching at a gallop.

Actually, the motor cycle does not lend itself so readily to mass-production as the motor car, for the simple reason that it is too small for a squad of four men to work upon it simultaneously. Even by 1950 its assembly methods were to look clumsy by comparison with, for example, the Standard conveyor lines at Coventry, whence Ferguson tractors emerge, so to speak, in the winking of an eye.

But the 1920 methods were incredibly more efficient than the 1914 methods, with the result that, when inflation died down, Britain produced by the thousand motor cycles infinitely superior to any of her pre-war types, and that at far lower cost, in spite of the fact that specifications by then included full chain drive, three-speed countershaft gear boxes and, very soon, full electrical equipment. In sober fact, that is a feat which no other British industry surpassed, and only a very select few even equalled.

Nevertheless, the dice were loaded heavily against the motor cycle industry in 1920. It was administered with as much vigour and intelligence as is common to man—indeed, with more than that. For a brief season it reaped its deserved reward. But the massed engineering industries of the world were operating with astounding energy on similar lines, if no country could quite parallel the feat of our motor cycle industry.

It is obvious that increased output required larger markets to absorb that output. There were, of course, even in the first post-war decade, plenty of men all over the world eager to buy British motor cycles. But a majority of them resided in countries with an adverse trade balance. Such nations cannot afford to import luxuries. In fact, few of them could afford to purchase the necessities of life for more than a comparatively low standard of living. Tariff walls were hastily constructed. We ourselves erected a $33\frac{1}{3}$ per cent tariff against the import of American cars into our islands. Currency restrictions were stringently imposed.

One fact is worth a million words. One friend of mine, spell-bound by the demand for motor cycles, rented a small factory and devoted his small capital to building a charming little two-stroke motor bicycle of excellent design and high quality. He started production before the chancellors of all the small nations realized they were heading for bankruptcy. I met him at Olympia on the opening day. He was beaming with pride and joy. He feverishly showed me order after order—in particular, an order for a hundred machines for immediate delivery to a single buyer in a small European country. We met again a week later. He was in the depths of despair. The chancellor of that country had refused an import licence!

That was the general atmosphere in which the industry laboured from 1919 onward. In 1929 came the world depression which momentarily reduced even the United States to beggary. There were long periods in which Britain contained 2,000,000 unemployed; periods when that figure threatened to exceed 3,000,000. The pound was devalued.

Against this background the industry registered its main triumphs —at the cost of the failure of many of its lesser firms. That depression had not lifted when the threats of the Fascist and Nazi dictators were superimposed, and our path led remorselessly to Munich— and a second world war. History must dwell on these economic and political menaces before justice can be rendered to the solid and brilliant achievements of our industry.

Another factor, indirectly due to war, was to exert wide and deep influence upon motor cycling between 1919 and 1939, with a pressure which increased as the years passed. The pioneer motor cyclists had been recruited principally from three classes: The trade, and especially cycle dealers, and their close associates; the *petit bourgeois*—youngish people, of moderate income, yet not ranking as " gentry "; and a type of whom the undergraduate with good private means is a fair representative. The University motor cycle clubs soon became very strong. Boys at the expensive public schools yearned to own motor cycles.

Between 1919 and 1939 the latter class became impoverished, and inclined to transfer its allegiance to small cars, so that motor cycling broadly tended to become a " class " pastime. (That process was most strongly marked in the United States, where cheap mass-produced cars proved far more attractive to young married people and to courting couples than any motor cycle.) In 1914 a baby car cost upward of £160, was expensive to run, and not remarkably reliable. In the 1919–1939 period the price of a new baby car dropped considerably—a Morris 8 h.p. was at one time listed at £100, while used baby cars in good condition became available in quantity at prices from £50 upward.

Since the motor car had simultaneously abolished the chaperon, and procured far greater freedom for marriageable girls, young folk in the more monied classes began to think in terms of four wheels rather than two wheels. Solo motor cycles lost some of their grip on the young male. The three-wheeled passenger machines lost a percentage of their market.

As this trend stiffened, the typical motor cyclist could only be briefly defined as a " prosperous artisan ". Such a definition was by no means wholly accurate, and certainly far from exhaustive, but it is as near a two-word rating as our language provides. From that definition flows a conclusion that in the periods when the number of unemployed exceeded 2,000,000, the motor cycle market became definitely emaciated. On the other hand, since this period produced a marked " re-distribution of wealth ", the number of well-to-do families able to provide a motor vehicle for their adolescent children during the later stages of a long education shrank steadily. Simultaneously, provided the nation was prosperous, the percentage of " prosperous artisans " increased proportionately.

After the second World War this condition underwent a certain modification, since the type of citizen who bought a new or second-hand baby car in 1929 could now not always afford it, especially when meagre petrol rations limited the mileage. Such people began to return to the motor cycle fold, and perhaps bought a 50 c.c. " motor-assisted bicycle ", an autocycle, or a 150 c.c. LE Velocette. This applied the brake on the tendency for motor cycling to become the monopoly of a single class. All these variations exercised an effect on the industry as subtle as it was steady and important.

From 1919 onward, motor cycling entered a completely new phase. For the first time any standard roadster could be trusted to carry its rider anywhere, thanks to the adoption of weatherproof transmissions and gear boxes. The subjoined table indicates the extent of this revolution by contrasting the 1913 Show with its 1920 successor; the figures indicate the number of each type:—

Type	1913	1920
Belt drive	80	10
Chain-cum-belt	24	61
All-chain	49	85
Shaft	2	3
Hub gear	56	0
2 speed (countershaft) ..	54	54
3 speed (countershaft) ..	27	56
Spring frame	3	15

The belt was extinct except on lightweights. Combined chain-

and-belt drive was dying out. All-chain drive, with a three-speed countershaft gear, had conquered the transmission battle by sheer logic during the meditations of the gap caused by war. Cost alone obstructed the general adoption of rear springing, a feature destined to recur in 1950—after all, what car designer would dream of using a chassis devoid of rear springs? By the end of the year, electric lighting with some form of dynamo was gaining ground. Lubrication continued to rely chiefly on the hand pump with a sight-feed drip.

These revolutions in design created an utterly new atmosphere among riders. For us, 1919 was an *annus mirabilis*. We knew that tomorrow would produce even better mounts, but the current types were thoroughly satisfactory . . . cheap, fast, dependable, fine climbers, durable. If in 1920 we were to buy a new machine for 1921, the change would be pure extravagance. From henceforth a man could buy a motor bicycle in the same spirit as he bought a sewing machine or a wheelbarrow—" for keeps ". The connoisseur and the spendthrift continued to switch mounts annually just for the fun of it. But, from now on, thousands of " utility " owners bought a model and ran it for ten years, twenty years; a few even kept them running right through World War II.

Our sensations corresponded to this atmosphere. In the eighteen months following the Armistice I retained a pre-war A.B.C. (500 c.c.) and a pre-war Levis two-stroke. I made short buys of a Scott; a sports model Norton (single gear, belt drive); a Royal Enfield; and a Triumph. I carried out Press tests on perhaps twenty other models, especially on new Douglas types. When I went out, I faced the risk of tyre and lamp trouble. Otherwise, I anticipated a non-stop, no matter how hilly the route, and I usually got it. (The Levis and the Norton could not, of course, climb precipices.)

However, even the enthusiast had his troubles in quite a different sphere. The worst headache was selection, with 203 different models in *The Motor Cycle* Buyers' Guide for 1920 and more coming on the market weekly. The second headache was price. In March, 1920, most list prices were " provisional ", and might steeple before one got delivery; for example, the 3½ h.p. Ariel was " provisionally " catalogued at £105. One consequence of this inflation was a perfect flood of lightweights, many engined by Villiers and employing the new Villiers flywheel magneto. These were fiercely challenged by fleets of rather horrid little scooters, of which a single factory laid down machinery for a 40,000 output.

Sidecars boomed, with so many war brides newly reunited to soldier-husbands, and gratuities scorching the latter's pockets. The sidecars had to repel a spirited challenge from the new " spider-quads ", " cyclecars " and " monocars ". But the shrewder heads in the industry never took either the scooter or the cyclecar at all seriously, though hosts of simple-minded buyers burnt their fingers.

Labour troubles were both frequent and acute, and materials were still as scarce as they were expensive. Nevertheless, in 1920,

100

the factories contrived to enter 61 machines for the T.T., and to put large teams in the major trials. The Scott won the manufacturers' team prize in the A.C.U. Six Days' Trial, in which—*mirabile dictu*—really steep hills were included and *observed*—no penalty for footing, but a five-mark debit for every stop. This stringency was a shade premature, as the " chamois " type of rider has as yet hardly been developed, and by-roads were vile past description. Mortimer Batten wrote that the course and weather had reduced some of the weaker riders to a state bordering on " hysterical collapse ", whereon the officials relented a little, converted Park Rash into a " bonus " hill, pretended not to " observe " Summer Lodge, and sent the trial *round* Rosedale Abbey instead of *up* it!

One shudders to imagine what such a 1950 chamois as B. H. M. Viney would of think such pusillanimity; but real rough-riders hardly existed in 1920.

Mournful memories are stirred by one photograph. In August, Geoffrey Smith captained a mixed team of amateurs and trade riders against a similar Dutch team. The two teams were photographed massed on the Rhine Bridge at Arnhem, which was to run with British blood in 1944.

To sum up, a new era of joy-riding opened in this Fourth Phase of our movement. Happy, carefree travel was now available not merely to an athletic owner prepared to train himself as a semi-mechanic, but to the plain John Citizen, largely ignorant alike of electricity and of engines. Except in the brain of the engineer, it seemed that any further modifications or inventions could only rank as " frills ". The story of the Fifth Phase will indicate that the machines of 1920 were not quite so good as that.

CHAPTER 14

THE FIFTH PHASE—1920 to 1930

1920 WAS A YEAR IN WHICH COMPLACENCY was the real enemy. We surveyed long ranks of British motor cycles gleaming on their dais at Olympia. We saw them contemptuously scorching up our most atrocious hills. We watched them lapping the T.T. course at 55 m.p.h. Foreign competition was by no means formidable. Riders felt as if, after many vicissitudes, we had attained finality. If the industry had yielded ever so mildly to pride, stagnation might have tightened its frozen grip on all progress. Fortunately, designers are men of science and, as such, are characteristically humble. They are profoundly aware that the area of knowledge which they have mapped is a microscopic islet in a vast ocean of ignorance. In the midst of their 1920 triumphs, engineers were acutely conscious of unfulfilled tasks.

They hoped that labour would acquire wisdom and permit sustained economic production. They trusted that financiers would puncture inflation and stabilize currencies. They hoped that exaggerated nationalism would cease to construct arbitrary barriers against the flow of commerce. Whether other specialists toiled efficiently or not, the motor cycle engineer shouldered his personal responsibilities.

Prices must be heavily slashed if the small man was to enjoy such pleasures of private motoring as cars bestowed upon his wealthier brothers. Speed had run ahead of steering—a nasty phenomenon known as " speed wobble " had to be diagnosed and cured. Brake power was inadequate for modern speeds and modern congestions; moreover, brakes wilted too quickly under hard use. It was time for the motor cycle to be electrified—the age of gas lamps and squawk horns was dead in the car world, but dying too slowly for two-wheelers. Any car designer who adopted a spring-less rear axle would be hurried into the asylum, but not one motor cycle in 10,000 possessed any form of rear springing, apart from the cushioning effects of a fat tyre and a large saddle.

Certain items of air-cooled engines—notably, the cylinder bore, the valve faces, and the piston rings—wore far too fast, confronting the owner with the choice between costly renewals and rattles plus inefficiency. Like their brother scientists who laboured to popularize radio, they faced acute problems of space and price. Economists prophesied that a world-wide depression must follow the post-war boom and that it might last for years. Maybe, nothing but novel and more economical methods of production would enable the motor cycle to survive at all. As yet, they knew nothing of the dole and the Means Test, which were to blacken the imminent decades.

Behind such financial and technical questions lurked two petty posers which swelled their toil. Many optimists were loudly heralding the almost immediate triumph of two tolerably novel versions of the motor cycle—the cyclecar and the scooter. Every factory wondered whether to exploit or deride these innovations. The scooter had two specious assets. First, it need not cost more than half the price of a standard roadster. Secondly, it was being enthusiastically taken up by the " nobs "—a surprise new market, for, with the exception of a royal prince and a royal duke, hardly anybody of lofty social standing had ever condescended to enjoy motor cycling.

The writer, as a humble journalist, was set to solve these same two problems. He solved them practically. He seized every chance to handle the newcomers, and swiftly concluded that scooters were absurdities, and that the cyclecar, the spider quad and the monocar stood small chance of survival in competition with the baby car of full motor car specification. I rode countless scooters. I drove perhaps thirty cyclecars. Only the evergreen Morgan, which was once libelled by the label of " cyclecar ", survived its test with flying colours.

One more problem of a less obvious character clamoured for solution. Hitherto, practically all four-stroke motor cycles had been lubricated on the " total-loss " method. A charge of lubricant was pumped into the crankcase, distributed mainly by flywheel splash, and anon reinforced by another pumpful on a mileage reckoning. Already most cars carried a gallon or two of oil in a sump which was circulated to each engine component according to its need, filtered, returned to the sump, and used over again. The simple motor cycle method had two grave defects. The supply was dependent on the memory of the rider, who might be stupid; and it bore no automatic ratio to temperature, to distance, or to load. Whatever oil was present in the crankcase was always extremely hot.

Granville Bradshaw had expatiated on the ability of oil to absorb surplus heat from hot metal by sinking the cylinder barrels of his engines deep into a large crankcase plentifully supplied with oil. A simpler method was available—the " dry sump ", employing two pumps: a scavenge pump, which swiftly sucked out the used oil and wafted it to a cold tank astern, and a feed pump, which continuously supplied filtered oil in graded quantities to every bearing according to its requirements. By this system any desired gallonage could be forced through the engine per minute or per hour. Such a reform could not only assist cooling, but would also retard the wear of heavily stressed parts, and metallurgy could complete the ideal durability.

Make no mistake: in 1920 the average private owner considered his brand-new motor cycle to be already perfect. If he could have seen, in imagination, the Olympia Show of 1930, he would have been both thrilled and disillusioned. The difference between the amateur and the engineer was that the engineer was already thinking of 1930.

Came a long period in which the engineer cherished an ever-deepening grudge against the economist, who allowed currencies to oscillate and markets to swell and dwindle so bewilderingly; against the politician, who utterly failed to make mankind behave sensibly; and against labour, who—often with genuine justification—regarded force as the one hope of ensuring equitable division of the profits of industry.

Surveying these three professions with genial and indulgent irritation, the engineer toiled away at his purely technical job with such small liberty as the salesman could grant him. In the middle of this decade, his liberty was narrow indeed. Factories were compelled to produce a monstrous regiment of rather crude light-weights, because only a small percentage of the British motor cyclists could any longer afford new roadster machines.

Indeed, at one period *The Motor Cycle* was compelled to feature articles under such titles, " Why Not Buy a Used Machine? ", aware that too few of its devotees could afford new prices, even when some firms offered fantastic value. (In February of 1930 the Triumph Co. contrived to market a 173 c.c. single-cylinder two-stroke, with two-speed countershaft gear, flywheel lighting, all-chain drive, and a weight of 165 lb, for £24 17s 6d! Rival firms were reduced to similar expedients.)

The trouble was that " prosperity was always just round the corner ". Few folk thought that bad days had come to stay. The sermons of production engineers, who inculcated the gospel of flow-producing a single model, could never be obeyed. Customer A demanded " all the works " with an open cheque book. Customer B, so retailers reported, was keeping his 1927 machine, or had bought some second-hand model, or was inquiring about a 250 c.c. model at £30. That was why the 1930 *Buyers' Guide* revealed that, on an average, every factory was listing 5·33 different models covered by a price range of £20 to £160! In such trading conditions the production engineer was a voice crying in the wilderness.

I shudder to recall what a weird variety of models I owned or tested during this decade. Some are better forgotten, others I can no longer recall in detail, and a few were supremely excellent. Some sixty were the scooters and the cyclecars. Others included the Harper Runabout (a £75 old man's tricycle); several Scotts; a whole fleet of Douglases and Triumphs; Royal Enfields; Dunelt two-strokes; two four-cylinders de luxe (Matchless and Ariel); A.J.S.—both large and small; several Brough Superiors; Villiers-engined machines in variety; and a host of others on brief loan. Be it plainly stated that none of these had any major faults whatsoever.

Towards the end of this critical and arduous decade, a select handful of shrewd judges began to preach yet another new gospel. It is impossible to exaggerate the popular emphasis laid upon *speed* in this period. The Senior T.T.-winning speed climbed from 51·79 (by Sunbeam in 1920) to 74·24 m.p.h. (by Rudge in 1930). Le Vack, J. S. Wright, Eric Fernihough and Ernst Henne periodically risked their necks to raise the world's fastest speed by a motor cycle. Whenever somebody added a fraction of a mile an hour to a world's record, another lad jumped in and added a fresh fraction, until the struggle smelt like a racket in the public nostrils, as if each rider had deliberately refrained from adding more than decimals to the figure so that he could earn fresh laurels presently.

J. S. Wright had the excruciating temerity to cover a flying half-mile within the narrow confines of Brooklands track at no less than 135 m.p.h. By November, 1930, Wright was the temporary holder of the world record at 150·736 m.p.h. G. E. Nott (Rudge) raised the hour record to just over 106 miles on Montlhéry track in the same year.

The B.M.C.R.C. celebrated its twenty-first anniversary in 1930, and had the audacity to organize a 200 *mile race for sidecars*! (The entry, mercifully, was small. Only the three placed men finished in the three classes, 350 c.c., 600 c.c., and 1,000 c.c.; and one unfortunate was killed.) Cinder racing had a terrible year, partly owing to continuously bad weather, partly to mushroom, makeshift tracks, and partly to miserably poor management. The A.C.U. stepped in with a firm hand, and revived a sport which, although it seemed doomed for the moment, had contrived to commandeer at least a weekly page of *The Motor Cycle*.

The previous paragraphs may serve to indicate a genuine risk, liable to produce crops of road fatalities. So alarming did the emphasis on speed become towards the end of the decade that *The Motor Cycle* made a premature attempt to guide popular taste in more rational directions by offering £500 for prizes in tests designed to foster an " Everyman " motor bicycle. Assisted by rather a small body of enlightened opinion, it pointed out that many sensible folk of both sexes found all the requisite speed in pure roadster models, which were still grievously deficient in aspects precious to John Citizen. Five of these were nominated, namely: (1) easy starting (or, in slang, " tickle " starting); (2) accessibility; (3) ease of cleaning after a dirty run; (4) personal comfort; (5) silence.

The sympathetic A.C.U. responded by announcing a special trial of " Everyman " models. This was never held, since an entry of 25 would not defray the promoters' expenses. But the appeal had issue in mild and sporadic forms. New Hudson produced a machine which was " totally enclosed " as high as its engine's waistline. Matchless and Ariel marketed four-cylinder engines. Ariel and New Imperial introduced triple silencers. But not until the LE Velocette was introduced 18 years later did a genuine Everyman model actually appear on the market. Not for the first time *The Motor Cycle* had forged ahead of public opinion.

105

At home this decade may be fairly summed up as a period in which the British motor cycle industry was possibly the most successful of all our technical and commercial endeavours. Other industries might claim that since the 1918 Armistice they had improved the quality of their products out of recognition, and simultaneously kept their prices low. But in this period the motor cycle industry had transfigured its goods in terms of quality, and had widely reduced its prices below pre-war levels.

Internationally, the comparison was equally startling. During this decade American machines had lost ground, simply because of the crushing competition of ultra-cheap cars. Their output had dwindled, their design had stagnated. Many factories had closed. Almost alone, the Indian and the Harley-Davidson were fighting an unequal battle against cars which were cheap to run, cheap to buy new, and ridiculously cheap when re-sold as " used ".

On the continent of Europe the aftermath of war imposed even heavier handicaps than in Britain. Devastated nations contained only a small percentage of citizens who could afford to buy motor cars. That pressure created a new emphasis on the cheaper two- and three-wheelers. But the prices of even these simple vehicles were too high for most pockets. In this dilemma Continental manufacturers adopted a two-pronged policy. They frankly copied the best British roadster motor cycles for sale to such customers as could afford such mounts. Not only were leading designs unblushingly imitated, but British components were freely duplicated —our engines, gear boxes, layouts, control wires, etc.

Towards the end of the decade originality had freer play, and national genius began to find scope, particularly in Germany and Italy. At lower financial levels the impoverished citizen was tempted by incredible numbers of motor-assisted bicycles, turned out by the thousand or even by tens of thousands. These handy little vehicles gave their owners the freedom of the road for purposes of pleasure, and also rendered him or her mobile from an industrial viewpoint. Governments on the Continent realized this asset, and liberated the lightweights from all tax and insurance handicaps.

Presently little clouds, no larger than a man's hand, indicated that Germany and Italy were about to challenge Britain's speed supremacy, which had almost become monotonous. Early in the decade, British machines and riders acquired almost a habit of winning the 250 c.c., 350 c.c., and 500 c.c. classes at every European road-race meeting, though we never took the lightweight (250 c.c.) events quite so seriously.

This invincibility was not to last for ever. For example, in 1927 Arcangeli, on a Guzzi, ran 2nd in the 250 c.c. T.T. In 1929 Pietro Ghersi, also on a Guzzi, headed the field for the first five laps— out of seven—and was unlucky not to last out the race and so score the first foreign victory on Manx soil since 1911! Our traditional supremacy was imperilled at long last.

Meanwhile, on the Continent, our lads were having grim fights to retain their laurels. The B.M.W. Co., of Munich, had evolved a thoroughly original design of outstanding merit. It used a horizontally opposed twin-cylinder engine, mounted well forward in the frame and athwart it, a location which conferred a low centre of gravity. The machine was cleaner in outline than any British rival. The final drive was by a propeller shaft. Maybe, the layout was not wholly perfect for a popular motor bicycle, since the engine was vulnerable in heavy slides or tumbles, and the design was definitely costly. But it was at least as good as any British contemporary —some honest folk thought the model produced in the late 1930's superior to our best.

Henne, in record attempts, handled it like a fiend out of hell, and repeatedly broke the world's fastest two-wheel speed record on it. We regained it time and again, but the irrepressible German promptly brought his blown B.M.W. out once more and beat our previous best. In the 1929 International Six Days' Trial the final test consisted of an hour's sprint round a short lap at Cointrin aerodrome, designed to probe the finishing condition of all machines which had survived a gruelling 1,000 miles of Alpine road. Two minor scions of the B.M.W. factory utilized the chance to set up higher averages than any of the British competitors. In the phrase of Fougasse, we had been warned!

During the next decade we were to realize that, though both Germany and Italy might still lag behind us in the general quality of roadster machines, both of them had become very formidable in the sphere of sustained speed.

Speed at such high levels as a 75 m.p.h. average round the Isle of Man T.T. circuit, or 100 odd miles in the hour on Brooklands track, or a flying kilometre at Arpajon or along a German *autobahn* is a matter of sport, of publicity, and of prestige. Its importance is easily exaggerated. But such feats admit of deductions. If a nation's engineers consider pre-eminence in such fields worth lavish expenditure of brains and money, and they are nevertheless outstripped, the inference is that the victor disposes of better brains. It is foolish to belittle them, however silly it seems to enclose a man in a streamlined egg and convert him into the likeness of a military projectile. We did not submit to Henne and his B.M.W. at all meekly. We never had any very solid excuse for the repeated lickings which he administered, though it is true that we had no strip of road or track in our islands which permitted us to try out our projectiles on our own soil.

In minor aspects, there were definite happenings during the 1920–1930 decade. The cyclecar followed the scooter into deep oblivion, which had long since absorbed the tricars. That concentrated essence of genius, the Morgan, retained an almost solitary sway in the sphere of three-wheelers. The sole really popular survivor of the three-wheelers, Morgan only except, was the sidecar, which continued to appear in great number and variety, since the ugliness of another brilliant design, the Scott crab, outraged popular taste.

Engineers still raised mild eyebrows at the survival of the lop-sided sidecar outfit, but they accepted the popular verdict and strove to make the best of it, notably by providing solid frame attachments for it. In fact, it could claim definite merits. It was a two-track vehicle and, therefore, more comfortable on inferior roads than any three-tracker. It was very light. It was extraordinarily manœuvrable—possibly more so than any car or bicycle. It was detachable, and so formed two mounts in one; the owner could switch to two wheels in a very few minutes. It was well sprung. It was practically immune from skids. And it was sociable —the wife sat at her husband's ear, and baby found her lap cosy. It is not likely that any other version of the passenger motor cycle can ever oust it.

Simultaneously, a cheaper and lighter method of accommodating a companion came into its own—the pillion seat. Insurance companies are not fond of the pillion seat. But in all soberness it is entirely safe in sensible hands, and modern versions are extremely comfortable. Its use converts a solo motor bicycle into an efficient passenger mount with only a few pounds increase of the " dead " load. During this decade it leapt into popularity in great variety, with its cheapness and simplicity as its main assets.

The worst that can be said against it is that if a fool at the helm takes wild risks, he is liable to injure or kill two people instead of one, and even at that the pillion occupant stands an excellent chance of being flung clear. If anybody is prejudiced against it by unhappy experience with a pedal-cycle tandem, let him realize that it retains the short wheelbase of the solo model (which spells easy steering and freedom from skids), while the " live " load is far more concentrated than on the more widely spaced seating of a tandem.

In sum, the story of the 1920–1930 decade is one of great technical triumphs against a sinister economical and political backdrop.

Little has been said of personal riding experiences during this decade. My silence is easily explained. This chapter has been written on a typewriter purchased twenty-five years ago. During that period it has displayed no faults which irritated me into an impatient wait for an improved machine. It has never given a mite of trouble. It functions so perfectly that one forgets it is a complicated machine. All it demands is an occasional clean, a spot of oil, a periodic change of ribbon. Its behaviour by no means reminds one of the motor cycle of 1920, which could on occasions be extremely tiresome and expensive, though infinitely less so than the motor cycle of 1910.

But by 1930 a good motor cycle had ripened into almost the automatism of a typewriter. Any serious failure came as an absolute shock. We filled their tanks. We cleaned them. Occasionally we were delayed ten minutes on the road by a puncture. Every 3,000

108

miles or so we removed carbon deposits from the engine. Chains and brakes required a simple adjustment every so often. *But there were no mechanical road incidents to be recorded in the log.*

Naturally, each long trip had its special features. But these were not dictated by the machine. Maybe, we had a brush with the police. We encountered fogs or floods. We had an amusing scrap over lonely roads with some chance-met stranger. At journey's end the motor cycle was not the topic of conversation with host or wife. Its faithful service was now axiomatic, and therefore—human nature being ungrateful—it passed unmentioned as often as not. If I take the Flying Scot to Edinburgh, I do not report to my Scots host that its engine achieved a speed of 80 m.p.h. near Grantham, or that it covered its 400 miles without a breakdown.

December, 1931, did not find the motor cycle perfect. But it found it so good that only imaginative users still pined for something better.

CHAPTER 15

THE SIXTH PHASE—1930 to 1950

THE TWENTY YEARS SUMMARIZED IN THIS CHAPTER view the motor cycle against an appalling background of industrial problems and of a war which cannot reasonably be confined within the six years which it occupies in the history books. Most wars are more or less imminent for several years before the first shot is fired, and their aftermath convulses humanity for many a year after the guns have returned into store. From such angles this period hampered the natural development of the motor cycle in a myriad ways.

Nevertheless, from the purely technical angle, war accelerates most engineering and scientific developments, for modern war is basically mechanical. When a nation is fighting for survival, it ceases to grudge expenditure on research. Hence the period 1930–1950 begins with nine years spent under a progressive menace, which cramped technical progress, followed by six years during which effort was focused on other aspects of engineering science. The two years immediately following VE Day were necessarily devoted to the transition from war to peace. But the last three years of the period were destined to prove quite amazingly fruitful, even in the teeth of marked financial inflation and under the gravest threat of national bankruptcy which Britain has ever faced.

A strong critical school was audible in the field of motor cycle design in the year 1930. We had long since triumphed over all our early difficulties. The current motor cycles were cheap, speedy, reliable, fast climbers, reasonably comfortable, demonstrably superior to those of any other nation. Their fundamental durability was not generally realized, since enthusiasts seldom " rode a machine to destruction ", but scraped and pinched to buy some new model long before their existing possession was worn out. Yet this durability emerged into the limelight, when production of new machines for civilian use ceased in 1939 at the outbreak of war.

To the general surprise, the private owner discovered during the war that his pre-war machine—whether it was a 1939 or even a 1929 production—continued to function with very little attention until post-war models became available in 1947 or thereabout. This very great merit—the result of sound design, good materials, and fine workmanship—had not previously received the praise which undoubtedly was its due. Indeed, 1950 found many riders of the quiet " utility " type still happily using models ten, fifteen and even twenty years old!

The strictures of the 1930 critics were independent of all these

110

specified virtues. They were based on an indictment that the dominant type of 1930 motor cycle paid overmuch deference to racing. That broad accusation was true, and is best interpreted by comparing the roadster motor cycle of the era with a motor car of similar date.

A few high points of this comparison may be set out here. The car was silent; the motor cycle was noisy. The engine of the car started at the touch of a button. The motor cycle engine demanded vigorous acrobatics of rather an awkward and ungraceful kind before it would start. The motor car was not only softly upholstered, but doubly sprung fore and aft. The motor cycle had rather a hard saddle, a front fork which was inclined to bounce, and an unsprung rear frame, which was prone to " hammer ". The motor car protected its occupants from every type of unpleasant weather.

The motor cycle lacked every possible kind of weather protection, and the rider was compelled to choose between adding leg-shields, windscreen and handlebar muffs in winter, or submitting his person to the filth of the road and the fury of the elements under such protection as special clothing could provide. The motor car engine was designed to tick over in neutral like a sewing machine, both at its owner's door and outside an office or shop. The motor cycle engine suffered from wretched manners when the machine was stationary, running unevenly at the best, with a tendency to stop.

The entire mechanism of the motor car was encased in metal covered with very durable enamel and plating, both of which could be hosed down quickly at prolonged and irregular intervals, during which patent wax polish protected the expensive finish from serious harm. The mechanism of a motor cycle was designed to withstand weather without technical injury, but could not safely be hosed down and, owing to the incredible irregularities of its surface, was more than awkward to clean. Though its superficial area was ridiculously small compared with that of a car, a thorough cleansing was a tedious and back-aching business. It was further asserted by the critics that though the motor cycle, being a simpler entity, was in a major sense more durable than any car, yet it was apt to suffer from more niggling and petty troubles than a car, and to demand more " tinkering " from its owner. In some of the motor cycles vibration was excessive.

These critics consequently waved a banner of reform. Their ideal pictured a motor cycle of tomorrow which should be a " tickle-starter ", boast a sewing machine tick-over, possess a modicum of intrinsic weather protection for the rider, be as silent as might be consistent with safety, have an engine devoid of a vibration " period ", be fully sprung aft as well as fore, and have its mechanism so far enclosed that it could be hosed down after a dirty run in car fashion.

This was certainly an ambitious dream. But reference to a later page in this chapter will prove that the ideal was capable of translation into terms of metal, even if the first real embodiment of the 1930 specification did not burst upon our vision till the autumn of 1948, when the LE Velocette graced the Earls Court Show.

However, much earlier in this period two considerable advances were made. The cult of the multi-cylinder engine grew by leaps and bounds. The Triumph machines, which on two previous occasions had blazed new and valuable paths, appeared with the so-called " vertical " or " parallel " type of twin-cylinder engine. Concurrently, rear-sprung frames, which were no novelty, came to be regarded as " musts " in at least two spheres. The racing men wanted them, for what was the use of extorting 50 b.h.p. from an engine if the back wheel was airborne for a large percentage of a race? The tourist wanted them for the sake of sheer comfort. It is unfortunate that their additional cost still limits them—with a few noble exceptions—to the more highly priced types. The additional cost of a spring frame varies from £5 on a lightweight to £25 on a full roadster.

The assimilation of a multi-cylinder engine to the narrow limits of a motor cycle frame is not child's-play. No successful motor car of today is content with fewer than four cylinders.

Altogether at various dates some forty engines of the four-cylinder type have appeared on motor cycles, from Colonel Holden's premature freak of 1897 to the Italian racers of today. Early designs in this class were unreliable, and so lengthy that they required a wheelbase too long for easy steering. Sounder designs such as the 1930 Matchless did not sell in sufficient quantities to encourage their makers.

The pre-war Squariel was indeed the first of a long and ancient line to score a real commercial success. Its engine consists, basically, of two units forming a square block, each unit having a separate crankshaft, with coupling gears to join them. Vee twin-cylinders are awkward to house, by no means free from a vibration period, and apt to suffer from differential cooling under hard work. So the Triumph designer adopted the vertical twin: first, because it fits glibly into the standard frame; secondly, because both cylinders enjoy the same cooling; thirdly, because it is cheap. It is also true that it really effects very little more than the substitution of two small single-cylinder units for one large single-cylinder unit. But the substitution unquestionably goes some distance towards providing a smoother engine with a less obtrusive exhaust.

The best of the two-cylinder layouts is unquestionably the " flat " or horizontally opposed twin, famous on the long line of Douglas models, creating a great sensation on the 1919 A.B.C., world-renowned on the German B.M.W., and scoring lesser success on several other makes. But it is an uncommonly awkward engine to house in a motor cycle frame, especially in the larger capacities. The LE Velocette showed in 1948 how comfortably it can be applied in the 150 c.c. size, but most motor cyclists want a larger engine, and in a 350 c.c. or 500 c.c. pattern its accommodation is a headache for the designer.

Nevertheless, the Triumph innovation with the parallel-vertical twin in the years immediately preceding World War II sounded the knell of single-cylinders for full-size roadsters with aspirations to quality. The first post-war Show indicated that the other leading factories were following suit. The Sunbeam Co. varied the prescription by twisting their engine round in the frame with one cylinder in advance of the other. They achieved this without any sacrifice of efficient cooling. In fact, in every respect they made their new power unit approximate with great fidelity to car types, even using a shaft as its final transmission element. Incidentally, the cost was not small.

Almost alone among the world's manufacturers, the Douglas Co. remained loyal to the flat twin, though they stopped short of adopting it in the 500 c.c. size, restricting their engines to 350 c.c. In any short survey of this period, the conclusion is that the critics of 1930 inspired a heavy stampede into the multi-cylinder field, led by the parallel-vertical Triumph, accompanied later by the post-war Sunbeam, B.S.A., A.J.S., Royal Enfield, Norton, Matchless and Velocette. With the new multi-cylinder engines came a host of rear suspensions, though owing to universal poverty and the high cost of fully sprung frames the second innovation was mainly limited to the de luxe class. The LE Velocette alone contrived to incorporate every single item of the dream " Everyman " specifications of 1930—shaft drive, lever starting, vibrationless 2-cylinder engine, rear springing, car silence, car tick-over, and a prospect of 20,000 miles without mechanical attentions or replacements.

Of course, 80 owners out of every 100 prefer engines of at least 350 c.c. Very few people buy machines with engines of 250 c.c. or less except for financial reasons. The exceptions to this generalization are mostly elderly men, women, or pedal cyclists in a slightly timid transition stage.

So far as the purely technical aspects are concerned, the roadster machines of 1939 ranked as practically perfect with the athletic, hard-riding type of owner. He uttered no complaints anent the exertion of kickstarting or the occasional discomforts of inferior forks or rigid rear frames. Roads were so good that large tyres conferred a reasonable degree of comfort. Brakes were both durable and effective. Automatic lubrication, comparable with that of car specifications, was universal. Engines employing side valves had detachable heads, which simplified decarbonization. The exterior of most machines had " smoothed up " considerably, so that cleaning was easier.

The chief outstanding question was whether an " Everyman " design could attract into the hobby countless thousands of potential customers for whom a rorty 70 m.p.h., 3 cwt model of 500 c.c. possessed no vestige of charm. Not all the folk who had abandoned the pedal cycle as they grew older and lazier, could afford cars. Lightweights of that period were not on a par with the roadsters in terms of quality and long life.

Moreover, in the field of speed our accustomed invincibility was more than threatened. We had long ceased to attach much value to speed in the lightweight classes, where the German D.K.W. two-stroke and the Italian Guzzi were now our masters, not to mention the Benelli.

More sinister was the contemptuously easy victory of the German 500 c.c. B.M.W. in the 1939 Isle of Man T.T.—a win scored on our pet ground. In a sense it was meaningless, because the rules permitted the use of superchargers, which have almost the effect of transferring a 500 c.c. engine into the 1,000 c.c. class. The Germans availed themselves of the opportunity offered by the rules, while our own designers rested content with unblown engines. True, the previous year Daniell on an unblown Norton had put up a faster lap than either of the blown German machines, but none in the 1939 race could worry them.

We were also warned in the 1939 Ulster that the Italian Gilera— then a supercharged 4-cylinder type—had the legs of us. Frith was streaking along all out on his Norton, when Serafini rode his Gilera alongside, grinned happily, and shot ahead to leave Frith helpless. Moreover, the 500 c.c. Guzzis were plainly threatening to outspeed our fastest 500s, though they had yet to acquire Norton reliability. Of our famous speed models, only the 350 c.c. Velocette still retained a firm grip of its class. Thus we felt far less comfortable in the field of sheer speed than in the roadster atmosphere. The B.M.W. held the world's fastest land speed record, and no British manufacturer was inclined to face the high cost of assaulting its figure (174 m.p.h.).

If speed was one of our 1939 headaches, cost was another. Ever since the 1919 boom had dissolved into the worst slump which ever hit this nation, unemployment and lack of spending power had hampered our virile industry. The question " How cheap? " had loomed at least as large in our councils as " How good? " The eve of each annual Show found manufacturers lying awake at night, wondering whether their principal rivals were about to unveil a cheaper popular model than their own. It was no time for lavish expenditure, or for luxury designs. The export trade was hard hit by currency regulations, by tariff walls, and by trade depressions in customer countries.

Even at home a high percentage of motor cycling enthusiasts were buying secondhand machines, and the more monied riders were keeping their machines for several years, instead of blithely trading them off each winter in part exchange for the new-season models. Cost was paramount. Meanwhile, Hitler's sinister shadow brooded over us, and the Government was increasing heavy taxation in the interests of national defence.

Then came the war. Every factory switched to military production. The output of motor cycles for civilian purposes was cut off almost as by the fall of an axe. Over 400,000 motor cycles were manufactured for Service use, but their design was simple, and designers had no leisure for post-war dreams.

114

The return of peace followed precedent, bringing insistent demand, gross financial inflation, high costs and a quite unparalleled system of governmental controls. When the engineering industries had been reorganized, only a very nominal percentage of the motor cycle output was allotted for home consumption. During this artificial and transient stage two features deserve special attention.

The first was primarily financial. We owed a formidable total of dollars to the U.S.A. In addition, they alone could supply many vital commodities, which must be paid for in dollars. Simultaneously the motor famine in the United States was as widespread as our own and starved thrice our population of its accustomed personal transport. Here was a chance to export British motor cycles into a market which had long been fenced by steep tariffs. Our industry rose nobly to the opportunity. For many years past. cheap cars had strangled motor cycle production in the States, Only two of their original motor cycle factories retained any importance—Indian and Harley-Davidson. They had crystallized a heavy clumsy design with huge and rather woolly vee-twin engines. The smaller and lighter British models proved entrancing novelties to American enthusiasts, and sold with remarkable freedom. But since America owns a vast mileage of superb highways and worships the goddess of speed, we had to concentrate on speed, to compete in their speed events, and to win them.

The second feature of real importance in this hectic chapter was the general adoption of a new type of front fork. The British pioneer in this field was the so-called " Teledraulic " fork introduced by Associated Motor Cycles, Ltd., on its Matchless and A.J.S. models. This telescopic fork, with hydraulic damping, owed something to the original Scott machine and something to the pre-war B.M.W. It unquestionably ruled out the minor inequalities of good roads in the most magical fashion. In the old days of girder forks and rigid rear frames a Senior T.T. winner sometimes finished his 260-odd miles in a state of semi-collapse. With a " tele " fork and rear springing he was fit enough to dance that same evening!

A third evolution rapidly followed the opening of the American market. Almost immediately they discovered that a similar speed craze possessed at least the more juvenile sections of the home market. Brooklands track had been lost for ever. The road circuit at Donington was still in obstinate War Office hands. But small tracks were leaping up like autumn mushrooms all over Britain . . . grass tracks, aerodrome circuits, and small, hard-road laps in private ownership.

In 1939 only two firms—Norton and Velocette—had raced on the grand scale. Both marketed a few high-speed models for private owners. But the new situation shrieked for expansion on these lines. The Triumph Co. decided to assemble five hundred " Grand Prix " machines of 500 c.c. for public sale, each ranking very near the qualifications for T.T. victory. Associated Motor Cycles, Ltd., worked hard on the development of a 500 c.c. twin-cylinder as a

" works " model, and simultaneously marketed a 350 c.c. machine (the 7R) which in delivery tune was almost capable of winning a Junior T.T. in competent hands.

Germany was temporarily out of the racing hunt, as the Control Commission limited her to 250 c.c. machines. But Italy was quite amazingly busy and effective in this sphere. In 1949 her new four-cylinder (unblown) Gilera was probably the fastest 500 c.c. on earth over a fairly straight course with not too many corners, while her 500 c.c. Guzzi was a possible winner anywhere, if still a little short of high-speed reliability. In the 250 c.c. class the Guzzi and the Benelli could honestly defy the world.

So 1949 produced the wildest outburst of motor cycle racing that history had ever known. Britain, despite her handicaps, acquitted herself magnificently. F. L. Frith, on a 350 c.c. Velocette, became world champion in his class. R. L. Graham, with his A.J.S. 2-cylinder 500 c.c., secured similar eminence in the bigger class. Eric Oliver (Norton-Watsonian) gained the world championship in the sidecar class. Tommy Price, of Wembley, won the world speedway championship, never previously held by a Briton. The 998 c.c. Vincent acquired a most enviable reputation in a field which has never been largely exploited by racing men. Only in the lightweight classes did we yield an easy precedence to foreign machines.

So much for the speed classes. In the medium-weight roadster field we remained supreme and, as yet, invincible. In a sense, this victory was cheap. France has not yet recovered sufficiently to be genuinely formidable. Italy is too poor and, for the moment at any rate, is concentrating with amazing success on lightweights and motor-assisted bicycles, which she produces in gigantic quantities and high quality.

Our conventional roadster models are better than ever, and the " tele " type of fork had endowed them with a degree of comfort and with roadholding qualities previously unknown. At the moment home sales are increasingly dominated by cost. We have quite forgotten that in happier days a very worthy Matchless 500 c.c. roadster was once catalogued at no more than £35. Today as the result of inflation, high wages and purchase tax, a good roadster may cost over £200. The Scott, which once sold at £45 in a simpler form, is listed at £250. A standard 998 c.c. Vincent is priced at £323, being a connoisseur's de luxe design. The demobilized soldier had spent his gratuity by the end of 1949, and large continuous markets at such price levels seem impossible in the teeth of our near-bankruptcy.

The lightweight market for folk content with normal traffic speeds is similarly expensive. A 125 c.c. machine, such as the B.S.A. Bantam, costs, with tax, £80. The 149 c.c. LE Velocette, the wildly acclaimed leader in the all but virgin " Everyman " field, is catalogued at just over £148, inclusive of tax.

In facing these price levels, the student must realize that tax absorbs more than a fifth of the figure; that few factories are producing at their real economic level, owing to shortages of materials, and possibly also of labour; and that shrewd managements are perhaps also recovering a portion of the cost of re-tooling after the war. The price levels are not necessarily permanent, though lately the prices of raw materials have increased sharply.

Furthermore, there has been the greatest redistribution of wealth in our history. The artisan classes receive higher *nominal* wages than ever before, together with a government promise of continuous " full employment " for all. Every economist is familiar with the distinction between *nominal* wages and *real* wages. If the nominal rise can be made to cover increased purchasing power within the ensuing decade, the ranks of motor cyclists in Great Britain will receive a vast influx. At present they number approximately 700,000. Should that total rise to 1,400,000 by 1960, the influx will exert an enormous effect on the industry. In January, 1950, the wage rise was more apparent than real, and labour as a class considered its high nominal wages to be in fact inadequate

Since the higher income classes were mostly impoverished, the home sales of motor cycles threatened to fall. This threat produced a wide and novel interest in lightweight motor cycles. There were, in the second half of 1949, definite signs of a minor boom not only in 250 c.c. and 125 c.c. roadster machines, and in 98 c.c. autocycles, but in those ultra-cheap " motor-assisted bicycles " which had sold by the 10,000 on the Continent during the Hitler and Musso-lini regimes, and which have also been manufactured on an enormous scale in post-war Italy.

The name of such designs on the Continent is legion, and their specifications vary over a wide range. Some of them are beginning to sell in Britain. A normal type employs a tiny engine of 25–50 c.c. capacity, driving either the front or the back wheel via a small friction wheel with a carborundum facing. Their petrol consump-tion may exceed 200 miles per gallon, a valuable consideration when dollars and petrol are both scarce. Their working life is as yet a question mark. Their average speed on give-and-take roads only exceeds pedalling rates by a very few miles per hour, while their climbing ability is obviously limited. On the other hand, they relieve a cyclist's muscles and, thereby, extend his range of travel.

All such considerations tend to convert the motor cycle industry into a hydra-headed monster. At one extreme it turns out a £323 120 m.p.h. machine like the 998 c.c. Vincent. Then there are the racing machines of 350 and 500 c.c. capable of maintaining an 80–95 m.p.h. average over severe circuits. Next below rank the standard roadster machines, weighing 3 cwt or thereabouts, capable of 60–80 m.p.h., with tomorrow's price levels an unsettled question. Lower down we find the roadster lightweights of 125–250 c.c., becoming popular on British roads. Still farther down the scale stand the 98 c.c. autocycles, which might be described as glorified editions of the motor-assisted bicycles, ranging in price in 1950 from £57–£70, inclusive of tax. At the bottom are the simplest

117

motor-assisted bicycles; engine units for fitting to bicycles are available for about £20.

Behind and apart stands the " Everyman " class, at present represented only by the LE Velocette, which is probably assured a very definite future, though the precise extent of its appeal may only be clarified when its cost is pared free of tax and of the effects of an inflation which may or may not be punctured rapidly. At the moment no man knows what will happen in this free-for-all battle for survival.

The claims advanced in this volume for modern design have long since been completely true of all the more expensive models. They apply in good measure to the 125 and 250 c.c. classes. Price considerations will debar many of the later improvements from the autocycle and the motor-assisted bicycle, both of which are modern throw-backs to the pioneer designs of 1900, though subject to a host of minor technical advances. Like the pioneer models, they retain pedalling gear, and require muscular assistance up our steeper hills. At the moment no machine below the 125 c.c. gear-box types can claim satisfactory climbing power, though the two-speed version of the 98 c.c. type climbs fairly well.

The answer to the many questions raised by this survey of current design can only be sought in the political and economic fields. It has little direct connection with the desires of the buying public or the objectives of the manufacturer. Britain will in any case be forced to tailor her garments in proportion to the available cloth, and at the dawn of 1951 she finds herself most uncommonly short of cloth!

Meanwhile, those of us who are familiar with the knowledge, skill and determination of this fine industry are confident that it will continue to produce the best available versions of such models as can construct a market in the new world which is now slowly emerging from the mists of war.

During this period—apart from the rigours of war—most of us savoured all the dear pleasures of the road in complete mechanical serenity. I can recall but one serious breakdown—unique of its kind in my long experience—a " diss ", or complete break, in the winding of a magneto armature somewhere in Kent, miles from garage or railway.

An innocent breakdown caused me gross discomfort and perhaps a shiver of fear within this period. One very wet winter I was returning home late at night. A main road bridge had been swept away. The next shortest way I had traversed that morning—it was flooded for nearly a mile along a ditch-lined road with no fences to indicate its meanders. Rain had fallen lightly all day. How deep would be the water at 11 p.m.? But the third route home was some ten miles longer. I was wet, cold and hungry. I chose the floods. As I sploshed into the first brown waters, I realized they were inches deeper than at my earlier passage. Foolishly I persisted.

In floods, of course, one proceeds slowly, avoiding a bow wave.

Inch by inch I could feel the water becoming deeper, and my head lamp shone loathsomely on a waste of brown ripples. Suddenly my engine quietly ceased to beat. In the next ten seconds my lamp went out. It is not possible to minister to a submerged dynamo, What should I do? There would be 6 feet of water in the ditches, if my feet wandered off the roadway. Of light there was none, for a low ceiling veiled moon and stars. Should I essay to push the model an estimated half mile through knee-deep water, or wait till tomorrow to charter a lorry for its rescue?

I did the only sensible thing. I waited till my pupils adjusted themselves to the gloom, when a very faint luminosity " made darkness visible " in the masonic phrase. I laid the model tenderly on its side at the very edge of the submerged road, so that no noc-turnal lorry should trample it. Then very, very slowly, with booted toes sensitive for the faint difference between hard road and sodden turf edging, I began to feel my way back to the higher road some half a mile distant. I made it. Next morning we went out with a lorry, and ultimately found the model after not a little groping. (I know I ought to have had a cork and a cord in my pocket, but I had neither.)

Finally, I must just mention one abominable word—" mask "! To all motorists who lived through the first two years of the 1939 war, when the war blackout was darkest, and lamp masks were least efficient, that word reeks with nausea. Later, the optical experts devised more efficient masks which allowed us some notion of whereabouts and obstacles without rendering main roads or car parks too visible to prowling Heinkels. But the original masks of the 1939–1940 winter were the abomination of desolation. They flung ahead a minute and pale patch of glimmer which barely showed up on the tarmac. Much less did it enable a myopic person like myself to spot a cow, a building, or a pedestrian dead ahead. More than once I was uncertain whether or no I was in my own street or outside my own gate. On another occasion, descending the Nailsworth " W " on a moonless night, I had a sudden qualm that I was running out of road. I was! My front tyre was within millimetres of the drop off the centre of a hairpin.

It is a tribute to the modern motor cycle that in the two decades covered by this chapter I can only recall one serious breakdown due to any flaw in mechanism. That single stop must be set against perhaps 150,000 miles of joyous carefree riding.

PART II—BACKGROUND

CHAPTER 16

THE MAGIC OF MOTOR CYCLING

ANY RECRUIT TO MOTOR CYCLING who mixes with fellow enthusiasts will be immensely impressed by two traits which are almost universal among us. The first is our enthusiasm. The second is our camaraderie. Enthusiasm in the form of a transient craze is a characteristic of youth. The schoolboy collects stamps today, keeps rabbits tomorrow, and chases autographs next month. He changes his hobby far more regularly than he washes his ears. But motor cycling usually develops into a life hobby, and is marked by an almost passionate element. At the T.T. week in the Isle of Man, or at the annual motor cycle Show at Earls Court, one may see fat old men with grey hair, or no hair at all, babbling happily of their days awheel.

We Britons are renowned as being a trifle snooty, slow to make friends, sitting silent in a railway carriage for eight hours, shy, inarticulate—in all respects, the precise opposite of the extremely forthcoming American. Especially are we snobbish in terms of class. If we are moderately friendly with men of our own status, we are apt to be shy and difficult with strangers, and especially towards people in another walk of life. All these barriers dissolve instantaneously between two men who own motor cycles; they ask to know nothing more than the link of a common hobby—a freemasonry is bred of their mutual interest. These two assets enhance the pleasures of ownership enormously.

But the basic magic of motor cycling is not dependent on friendship. As a nation we are not prone to analysis. If we ask a dozen motor cyclists why they are so passionate about our common hobby, few of them will find immediate words. There are, of course, plenty who will readily reply that they " like to get away " from something or somebody—maybe the grimy industrial district where destiny has planted them to earn their daily bread; maybe the " shop " conversation of a clique of fellow labourers in the same profession or industry.

As an " escape ", motor cycling especially appeals to the young. In youth we are all slightly intoxicated by the novel independence which results from going out to work. Father no longer wants to know exactly where we have been. Mother does not fuss over us to the familiar extent. We start to be men, and we relish the sensation. But in fact we have only exchanged one tutelage for another. At the works or the office we have to mind our step, and to submit to a new form of discipline under new masters. Such restraints and supervision are wholesome enough for the adolescent. But we nevertheless pine for at least brief spells of real freedom. A motor cycle wafts us swiftly into a world of liberty where, for a few delicious hours every week-end, nobody can push us around.

But the magic goes much deeper than that. After all, we are descended from primitive man, who lived dangerously, and in his solitary person tussled with all the historic enemies of his kind— cold, flood, starvation, wild beasts—a myriad threats to his very life. We retain most of the primitive instincts, and they accord ill with clocking-in at 8 a.m., labour exchanges, foremen, and the monotonous routine of a 48-hour week for 50 weeks in every year, promotion coming slowly, and jobs too often tedious with the wearisome sensations of eternal repetition.

If this sense of revolt is here expressed in terms of artisans, it is only because a majority of British male youth are artisans. The experience is similar if, for example, one is a junior bank clerk, counting other people's money all day long, and aware that the routine will last with slight progressive variations until one is eventually pensioned off at sixty.

Now, mount such a mildly disgruntled adolescent on the saddle of a motor cycle; put a few shillings in his pocket (and maybe a girl on his carrier); and send him off into the country, free to go where he likes and ride as he likes, subject to the prudential claims of his own and the public safety. All his cares and worries evaporate in the first mile. A slight sulkiness fades from his young features, his eyes begin to shine, and his heart leaps. On his return he is a different creature, alert, vivacious, human. He is the very spit of that distant ancestor who chopped his first boat out of a big log, or slew his first sabre-toothed tiger, and returned to the tribal caves or camp fire proud and happy.

Even that is far from exhausting the magic of the motor cycle. In a sense, demobilization at the end of a war is a long-pictured relief to the fighter pilot. For several years he has risen every morning aware that each day might be his last, or that he might survive it crippled, mangled, suffering, impotent. Yet, as he hands in his flying kit and goes off to seek civilian employment, he is acutely conscious of regret.

Never again will he swirl high above the clouds at five miles a minute, feeling in his every tissue the exhilaration of the dive on a victim, the wild zoom into the dome of heaven. Never again will he grope fast through the night, every sense keyed up to sight an enemy. Never again, maybe, will he thrill to quite the same consciousness that he is doing something one hundred per cent virile, worthy even of the final sacrifice, effective, important. As he settles down to the mid-period of a masculine life in which he

121

perpetuates himself and his race, toils and struggles for a mate and a child, his motor cycle will furnish him with some of those sensations of travel which were once mingled with so much fear.

We may deride simple physical sensations allied to muscle and motion, but they can be intensely satisfying, as we realize every time we see a high diver, a tight-rope walker, a gymnast, a great runner, yes—a ballerina. To those basic instincts the motor cycle ministers in high measure.

Moreover, the motor cycle is a powerful ally of health. Physical exercise is a keen problem in this modern age, when most of us, of both sexes, from about the age of eighteen onward are condemned to some phase of sedentary indoor labour. There are, of course, innumerable sports—hiking, cycling, football, cricket, tennis, golf, skating, dancing, and many another. The critics condemn us as a nation as they detect a growing reliance on " spectatorship ", of personal abstention from athletics, coupled with a curious habit of paying professionals to disport themselves publicly for our amusement. These critics lack sympathy. After a long indoor week of either mental or physical effort, many of us are no longer equal to playing games with any success or satisfaction.

It is no pleasure or relief, for example, to play week-end cricket if the player is inexpert, takes no wickets, drops a catch or two, is bowled in his first over. It was a very great physician who regretted that so many of his business patients play golf. He remarked that they necessarily play badly, as they arrive exhausted on the tee and, maybe, lack the training or the physical qualities required to play well. So, by about their twenty-fifth birthday, many hard workers abandon the popular sports because they no longer play as well as they did at twenty, and retrogression even in games is humiliating.

By contrast, motoring is a far better week-end hobby for such men (and women). Of the two forms of motoring the motor cycle is infinitely superior to the car—unless the car is an open two-seater, preferably of the sports type. The Americans have wisely recognized the " convertible " as the most rational type of motor car. But the motor cycle is better than a 100 b.h.p. convertible, since the latter carries at least one occupant who does not drive. The motor bicycle carries a driver and, frequently no passenger.

It is the driver who reaps the most pleasure and profit from motoring. The compulsory concentration on the road peels his mind bare of all professional, financial or domestic problems. It flings him into a world completely divorced from his Monday to Saturday routine. It claims all his faculties, faculties most of which were either dormant or at least otherwise employed during his working hours. It takes him into fresh scenes and pastures new. It invigorates him quite incredibly.

Moreover, a new theory about physical exercise is being born. The present writer, in youth, was doomed to work quite fantastic hours in the stale air and grime of London. His average week was nearer 70 hours than the modern 40–48. He soon found himself growing stale and heavy. He experimented with divers forms of exercise. Not only was he too weary to extort much pleasure from them, but they merely emphasized his tiredness. He tried cricket and football, for which he had to waste hours in travel, and from which he returned exhausted. His first successful experiment took the form of railway trips to Brighton, where the sea air was refreshing.

He found that a long afternoon in the saddle of a motor bicycle was of more benefit than an occasional week-end by the sea. Analysis soon suggested a two-fold cause. First, his brain was automatically scoured clean of all preoccupations by the task of conducting a crude and temperamental machine over difficult roads. Secondly, his entire body was exposed to a cool breeze— either natural or generated by the speed—and so became thoroughly oxygenated. Possibly the vibration of bad roads and an almost rigid machine was further beneficial. By comparison, gliding in the portable greenhouse type of motor car with somebody else at the wheel was a wretched substitute.

Finally, it may be noted that most users enlist the motor cycle as an ally of some other hobby. It is always, of course, an invaluable aid in retaining constant touch with scattered friends and relatives, with whom close touch is often lost when one enters a profession. It is as invaluable for most of the commoner hobbies, as for those which are not common. The bird watcher, the brass rubber, the angler, the archæologist, the glider, the mountaineer, every type of naturalist, the photographer—all these and hundreds more find the mobility conferred by motor cycling quite invaluable.

In actual fact, a very large percentage of motor cyclists find their main joys in extensions of their primary hobby, and would scorn to couple it up to any pursuit not connected with petrol. They attach far more importance to club life than car owners do. Their local club will have a full summer programme of trials and scrambles, coupled to a winter programme of lectures and social fixtures. They will travel far afield to events organized by other clubs, perhaps visit one of the many small grass-racing tracks, miniature road circuits or hill-climbs, attend car racing meets at Goodwood or Silverstone, spend a June or September holiday at the Manx motor cycle races, join a communal motor cycle tour on the European continent, and the like.

As was said earlier in this chapter, their enthusiasm is coupled with a camaraderie which almost seems to assert that motor cycling is the only worth-while sport, and that motor cyclists are the people best worthy of association.

CHAPTER 17

MOTOR CYCLES IN WAR

NO GREATER BLUNDER COULD BE PERPETRATED than to estimate the contribution of motor cycling to the national effort in two world wars by a catalogue of the motor cycles supplied to the Services.

Our major contribution in both wars consisted of *men*. Many thousands of athletic and mechanically minded youths dashed to the colours, and supplied the aircraft with many of their best pilots. At the outbreak of the 1914–18 war, motor cyclist despatch riders being in great demand, *The Motor Cycle* became the recruiting medium for this particular section. Later, when the War Office decided to form the Motor Machine Gun Service, men were gathered together to drive the Royal Enfield and Clyno sidecar outfits and *The Motor Cycle* filled the ranks. Still later, the policy was to employ heavy armoured cars and the M.M.G.S. was eventually transformed into the Heavy Machine Gun Corps. Similarly from 1939 onward motor cyclists provided many of the best recruits for all the more definitely mechanical arms of the Services.

Apart from fighting men eager for actual combat duties, we contributed an enormous number of older men to such arms as the R.A.S.C., the R.E., the R.E.M.E. and all the communication and signal units.

The second contribution was made by the surviving personnel of the factories, who stayed at home and provided every imaginable type of munition for the fighting forces. It is impossible to print a catalogue of these supplies. But it is worth mention that the industry disposes of enormous numbers of precision tools, manned by hands skilled in their use. One firm at least—B.S.A.—has long been proficient in the manufacture of small arms, and everywhere both staff and plant were kept fully absorbed in tasks of high priority and great delicacy.

Third only to our contribution of fighting men and of skilled mechanics came the provision of actual motor cycles.

In the 1914–1918 war, wireless was insufficiently developed for military communications, and despatch riders played an even more vital part than fell to them in 1939. At first the War Office hastily bought up secondhand motor cycles in quantity, and appealed for experienced riders in great numbers. Later on, to simplify maintenance in the field, the " used " machines were largely discarded, and the Army relied chiefly on two-speed Douglas and three-speed Triumph machines, while the R.F.C. (later, the R.A.F.) selected

P. & M. for similar duties. From 1914 onward, limited use was made of sidecar outfits by the Motor Machine Gun Corps, whose choice fell on Clyno, Royal Enfield, Matchless-J.A.P. and Scott machines.

A minority of riders found themselves in far-away places with strange sounding names. For example, one expert was sent to Russia, where he tackled the tough assignment of training peasants who could not speak his language to ride motor cycles in the dead of winter over icy surfaces on which he doubted his own ability to remain vertical!

The 1939–1945 war required an even more comprehensive mobilization of young athletes and of trained mechanics. Once again most of the younger riders flocked into the R.A.F., the Royal Corps of Signals and the Tank Corps. The human and mechanical resources of the factories were again reorganized for novel tasks of the utmost delicacy, and rose to the occasion magnificently. Some of the expert factory riders staffed special schools for training Army despatch riders. Incredible quantities of Triumph, B.S.A., Royal Enfield, Ariel, Norton and Matchless machines were built in specially rugged and simplified versions for military duties.

New corps with no parallel in the great armies of 1914 required novel transport. The airborne troops were all destined to find themselves landed on enemy soil. The industry produced for them two handy lightweights, the two-stroke James and Royal Enfield, which were sturdy enough to survive rough parachute landings and capable of being ridden or manhandled over roadless territory (These two models proved so excellent that their manufacture was continued for civilian service after the peace.) In addition, Welbike, a folding lightweight, was rapidly improvised. This, too, survived as a civilian autocycle and a modified version sold in thousands after the war under the name of the Corgi.

It is worthy of mention that the very qualities which the general public is apt to criticize in motor cycles during peace, have twice proved invaluable in national emergencies. The enterprise and dash which can be tiresome on crowded roads are indispensable to the handling of tanks and aircraft in war.

CHAPTER 18

SIX DAYS' TRIALS

THE MOTOR CYCLE HAS BEEN EVOLVED from crude origins by an immense variety of influences. Conscientious makers have continuously tested their successive experimental models alike on the bench and on the road. Private owners have played their part by reporting dissatisfaction to factory staffs. Clubs have organized innumerable road trials varying from easy Saturday afternoon competitions to such formidable events as the old M.C.C. London to Edinburgh and back in 48 hours.

The Auto Cycle Union, formerly the Auto Cycle Club, has always been the principal independent body to run public tests. It began modestly with short afternoon trials over mildly undulating routes, coupled with offers to superintend special tests on request. Before long it began to organize its famous Six Days' Trials, which steadily increased in severity and eventually led to the foundation of even more severe International Six Days' events. These last inspired fierce international competition. They came to be held within the territory of the previous year's winning team, and introduced an ever-increasing body of British riders to the ardours of the Alps and the Dolomites.

Side by side with these immensely varied road tests, a growing increase in the popularity of motor cycle racing provided tests to destruction of engines, coupled with intense demands on the quality of every auxiliary component—forks, brakes, transmission, ignition, controls—the entire range of components figuring in the construction of a machine. Brooklands, Donington and many a minor track combined to provide a vast mechanism of tests from which no unworthy design, metal or workmanship could hope to emerge unscathed, whilst merit was identified and rewarded.

Rome was not built in a day. At the outset makers foisted crude and almost untested designs on an innocent and gullible public. The designer bought a foreign engine—in France or Belgium. He modified a standard pedal cycle in a few obvious respects to form a chassis for an engine of which he knew next to nothing. One of his mechanics took the machine out on the road for half an hour, and perhaps made a few trifling adjustments. The purchaser was notified, handed over his cheque for £45 or so, and took the contraption away.

In those dark days the Auto Cycle Club possessed no experience, and was far too weak to impose such will as it possessed on the trade. When the notion of organizing public trials was first mooted on its committee, a policy of extreme caution was inevitable. Everybody knew that no existing vehicle would emerge from any *severe* trial with credit, if indeed it survived the distance at all. Such public failure would not only hamper a struggling industry, but would incline manufacturers to abstain from future tests of a public type. Obviously, the daily mileage must be short, the hills contemptible, and the regulations elastic. One of the main functions of the officials was to help to push competitors' machines up the mild hills, a task in which the spectators were encouraged to lend a hand.

The first great A.C.C. trial was held in 1903. The distance was ambitious—no less than 1,000 miles. But this was mercifully split up into ten 100-mile daily instalments. Each day's route started in the London suburbs and took the form of an out-and-home run to some town about 50 miles distant, such as Brighton or Canterbury. Grades like Handcross and the Hog's Back, near Guildford, were the supreme climbing tests. A speed test of five miles over the Crystal Palace track was audaciously included to show up any developed weakness in the surviving machines. Ludicrous as such a layout sounds today, it was perhaps dangerously ambitious, and might have produced a fatal debacle.

There was plenty of friction. The regulations were loosely drafted, and the marshals soon perceived that, at the legal speed of 12 m.p.h., certain competitors were attended by works' machanics riding pedal cycles, and transporting tools and spare parts. At the end of the first week some of the riders were so leg weary that their entrants sought permission to put up a fresh rider for the second week, for the 48-hour rest over the intervening Saturday and Sunday had failed to refresh the tired pedallers! Leave was granted, provided that the substitute jockey weighed no less than his predecessor. Twenty of the original forty-three starters survived to contest the five-mile speed test on the Palace track. Ample time was allowed for repairs and re-tuning before the final ordeal. The survivors attained an average speed of 28 m.p.h. on the track— no mean achievement for the times.

Thus early, defective brakes were identified as a main weakness in design and construction. This was hardly surprising, as most of the brakes had been bodily transferred from standard pedal cycles.

Proof of progress jumps to hand if we compare the timid absurdities of a 1903 trial with the standards of 1950. Four facts govern the layout of a modern Six Days', whether it is run in Britain or on the Continent.

The first problem is to find a route sufficiently severe to furnish a real test. It is very nearly true to say that no roads in England qualify for the purpose. Even in such comparatively mountainous areas as Wales and Scotland, the organizers are bound to incorporate sections which are little better than goat tracks. They must not, of course, include the freak precipices which figure in " scrambles " or in some of the more lurid " one-day " trials. The purpose of a solemn Six Days' Trial is to verify and publish the merits of standard machines, not to ascertain whether the riders are circus acrobats. Consequently, the route must be as severe as possible, provided always that it does not require a Blondin to keep a machine vertical.

Secondly, there must be ample hotel accommodation for at least 200 people, including officials and the Press.

Thirdly, there must be some kind of track for the speed test which serves as the climax. (In the bad old days lurking weaknesses were sought only by visual inspection of the stationary model. Nowadays, a good mileage on a widish throttle opening serves a similar purpose ruthlessly, separate speed minima being allotted to each class according to the engine size.)

But neither the severity of the route nor the racing circuits at the end actually endow the trial with its basic ferocity. The factor which tends to make the riders look a trifle haggard towards the finish is the *time schedule*. This is nowadays drawn so tight that it leaves no margin in which a competitor might tinker at his machine. A time schedule which is formidable in fair weather may prove cruel in heavy rain.

The 12 m.p.h. speed limit adopted in 1896 survived until 1903, when it was raised to 20 m.p.h. This later limit was abolished in 1930, though, under both the more liberal limits, many busy or dangerous sections of road were allotted lower limits. In 1934, hundreds of miles of road in built-up areas were scheduled for 30 m.p.h. limits. All these regulations prevented trials organizers from imposing a really tight time schedule. Competitors, mostly riding machines capable of considerably greater speeds, possibly of speeds double, treble or even quadruple the legal limit, pardonably scorched ahead after checking through a control, stored up reserve time outside the next check, and employed the leisure in repairs and adjustments when such were needed, or in polishing up their machines to look smart on entry to the next town.

There were two methods of eliminating such patchwork along the road. The first was the " secret " check. A hidden car, filled with timekeepers, ambushed the procession, and anybody who was ahead of time was penalized. The other and simpler method, comparatively devoid of friction, consisted in picking roads sufficiently difficult to make the legal limit quite onerous, without condemning the riders to acrobatics on almost unrideable surfaces. Finally, the fifth problem was to find out outright winners for various special prizes and trophies awarded to the individual registering the finest performance with each type of machine. This was usually done by means of " observed " hills. If a rider even made a single dab with one foot, he blotted his copybook.

Compare this ruthless, stringent organization to punish the tiniest slip with the old easy-going days when everybody, down to the feeblest competitor, was encouraged to win a gold medal, when the route was almost flat, no hills were observed, there was no

60 m.p.h. track race at the finish, and the time schedule permitted everybody to spend perhaps two hours a day on tinkering by the roadside without penalty.

At this stage I may perhaps quote examples of what happened in the generous period. On one occasion I won a top award, a gold medal, for a perfect score with a machine which completed the course devoid of brakes, minus a rear mudguard, with an engine so debilitated that it could barely exceed 20 m.p.h. On another occasion I was equally successful, although my engine had repeatedly seized up solid en route and I had used up no fewer than three complete variable gears.

Nowadays, the risk of punctures is the chief threat to success. This implies no slur on the modern tyre. Indeed, the puncture risk is almost infinitesimal on British roads, for the simple reason that only a very small minority of our population wear hobnailed boots, while horses are now scarce even on our country roads. Nails from boots and horses have always been the main cause of punctures. Britain's worst period for punctures coincided with the first decade of tarred roads. So long as road surfaces were loose, shed nails often lay flat amongst the mud, dust or grit. But when tarred roads first became extensive, hobnails and horseshoes were still common. A shed nail might lie flat on the smooth, hard, even surface, but a front wheel often jerked it into the vertical position, the rear tyre, maybe, picked it up and, before the rider had a chance to examine his cover, the point had holed the inner tube.

In Continental Six Days' events, punctures are still a genuine menace. Dwellers in the Alps and Dolomites still wear hobnails. In the mountainous areas of Europe the horse still supplies much of the agricultural transport. Punctures in such districts are still very common, and the time schedules of trials are so severe that the swiftest worker can seldom mend a puncture and keep time at the next check, unless the stop occurs early in a section and the competitor can make up his lost time by very hectic riding up and down the passes.

Thus, when we enter teams in the International Six Days', special measures are essential. The selected riders are drilled by experts in lightning tyre repairs. The machines are often equipped with quick-detachable wheels; nailcatchers may be fitted; and the inner tubes are usually treated with some self-sealing material. (None of these precautions is now indispensable on British roads.)

In the old days we usually carried a spare cover; it was possible to furl a 2-inch beaded-edge cover into a flat object, measuring about 8 × 4 inches and pack it under our overalls on the carrier. We took spare tubes—possibly of the butt-ended type, which could be fitted without removing a wheel from its forks, but sometimes of the standard endless type—wrapped round the handlebar or packed in special leather cases. When a puncture occurred too near the end of a section for time to be regained by reckless speed, we rode into the next check on a flat cover, and changed the tube as soon as we had signed out. I remember using six covers and several tubes within one week in the Highlands.

These six-day trials were more than a test. They served as a mobile demonstration to the general public, and attracted crowds at all the stopping places and, not least, on any accessible hills. The manufacturer whose wares made a good impression could rely on a flow of orders. Hence the entry of many inefficient amateurs was not too welcome to the factories. Not only did the amateur waste too much time on roadside repairs, but he seldom bothered to clean up his machine properly at the night stops. His low award in the results list (if, indeed, he finished!) did the maker of his machine no good, and the dirty appearance of the machine at all the town stops had a poor effect.

By contrast, a man like Billy Pratt, who managed the competition riding of the Phelon & Moore teams for many a long year, must have earned lots of money for his employers. These sturdy machines were not fast, but they were immensely reliable and, as they incorporated a two-speed gear many years before the industry as a whole abandoned the single-gear belt, they always shone in the climbs. Billy was not content with that. He trained his two team-mates to ride in close company with him. He held the master watch, and saw that the trio were always a few minutes inside their time limit. They carried cleaning material inside their headlamps, and they used to dismount round a corner just short of each control and furbish up their mounts to almost a showroom finish, before trickling with dignity up to the waiting timekeeper! This system reaped pleasant dividends, and such of Billy's rivals as could climb the hills and keep good time, began to imitate his fine example.

On the Continent of Europe the more intelligent foreign riders needed no such example from us. Abroad every reliability trial is regarded as a race by the local inhabitants—not without justice, for in the Alps and Dolomites the time schedule is usually so severe that the rider must use his brakes almost as much in climbing famous passes as in descending the further side; he would sacrifice many time marks if he pottered up the cols and admired the scenery.

A Continental rider will tackle a six-day reliability trial almost as if it were a race in order to spread the impression that he is the winner throughout He will attire himself in some showy uniform of rubber cloth—easily wiped spotless in a minute or so— and generally snatch every atom of publicity and hero-worship from the simple natives. At the end of such a European trial, the British entries can always be heard complaining that they never had a moment for admiring the gorgeous scenery through which they have passed, and vowing that they will revisit the district on a private tour next summer and bring the wife with them!

I have jumped ahead in my tale to emphasize the sharp contrast between the 1903 A.C.C. trial and its modern successors. The 1903 event was reminiscent of Lewis Carroll's caucus race in which everybody received prizes. In the 1950 version, even a second- or third-class award is hard to win. The survivors are very weary men when they have completed the miniature race which forms the climax.

Indeed, the pace is quite often much too high for safety so far as the Continental trials are concerned. After the Alpine car event in 1949 there were very serious complaints on that score. The cars had to maintain really high speeds up the innumerable hairpin lacets of the worst passes in Europe. Ordinary traffic was not suspended. The ascents were tackled by incessant gear changing, rushes at high speed up the short straights separating one blind corner from the next, crash-braking as the next corner arrived, where one could neither see nor hear what might be just around it, all on narrowish roads of steep gradient with a loose surface. There were collisions and serious accidents. The mileage might be as high as 400 or more in a single day.

Motor bicycles are at a vantage under such conditions as they occupy a comparatively narrow space on the road, and can dive past in a surprise encounter where two cars cannot possibly dodge each other. Also their brakes do not " fade " from excessive heat as the brakes of cars are apt to do, when screened by enclosing coachwork from the mountain air. The 1948 International Six Days' for motor cycles was based on San Remo, and was so arduous that the lads christened it the " Goat Track Derby ". Nor was it carried through without several serious accidents.

After these intentional digressions let us return to the British scene. The A.C.C. was able after 1903 to adopt a progressive policy. It had proved to the industry that it was competent to organize large trials. It had contrived to plan events which fostered the improvement of motor cycles without unduly pillorying their current imperfections. It was not possible to include really steep hills in quantity until the 1911 T.T. race had sent the industry into a veritable stampede after variable gears. Short of this, the A.C.C. did its best, along two separate lines.

First, it included at least one real hill per annum. As early as 1905, Birdlip was included—and at that date very few car owners were foolhardy enough to go near Birdlip in either direction. This audacious experiment was softened by allowing the men ample time on the hill, and providing plenty of pushers. So, although only three solo machines climbed it under power, none of the failures sustained heavy penalties. In 1906 the Land's End-John O' Groats course was used. This contains no real hills, with Red Hill, near Bristol, Shap, and Berriedale, up north, offering most trouble, though most competitors sighed for a variable gear on gradients in some of the hillier towns (for example, Redruth). The next year, Wales was the venue, and hill-climbing was mostly poor, although the route avoided the more notorious ascents.

By 1909 a minor change in policy became possible, and steeper climbs could be included in quantity. The adjustable pulley was becoming popular. The old fixed pulleys limited a rider to a gear of 4 or $4\frac{1}{2}$ to 1. The adjustable pulley could be screwed down to a minimum diameter dictated by the size of the crankshaft on which it was mounted. With a normal belt rim on the rear wheel, the lowest setting of such a pulley furnished a gear of about $5\frac{1}{2}$ to 1. Since these settings varied the belt length, it was necessary either to carry two belts of different lengths, or to use some ingenious metal fastener with a variable setting.

The A.C.C. catered for these devices by enlarging the time schedule for sections that included the steeper hills. We all scorched madly ahead to the foot of such hills, leapt off the saddle, screwed down the pulley, and then charged the hill. At the summit we changed back to the normal gear ratio. The existence of a small selection of variable gears, plus the immense convenience of even an adjustable pulley, was exerting its logical effect upon designers. In 1910 the A.C.U. became really venturesome. Its chosen route was basically the End-to-End road, embodying switches to Cheddar Gorge and Amulree. Out of seventy-one entries, twenty-one rode machines with variable gears, and all the rest used adjustable pulleys.

In 1911 the first three machines in the Senior T.T. all used two-speed countershaft gears. They were Indians, of American manufacture, and the long lethargy of the British industry died a very sudden death. The battle of the gears was won, even if the three years still separating us from the first World War were to be mainly occupied by transient experiments with multi-speed hubs, retaining the belt drive. Timid as this compromise may appear in retrospect, it was at least extremely plausible. Everybody was conscious of strong antagonism to unnecessary weight. The belt drive had been improved out of recognition. It was light. It formed an admirable shock absorber between the engine and the rear wheel. It was cheap. Three-speed hubs had already attained an excellent reputation on pedal cycles. To fit similar hubs of slightly greater strength on motor cycles was a simple and promising expedient.

For 1911 the trials moved to the Yorkshire fells, centring on Harrogate. Out of eighty-one entries, no fewer than sixty-five rode with variable gears. Unfortunately, the weather proved extremely dry, and nobody realized how poorly belts can behave on steep hills in drenching rain! One unrecognized fact was silently operating to banish the belt. The introduction of high-tension magnetos (which first figured on the Triumph machines in 1906) was accustoming riders to at least one absolutely dependable component on their motor cycles. By contrast with its immaculate service, the belt stood out in high relief as a tiresome anachronism.

For 1912 the A.C.U. moved to Taunton as their centre, with the ghoulish intention of taking us up some of the more infamous Devon hills. Beggars' Roost figured as the main crux. Countisbury was scheduled as a " slow " climb. There was also a day devoted to a " secret " route, selected by Somersetshire zealots. This innovation has ever since dominated a majority of trials on British roads, in the sense that it marked a decision. Henceforward, hard roads were deemed inadequate for a real test of motor cycles. The " goat track " policy was born.

I do not see that any alternative was possible, considering how short and easy our British main-road hills actually are. Theoretically, a trial of roadster machines should test the machine rather than its rider. The guiding principle should be the gradual perfection of models suitable for the man or girl who buys a sample for ordinary use. Only a very small minority of owners have a burning desire to imitate the chamois, or are prepared to risk damaging their expensive purchases by rough-riding.

The inclusion of moderate rough sections in the big events ensures that successful machines shall be trustworthy not only for the type of amateur who tours the main roads, but also for a farmer or a gamekeeper or a naturalist, who intends to desert the beaten roads for quite a proportion of his riding time. (Of course, the really lurid forms of acrobatics are still reserved for those competition riders who enjoy a Scott trial or a " scramble "—a " moto-cross "—or go pot-hunting in the Colmore Cup and other " toughie " fixtures.

The next couple of years saw more determined applications of all the new ideas, and culminated in a riders' strike in July, 1914. The competitors had not expected quite such ferocious ordeals. The climax came on Litton Slack, which happened to be bone dry when the A.C.U. route-finders investigated it, but was wringing wet when a close-set procession of 132 starters arrived in pouring rain. Litton Slack is not climbable in close company under such conditions. There was a most fantastic jam on the hill. When at last the medley was sorted out, and everybody had been pushed up, they were all behind time, and many sustained heavy falls in a mad blind to the next check. Finally, the officials had to eat humble pie, and the week ended in angry farce.

On August 4 we found ourselves at war with Germany, and rough-riding became an affair for uniformed despatch riders on mud-covered *pavé* in Belgium and France.

Two reasons compel the writer to skim very briefly over the Six Days' Trials of the period between the two world wars, together with the five years succeeding World War II. One reason is lack of space. This book contains 100,000 words, into which half a century of varied and incredible effort must be compressed. The other is the fact that by about 1920 the struggle for amazingly lofty standards of speed, reliability, hill-climbing, manageability, and comfort had already been won. From that date onward the public was being supplied by some sixty different makers with an immense variety of completely roadworthy motor cycles in some 250 different types.

The Motor Cycle Buyers' Guide for the year 1932, for example, listed 254 different models of all shapes and sizes, including— unbelievable as it seems in these days of inflation—a 500 c.c.

133

Matchless roadster, scaling no more than 224 lb with full touring specification, catalogued at £35!

I do not pretend for one moment that design became stagnant in 1920, or that it will ever reach its climax. The industry has laboured under a myriad handicaps since VE Day, but in that brief period it has produced, together with half a dozen quite novel specifications, a front fork (the hydraulically controlled telescopic type) conferring a degree of comfort hitherto unknown, and a number of multi-cylinder machines with smoother engines than any other nation yet offers to its public. My point is that the fundamental reliability of British motor cycles, like Cæsar's wife, is above suspicion.

Ruthless reliability trials were once essential to the progress of design. Novel items will eternally continue to appear. Some of them will rank as details of minor importance—possibly the pedal gear change, which outmoded the gear lever about 1934, comes in that category, though it enhances the safety factor appreciably. Others, like the telescopic fork, rank higher, as a great asset in comfort and roadholding. But the mere maintenance of sheer reliability may now safely be entrusted to the brains of designers, the conscience of manufacturers, the eternal friction of competitive industry, and the educated demands of public opinion.

Reliability trials, even the major national and international events, have ceased to be indispensable. They are inclined to dwindle, except in the eyes of passionate enthusiasts, to the level of friendly and sporting rivalry. Doubtless they still contribute items of criticism and of advancement to all concerned. Yet, in the basic sense, they are almost anachronisms. Their organizers practically confess as much when they introduce so marked a " chamois " element.

The private owner asks for a cheap, dependable, comfortable mount, which will start easily, give him the minimum of trouble, and prove durable on his daily occasions. In such aspects the trials organizers are unable to separate one machine from another to any great advantage. So they almost unanimously switch to other objectives, and now award their trophies to the man, rather than the model—to the acrobat who never falls off, and can storm up disused goat tracks without dabbing a foot.

Apart from deep mire, rock steps, watersplashes and boulder-strewn torrent beds, the modern Six Days' presents a spectacle of contemptuous, monotonous progress by a band of unperturbed experts. This may offer a mildly dull spectacle, but is at least a remarkable tribute to the achievements of the industry.

For further triumphs we must look mainly to the sphere of speed. If any man quarrels with such opinions, let him switch his mind across to the sphere of motor cars. No longer are any tests of *pure reliability* organized to improve the breed of motor cars. 1949 included only one event which could by any stretch of the imagination be described as a test of car reliability. This was the

Alpine trial. Only one car emerged with a clean sheet—*one* car in an age when nobody expects roadside trouble with a modern car. But the conditions stultify any plea that the trial took stock of reliability. One day's run consisted of four hundred and forty five miles between sunrise and sunset, leading over Alpine roads, in which the contestants were set to *race* up famous passes at high speed, under conditions which imported a very definite element of danger, resulting in serious damage to many vehicles and to some drivers and crews.

Pure reliability trials have almost ceased to be necessary.

As already hinted, the International Six Days' Trials rank in quite a different category. Most Continental venues automatically furnish countless miles of steep, twisting ascents, followed by steep twisting descents. Either climb of the Stelvio Pass, for example, entails at least ten miles of continuous climbing, together with approximately fifty acute hairpin bends, many of which are absolutely " blind ". The road surface on such cols will vary from the very loose to the decidedly slippery, according to the weather.

A tight time-schedule will compel the riders to travel very much faster than is either natural or pleasant. It will be necessary to use the brakes hard and regularly on the ascents no less than on the descents, and to face definite risks of collision with vehicles from the opposite direction on any of the blind bends. Both ascending and descending, the men accelerate hard out of each hairpin, and brake hard at the approach of the next bend. Men like Henne have been known to average 40 m.p.h. across such passes. Some of these passes are extremely narrow and fringed by dangerous precipices, and the compulsory stoppage of a sidecar competitor or an official car just round the next blind corner may block the entire roadway. Some of them are disfigured by tunnelled sections drilled through solid rock. These are pitch dark, invariably dripping wet, very slippery, and twist almost as freely and viciously as the open sections. The sudden transition from dazzling sunshine to inky gloom cannot be appreciably eased by switching on a headlamp —the human eye is incapable of such lightning adjustments.

The weather is normally far more temperamental than in Britain. I have tackled such cols in heavy mist with a visibility of maybe ten yards. I have ridden " landings " on these climbs drenched by an almost tropical cloudburst, emerged into sunshine and seen a second cloudburst and another thunderstorm waiting for me 1,000 ft higher up.

In the earlier days our engines and especially our carburettors resented high altitudes. The best cars in the world were apt to boil furiously at 5,000 ft, and although that tendency has long since been overcome, few engines relish the altitude of such a place as the summit of the Stelvio. The riders may alternately be parboiled by temperatures almost unknown in Britain, frozen to the marrow on mist-clad heights, and drenched to the skin, nor does time allow them to alter their clothing to suit such extreme variations.

135

In the 1931 trial, starting from Merano in the Dolomites, the organizers cut out a set lunch at midday, with the idea of relieving the competitors from too long a day in the saddle; a roadside buffet lunch was substituted, and any unlucky wight who fell behind schedule rode from breakfast to dinner with nothing to eat. The final speed test was at Monza track in northern Italy.

In that area the trial was greeted by quite the most vicious exhibition of weather I have ever encountered in Europe. It was actually terrifying. The rain pounded down upon us in solid sheets, compared to which any English " stair-rod " downfall was meek and gentle. Haystacks became windborne. The local buses were blown off the road. The alfresco lunch, waiting for us at the track, was wafted over the surrounding countryside. Even semi-T.T. engines, tuned with an eye to bonus marks in the track speed test, were barely able to make headway when the gale was in our teeth, and when the wind attacked us from a flank, it was occasionally necessary to take shelter for a few minutes, as otherwise it would have been impossible to remain vertical or on the road. Finally, the storm eased, and the sun came out. Then the sodden riders with empty stomachs went out on to the concrete track to attempt, in the case of team men, an 80 m.p.h. average in search of bonus marks which decided any tie on the marks for road reliability.

When nature, unaided, furnishes such arduous conditions, it is seldom necessary for the organizers to go out of their way and use goat tracks or ask us to emulate the chamois. But it is never safe to assume that the entire trial may not be suddenly switched off ordinary mountain roads on to some such hill as our own terrors at home—say Post Hill or Simms Hill.

In one International Six Days' on the Continent we all lunched in civilization and, with stuffed tummies, departed in expectation of normal going. Within minutes we found ourselves stalled *en masse* in the worst hill jamb recorded in the annals of our sport. A beautiful main road of easy gradient led up the Ettalerberg, near the scene of the famous Passion Play at Oberammergau. This road had struck the promoters as far too easy. So they switched us down a by-way on to an old packhorse route or smuggler's track, unused for many a long year. The leaders sailed up its foothill happily enough. Suddenly, what poor surface existed changed to a deep sunken gradient which merely survived as the rough bed of some winter torrent. High banks topped with wind-stunted foliage converted it into a long tunnel, rising almost vertically with a grade of perhaps 1 in 3. Unseen in the gloom, a series of rock steps, littered with boulders, blocked our path.

We were all tightly bunched by being started three a minute only a few yards short of the hill. The sidecars were mixed up with the solos. The front men stuck on the first rock step, and the entire trial piled up, almost knee-deep in dust and rocks. The gloom of the trough was thick with powdery dust and burnt lubricant.

One man made a clean ascent—George Rowley, on an A.J.S.

136

He had the luck to arrive at the rock steps early in the proceedings and, by superb riding and quick intelligence, flung his machine at the rough bank of the cutting, used it as banking and, taking his neck in his hands, charged the crux of the climb at high speed, dived through without hitting anybody. Many of the others had to push through the sweating, heaving crowd amid a polysyllabic bellow of curses in a dozen different languages. Had such a problem climb figured in any trial at home, the men would, of course, have been sent up at intervals.

Mussolini was never so unpopular as when he gave special permission for one of these International trials to be sent along the half-finished road along the western banks of Lake Garda. This road, now one of the loveliest in Italy, zigzagged for miles a hundred feet or so above the beautiful lake in a series of acute Z turns. It had just been metalled, but no roller had as yet disturbed its serenity. The broken stones were perhaps 6in deep. None of us had the vaguest notion as to how many kilometres this foul surface might continue. The stones looked sharp enough to hack our tyres to smithereens and, in fact, many sustained punctures along it, while others suffered from concussion bursts. Under the time schedule we were forced to take it fast, and it seemed interminable.

Furthermore, the gangs of labourers, stripped to the waist and charred nearly black by the Italian sun, had not been adequately warned of our coming. As the road was barred to all ordinary traffic, great poles on trestles blocked it to public access at all junctions with existing roads, and some of us met these poles at a few seconds' notice around blind bends on a surface on which it was really difficult to remain vertical, and out of the question to take the risk of a crash stop.

In all these Continental trials the route is naturally unknown to the British (and to some other) competitors, though usually familiar to the men representing the nation in whose territory the trial is held (who are normally the victors of the previous year and, therefore, a pretty tough crowd to beat!). Additionally, we have to transport our machines to that country. They may thus have undergone perhaps 1,000 miles of hammering before they reach the start, and at the back of our minds lies the realization that, after the finish, we will have to get them back another 1,000 miles to the Channel ports.

A single day's section may extend to 300 miles in ten hours, including a total ascent of 20,000 ft, and be punctuated by such incidents of weather, hunger, peril and effort as are here outlined. At the end the British daily Press may or may not deem a British victory in both the Trophy and Vase classes as worthy of six lines of small print in some odd corner.

But our competition riders, professional and amateur, are so tough that dozens of them outside the enviable individuals appointed as our official representatives by the A.C.U., annually travel to these distant venues, and never fail to distinguish themselves and their mounts against any opponents. All honour to them. These pages are written partly to extol their pluck and technical ability, together with the quality of the machines which earn our nation so much prestige and so many foreign markets.

This brief narrative is further justified for comparison with those years in the first decade of the century, when a home Six Days' trial was compulsorily routed to detour all real gradients and conducted under regulations designed to camouflage the crude quality of our pioneer products.

The layout of the 1949 International Six Days' indicates the strenuous character of these affairs. A route of some 1,250 miles, including plenty of " goat track ", was laid out in the Welsh mountains. This was divided into about sixty sections, at the end of which a rider must be on time. The schedule was so arranged that almost any petty trouble would make a rider late, and cost him reliability marks. At the end, an hour of high speed on the closed Eppynt circuit tested the finishing condition of his mount. The prescribed speed varies with the different sizes of engine, and was 44·6 m.p.h. for the 500 c.c. models. The 237 competitors included many individual entries, but the main awards always go to teams, for whom three competitions were arranged, namely, (1) the International Trophy, for teams of five, riding machines made in their national territory; (2) the Silver Vase, open to national teams of three, riding machines of any manufacture; and (3) the Club Team Competition.

As the riders in these events, other than the club representatives, are all assumed to be experts, they were set to ride to a time schedule 10 per cent. more severe than that imposed upon individual entries. The British team won the Trophy; was second in the Vase (through no fault of its own); won the club team prize; and gained the only manufacturers' team prizes to be awarded—no fewer than four of them. (These last are given to each manufacturers' team that completes the course without loss of marks.)

As we live in a commercial age, it is fair to admit one exception to the verdict just pronounced upon reliability trials. Manufacturers have to sell their goods. Advertisement—that many-headed hydra—is the main instrument of sales. The best advertisement is a satisfied customer. He may be an excellent salesman for the motor cycle which he rides without ever singing its praises, since the mere spectacle of his happy daily progress sinks into the public mind. Space in newspapers and magazines is another major instrument in sales. But it is the belief of all motor manufacturers that publicized feats are essential to maximum sales. It is for this reason that the oil barons and most manufacturers of motoring components and parts are prone to subsidize motoring competitions in various forms.

Since speed makes a special impression on the public mind, speed contests receive the maximum publicity. But the fact that the X.Y.Z. motor bicycle defeated all comers in some reliability trial contributes its inexorable mite to any sales campaign. Still more efficacious is the fact that the Norton beat all American comers, together with several British rivals, in the Daytona races of March, 1949 and 1950, or that a British team won the Trophy in an International Six Days'. The former indicates reliability at racing speeds. The latter keeps speed in the background, although speed is actually involved in it.

Any motor cycle manufacturer would rather win the Senior T.T., or set up a new record for the world's best time on two wheels, than see one of his machines in the victorious Trophy team. In short, speed has wholly eclipsed pure reliability as a sales instrument, and this fact is a further explanation for the reduced importance of both the major and the minor reliability tests.

The main credit for the organization of motor cycling in its sporting aspects between the wars must be awarded to T. W. Loughborough, who was Secretary of the Auto Cycle Union from 1912 to 1946. At his appointment the A.C.U. was a somewhat spineless body. A man of great vigour and sound judgment, he collected committees of keen and knowledgeable men, and displayed real genius in combining the force of an autocrat with the persuasiveness of a democrat. He was alike the inspiration behind club life, reliability trials, racing in all its phases—the T.T., Brooklands, the " small " tracks, Donington—and crowned his career by salvaging the cinder speedways from threatened ruin, and establishing them on a firm foundation without the aid of the tote or the bookmakers. Nor did he confine his energies to this country, for no individual carried more weight with the International Federation of Motorcyclists than he.

CHAPTER 19

RACING

(and Especially the T.T. Races)

MANKIND HAS ALWAYS RACED, and will continue to race until the end of time. The habit is clearly based on primary impulses, including the desire to excel other males and to impress females. There are proofs that foot racing was popular among semi-primitive peoples. Today, men race horses, dogs, boats, pigeons, yachts, aircraft, cycles and, on foot, against each other. Prisoners of war have been known to race cockroaches when all else failed. As long as motor cycles are made, men will certainly race on them, no matter what the cost nor how valid arguments against the hobby may become.

Evidence of this irresistible tendency were numerous after VE Day. Brooklands track was lost for ever. Donington, our small but very intriguing road circuit in the Midlands, was doggedly retained by the War Office. There was no hope of Parliament changing its traditional hostility to closing public roads for motor racing. Land, labour and money were all lacking. Yet within four years an incredible number of " small tracks " leapt into being all over the country, ranging from quondam airfields to private park lands. The general public remains entirely ignorant of the multiplicity of such fixtures. For a single week in September, 1949, the motor cycle Press announced no fewer than eighteen local speed events on British soil. The figure is exclusive of speedway racing at the various stadia, and consisted mostly of grass-track and scramble events.

The justification of all motor racing is hotly debated from time to time. Its opponents complain that it kills and injures a certain number of men; that it is costly; that it tends to develop the wrong types of motor; that it is scientifically useless; and that it encourages a worship of speed which infects road users, and tends to increase the number of road accidents.

The supporters of racing are thus confronted by a formidable indictment. The best retort comes from a manufacturer. The director of a non-racing firm asked him why he raced. He replied, " I cannot afford *not* to race. My duty to my customers demands that I give them the best machines possible. This implies that I must perfect roadholding, steering, brakes, control and reliability by all means in my power. My experience is that every race teaches me something new."

The T.T. races have been much maligned. But it is indisputable that they transformed the primitive motor cycle from a flimsy toy into a well-nigh perfect two-wheeler, in which it is now almost impossible to fault any feature essential for safety.

The justification for racing may now be analysed as follows: (1) Men race because they just cannot help it; (2) they race for fun; (3) they race for motives of research, to perfect the numerous components involved in a design; (4) they race for fame; (5) they race for trade; (6) they race for the national safety.

The last two justifications require explanation. The motor industries are fiercely competitive, and their success is very largely based on shrewd publicity. Man, being a speed-loving animal, is peculiarly magnetized by speed. After VE Day we made a vigorous effort to sell our motor cycles in the U.S.A. We established a phenomenal demand in the States for our machines, largely based on their speed. Using smaller engines than were standard in the U.S.A., our motor cycles showed themselves equal or superior in performance to the big Harleys and Indians.

One illustration of the bearing of racing research on national safety occurred in 1914. The German Imperial General Staff had foreseen that the next war would bring aircraft into action. Their government instructed their engineers to spend vast sums in developing certain racing cars. When war broke out, those engines dictated the design of the power units for German aircraft, which secured the mastery of the air until, two or three years later, we had had time to develop even finer British engines.

The humane argument against racing is the most moving, and perhaps the most deceptive. Nobody approves the early sacrifice of young and potentially valuable lives. But racing has probably saved far more lives than it has curtailed. The T.T., for example, has perfected roadholding, tyres, steering and brakes. It has emphasized the part that rear springing plays in roadholding, with the result that rear suspension is now being added to the standard specification of roadster machines as widely as price permits. It has abolished the manual gear-change, which compelled a rider to remove one hand from the steering bar (and perhaps to take his eyes off the road) in favour of a pedal device, which frees both hands for steering and requires no downward glance.

Neither of these effects was widely anticipated 15 or 18 years ago, and other similar products of racing are still hidden in the womb of the future. These improvements have saved far more lives than they have cost. Irresponsible youths will ride fast on the roads whether races are organized or not. But racing will continuously supply them with safer machines, on which accidents will be less probable.

It is occasionally pleaded that although these facts justify the racing programme, yet racing tends to develop the wrong type of roadster machine. There is some meat in that argument, but it also bristles with fallacy. Nobody imagines that the car industry

141

is likely to supply the public with four-wheelers resembling Raymond Mays' E.R.A. racers or with modified versions of the spidery 500 c.c. Cooper projectiles. Such cars may be described as laboratory experiments, from which engineers derive knowledge later to be incorporated in milder touring designs.

A modern Senior T.T.-winning motor cycle is grotesquely ill adapted for road work. It has four gears, on which it will touch 80, 90, 100 and 120 miles an hour respectively. Owing to an extractor type of exhaust system, coupled with abnormal valve timing, it will hardly run evenly at much less than 5,000 r.p.m. Such features may seem fantastic.

Under normal road conditions they would be ridiculous. But in a race they serve two technical purposes, quite apart from the publicity, spectacular and fun aspects. The races test design in its every detail. They advance metallurgy in a hundred ways. They furnish the speeds which supply searching tests of every component— tyres, brakes, steering, gear boxes, suspension, and the rest. The proof is simple and undeniable. The roadster machines sold by the factories which develop the T.T. winners bear no close resemblance to their racing cousins, but owe to those projectiles the very qualities which make them the best roadsters in the whole world.

Most of the racing firms show themselves extraordinarily flexible. For many years past Veloce, Ltd., of Birmingham, have enjoyed a world reputation for marketing the best and fastest 350 c.c. sports and racing models. Some of their customers through these years were puzzled because the firm simultaneously displayed great interest in a design at the opposite pole—a small, light roadster of almost " pansy " type, namely, a two-stroke rated at $2\frac{1}{2}$ h.p. The discrepancy was explained in 1948 when the firm suddenly launched on a surprised public the new LE model described at length in Chapter 27.

The directors had always held that hitherto motor cycles had failed to attract an immense potential public, composed of mild, weak or elderly men, and of multitudes of women, who could not afford cars, who disliked the physical exertion of pedalling cycles for any great distance, who were affronted by the heavier types of motor cycle, but who would welcome a light, comfortable, silent, no-trouble " potter bus " (that is, a sedate machine, which requires no athlete to manage it, and will take its owner anywhere at low cost with great dependability). The LE is the indirect offspring of the rorty KTT Velocette, which ranked as world speed champion for 1949 and 1950 in its class. The knowledge garnered in racing experience qualified the designers to produce the quiet little roadster.

From that climax it is easy to retrace the technical history of the motor cycle back to 1900, to see how clumsily we blundered into the racing game, and how mercilessly the hard facts of the racing ordeal ultimately guided us to a host of correct conclusions.

Previous to 1896 our road laws condemned our engineers to concede a start of several years to our French, Belgian and German rivals, who had amassed considerable knowledge while we remained abysmally ignorant. As I have recorded earlier, our engineers knew no more than the stationary gas engine could teach them. They had no tyres suited for anything heavier than a pedal cycle. They knew little about bearings or valve steels, or piston materials, or cylinder casting. Their knowledge of brakes was limited to the flimsy pads of a pedal cycle. They knew little about ignition or carburettors. Many such fields were fenced by foreign patents, and patent law was obscure.

For the moment we were outclassed. Comparatively few people realized that the petrol engine was about to revolutionize road transport, to invade the railway monopoly, to open the door for the conquest of the air.

Out of this pit of despond our engineers began sturdily to climb the steep mountain of research. A marked characteristic of racing research is that it *accelerates* progress. Even today three hours of a race run at an average speed of 90 m.p.h. over a mountainous course may teach a designer more than 50,000 miles of experimental road work. Some car manufacturers sidestep the acid test of racing by sending their experimental models across the Channel to cover a huge mileage under relays of drivers over roads unhampered by speed limits or acute congestion and across the high passes of the Alps.

Simultaneously, sample engines are run day and night on the bench. Many popular cars of the day were tested by this method. It is good, but it is less exacting than racing, in which a designer submits his machine to tests far more devastating than public roads can furnish.

Our motor cycle racing policy betrays a definite evolution, which is worthy of analysis.

At the dawn of the century we knew that Continental designers were acquiring their special knowledge from racing on public roads (for example, the Paris-Madrid race). No parallel opportunity was feasible here. We began by entering our crude motor cycles for a Continental event known as the International Cup. It was open to teams of three riders from each nation, riding machines weighing not more than 110 lb, and contested on the soil of the previous year's victor. The 12 m.p.h. limit still fettered English roads. We organized simple eliminating tests for our own entries in the Isle of Man or in private parks.

Naturally, we were outclassed, though our failure was distorted alike by our ignorance of Continental roads, and also by the wiles of our rivals, who enforced their printed regulations pitilessly against us, but permitted their own nationals to be assisted by non-competing mechanics carrying plenty of spare parts!

Brief experience of this programme rapidly convinced us that the basis was just plain silly. The rules placed a ridiculous emphasis on lightness. At the start, all competitors were busy with brace and drill perforating saddles, clips, belt rims, and so forth, to get down the weight. Fractures were frequent, and the specification was

143

absurdly flimsy. (I speak feelingly, for I once entered three 8 h.p. twins weighing 110 lb apiece in a preliminary selection test!) We became very critical of the Continental theory that the ideal motor cycle consisted basically of a pedal cycle on which was hung the biggest available engine.

The following is a brief summary of this short-lived " International Motor Cycle Cup Race ", first organized by France in 1904. Largely owing to friction concerning administration it died a natural death at the end of 1906. It was open to (a) teams of three riders (with a fourth man in reserve) representing their nation, and (b) machines not exceeding 50 kilogrammes (approximately 110 lb) in weight, exclusive of oil, petrol, spare parts, and accumulator; an extra 3 kilos could be claimed for magneto ignition.

For the 1904 Race, Britain nominated H. J. Harding (Lagonda), W. Hodgkinson (J.A.P.) and T. Silver (Quadrant). France, Germany, Britain, Austria and Denmark entered. The result was: 1, Demester, France, on a Griffon; 2, Toman, Austria, on a Laurin-Klement; 3, Lamberjack, France, on a Griffon.

For the 1905 race, Britain held eliminating trials on a Manx course, near St. Johns, which produced the following team: 1, J. S. Campbell (6 h.p. Ariel-J.A.P.); 2, H. A. Collier (6 h.p. Matchless-J.A.P.); 3, C. B. Franklin (6 h.p. J.A.P.); reserve, H. Rignold (8 h.p. J.A.P.). The race was run on public roads near Dourdan, the five laps totalling 270 kilometres (approximately 167 miles). First was Wondrick (Austria), on a twin-cylinder Laurin Klement, in 3h 5m 15s; 2, Giuppone (Italy) on twin-cylinder Peugeot, in 3h 35m 2s. The only other finisher was Demester (France), on a twin-cylinder Griffon, whose time was 3h 13m 2s, but he was disqualified for changing his back wheel.

The 1906 race was held in Austria (as the result of Wondrick's 1905 victory) over a four-lap course totalling 248·8 kilometres near Patzau. Lord Derby lent the A.C.U. a course in Knowsley Park for their eliminating trials, where the three fastest men were: 1, C. R. Collier (Matchless-J.A.P.); 2, H. A. Collier (Matchless-J.A.P.); 3, C. B. Franklin (J.A.P.). The results of the race were: 1, Ed. Nikodem (Austria), Puch, 3h 13m 45·4s; 2, Louis Obruba (Austria), Puch, 3h 29m 41·6s; 3, H. A. Collier (Britain), Matchless, 3h 39m 53·6s; 4, Retiene (Germany), Progress, 3h 55m 21·2s.

All the defeated nations promptly protested against the Puch team on the ground that they were assisted by Puch riders travelling the lap in both directions with sidecars full of spare parts. The protest was never heard, and the international series was consequently abandoned.

The Manx Parliament proved more flexible than the British. Possessing Home Rule, the Manx House of Keys agreed to subsidize the event and to close nearly 16 miles of gently undulating road for us, provided we dated a race either before or just after their summer season. Realizing that spring forks and substantial fittings were impossible under the European scheme, we christened our race the

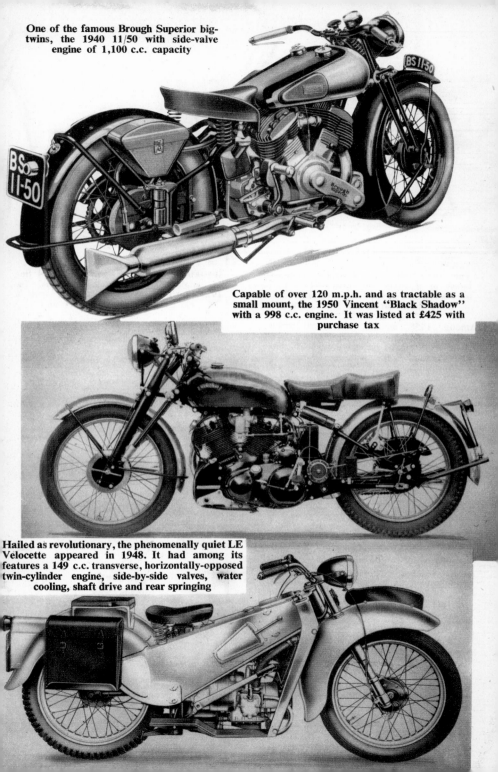

One of the famous Brough Superior big-twins, the 1940 11/50 with side-valve engine of 1,100 c.c. capacity

Capable of over 120 m.p.h. and as tractable as a small mount, the 1950 Vincent "Black Shadow" with a 998 c.c. engine. It was listed at £425 with purchase tax

Hailed as revolutionary, the phenomenally quiet LE Velocette appeared in 1948. It had among its features a 149 c.c. transverse, horizontally-opposed twin-cylinder engine, side-by-side valves, water cooling, shaft drive and rear springing

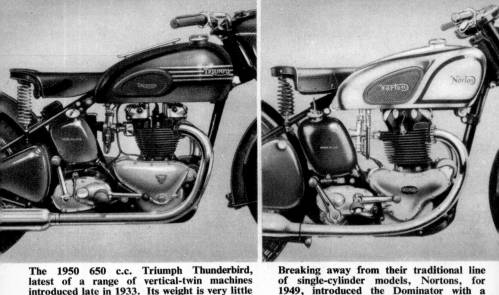

The 1950 650 c.c. Triumph Thunderbird, latest of a range of vertical-twin machines introduced late in 1933. Its weight is very little more than that of the 500 c.c. models

Breaking away from their traditional line of single-cylinder models, Nortons, for 1949, introduced the Dominator with a 497 c.c. vertical-twin power unit

Among 1950 models, the shaft-driven Sunbeam stands out with distinction. The vertical-twin engine has its crankshaft and cylinders in line with the frame

An unusually comfortable machine to ride, the 500 c.c. Matchless G9 twin, with its spring frame, made its début at the 1948 London Show

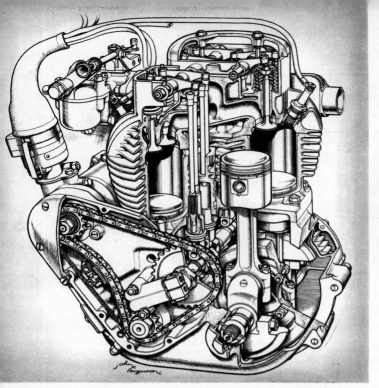

A sectional view of the 997 c.c. Ariel Square Four engine. The two crank-shafts are geared together. Cylinder block and cylinder heads are in light alloy and the rocker boxes are integral with the cylinder-head casting

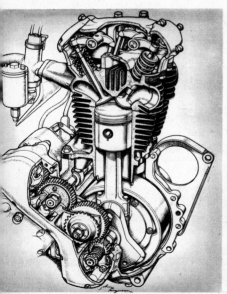

The 650 c.c. overhead-valve vertical-twin B.S.A. introduced for 1950. A single-piece crankshaft is employed, the central flywheel being threaded into place

Partly-sectioned drawing of the 500 c.c. vertical-twin engine fitted to A.J.S and Matchless machines in 1950. Separate cylinder heads and cylinder barrels are employed

Start of the London-Land's End trial of 1909. (Left to right) Dr. Gibbons, F. T. Bidlake (timekeeper), F. J. Jenkins, J. V. Robinson, C. C. Cooke, H. Karslake (Dreadnought), H. Gibson (Triumph), C. Jarrott, W. Cooper (Bradbury)

Controls and equipment of 1908. Typical features shown include the acetylene lamp, bulb horn, speedometer, watch and control levers. The long rubber handlebar grips will be noted

In the days when sidecar outfits were as common as solo mounts. Note the fancy canework of the sidecar door

B. H. Davies with his early Excelsior (1903). The machine had horseshoe brakes, surface carburettor and hand oil-pump beneath the saddle

Miss Muriel Hind (Mrs. Lord), who rode Singer and Rex machines in competitions for many years

J. Marshall winning the Isle of Man Tourist Trophy race of 1908. His mount was a Triumph and his average speed 40·40 m.p.h.

In the days when the police looked on. A speed event on an open road at a meeting of the Coventry and Warwickshire M.C. in 1905

(Right) A 2¾ h.p. V-type Humber ridden by G. Geoffrey Smith in the Anglo-Dutch International Trials of 1912 and 1913. At that time Editor of "The Motor Cycle", he is now a director of Associated Iliffe Press

A scooter of 1919. This model was fitted with a 1½ h.p. four-stroke A.B.C. engine

In addition to the great part played by motor cycle despatch riders in the first World War, gunners were equipped with machine-guns mounted on reinforced sidecar chassis as shown on this Matchless outfit. Royal Enfields and Clynos were also used

A scene in Brooklands paddock at the first open meeting in 1908

Forecars were the fashion in the early days. With the large windscreen and flexible cane body, real comfort was achieved

Ivan Hart-Davies (3½ h.p. Triumph), who broke the Land's End-to-John O' Groats record in 1911 with a time of 29 hours 12 minutes

The first ascent of Porlock in 1911 by a sidecar, showing Frank Smith (Clyno) on the second bend. The then Editor of "The Motor Cycle" was passenger

Beggars' Roost in the 1934 London-Land' End trial. At Easter hundreds of spectators gather at this spot to watch competitors thread their way up the rough, steep incline

(Below)
Part of the great crowd which invaded Brooklands on "The Motor Cycle" Clubman's Day in 1930. The attendance was estimated at 25,000

They're off! Clubmen on the closely-packed stand watch the start of the 500 c.c. sprint

Tourist Trophy, sketching a liberal specification under which any maker could enter his notion of a reliable roadster. We imposed no absurd weight limit. But we ensured approximation to commercial factors by limiting engine dimensions to reasonable figures, and by imposing a fuel ration.

Thus early our ideal was definite . . . to foster a sturdy, economical roadster, which should attain a fair speed on the flat, and carry its rider up ordinary gradients. (It would have been unwise at that date to put a premium on really high speeds, or to insist on the ascent of 1 in 5 hills.) The Marquis Mouzilly de St. Mars offered a trophy for the first T.T. run in June, 1907, through his friendship for the late Etienne Boileau (London Editor of *The Motor Cycle*, then published in Coventry).

The race was organized by the motor cycle subcommittee of the proprietary A.C.G.B. & I. (Automobile Club of Great Britain and Ireland—later the R.A.C.). This committee, then known as the Auto Cycle Club (later the Auto Cycle Union) worked to a very narrow budget, and opened a subscription list to finance the race. When I first saw that list, it amounted to no more than £50, of which a single subscriber had contributed £25!

There were two classes, for single and twin-cylinders respectively. The lap, measuring 15 miles 1,430 yards, started from St. John's, and ran via Ballacraine over Creg Willeys Hill into Kirkmichael and back via Peel. This was to be covered ten times, but anticipating the fatigue of the riders (who would have to pedal hard up Creg Willeys) a ten-minute rest was allowed after five laps! The machines entered for the 1907 race were supposed to be identical with those sold to the public. The fuel allowance was 14 pints 1 oz for singles, and 16 pints 17 oz for twins. (Pedals were barred for the 1908 race.)

The race was a gigantic success. Seventeen singles and eight twins started in pairs at two-minute intervals. Eight singles and three twins finished. C. R. Collier (Matchless-J.A.P.) won the race at 38·22 m.p.h., using pedals for acceleration and a few of the steeper gradients, from J. Marshall (Triumph). Rem Fowler (Norton) headed the twin-cylinder class at 36·22 m.p.h. Several riders averaged better than 100 miles per gallon. Nobody was injured or killed! There was plenty of trouble with belts, pistons, tyres, valves and brakes. Several men fell off through over-audacious cornering. Signals were given by footmen who trotted alongside the labouring machines up the gentle grade of Creg Willeys, and told the competitors at length precisely how they stood!

When the race ended, the fifteen manufacturers concerned had plenty of headaches. They knew, in ample detail, what modifications they must plan for the 1908 races. *Racing had begun to fulfil its primary function—to supply information upon which subsequent research should be based.*

From that day to this the T.T. races have continued to serve that primary function. They were interrupted by war in 1915, 1916,

1917, 1918 and 1919, and again in the 1940–1946 period. In 1924 no fewer than five separate races were held—for 175 c.c., 250 c.c., 350 c.c., 500 c.c. (solos) and 600 c.c. sidecar outfits respectively.

In 1911, largely under pressure from *The Motor Cycle*—desirous to see variable gears in the events—the races were transferred to the so-called " Mountain " course, now world famous. It covers 37 miles 1,290 yards, and ranks as the most famous racing circuit in the world. It is no longer used by racing cars simply because the road is not wide enough for safe use by large vehicles. It embodies the climb over a 1,400 ft shoulder of Snaefell Mountain, together with every imaginable type of bend and corner from the hairpin which brings men to a crawl up to the speed bend which an expert can round at 100 m.p.h. Nowhere can the rider see a clear mile ahead. Each corner is so linked with the next that the exit from one bend must be calculated to furnish the optimum entry into the next. Literally hundreds of gear changes may be involved in a single lap.

The effects of forty odd years of T.T. racing research are self-evident alike in the spectacle of a modern T.T., in the daily use of roadster machines embodying the lessons of racing, and in the statistical records.

In the past, such racing became highly specialized, and extremely costly. Moreover, between the wars the number of ace riders capable of taking a machine round the long lap at an average speed of close on 90 m.p.h. seldom exceeded three or four. A manufacturer who failed to contract one of these chosen few stood no real chance of victory. Hence, many manufacturers abstained altogether, or entered a machine or two merely to see how they stood up to the ordeal, though well aware that, even with better riders, they had no chance to win.

Nevertheless, the effects of research covered the whole industry. A myriad items were developed by specialists—steels, tyres, gear boxes, ignition devices, brake linings, steering design, rear suspension, carburettors, chains, sparking plugs and so forth. All these were immediately placed by component firms at the disposal of every maker, whether he himself raced or not.

By 1949 a novel situation developed. There were signs that the small select coterie of star riders was expanding at a high rate. Brooklands Track had been closed after long and yeoman service to the entire motor industry. The small circuit at Donington had been requisitioned by the War Office as a vehicle depot. But new tracks had been opened—Eppynt, Haddenham, Blandford, Cadwell, Scarborough, and many another. Virile young Britain was eagerly making use of its opportunities. During 1949 fourteen week-end meetings at Brands Hatch grass track drew 150,000 spectators.

Simultaneously two firms in the industry began to market genuine racing models, at a reasonable price, in quantity. This policy, initiated by Velocette as far back as 1928, was now adopted by Triumph and A.J.S. The Triumph Co. released their Grand

Prix model, capable of 120 m.p.h. in delivery tune. Associated Motorcycles, Ltd., followed with their 7R 350 c.c. racer. In addition, the famous " Manx " Nortons continued to be available to private buyers.

Success in motor cycle racing offers substantial financial rewards to young mechanics seeking to improve their monetary status. The winner of a Senior T.T. pockets close on £1,000 in prizes and in bonuses from the makers of his equipment.

The summer Continental programme includes a host of similar race meetings, at which starting money, cash prizes, and additional equipment bonuses may be earned. All this experience and training tends to develop a far larger body of high-speed experts. The signs indicate that motor cycle racing is on the upward crest of a boom, with the result that research is more intense and concentrated than ever before. This is reflected in greater racing reliability.

Any visitor to the Isle of Man during or after a T.T. meeting may now perceive a polished black line about 2 feet wide continuous round the whole 37-odd miles of the circuit, traced by the wheels of the riders and indicating the perfect line into and out of every corner—and the name of its corners is Legion. In June, 1950, the rush to compete was so furious that the officials were compelled in the interests of safety and of race management to limit the entries in each event to a maximum of 100.

In the Junior Race for engines of 350 c.c. 100 started, and 63 finished. The winner—A. J. Bell, Norton—averaged 86·33 m.p.h., his fastest lap being covered at 87·31 m.p.h. The slowest of the 63 finishers averaged 67·81 m.p.h. The vast majority of the machines were stock models, as sold at any retailer's showroom. The Senior Race for engines of 500 c.c. fell to G. E. Duke (Norton) at 92·27 m.p.h., who led from start to finish and established a lap record for the course at 93·33 m.p.h.

The contrast between this mighty spectacle and the slightly puny and laughable affair of 1907 is stupendous, especially as the only permitted fuel was " straight " petrol. On a petrol-benzole mixture the speeds would have been substantially higher.

I have no wish to minimize the contributions to engineering science ascribable to the defunct Brooklands Track, or to Donington, or to bench tests against the dynamometer. But none of them could accomplish what road racing has achieved in developing engines and machines. On the outer circuit of Brooklands, engines ran on one gear at one speed over the whole lap, whereas in the Island the engine speed is constantly varying, the brakes are in frequent and violent use, and the entire machine is steadily punished. The men who rather hesitatingly organized the first mildly ridiculous T.T. built better than they knew.

Nor must the international aspect of road racing be overlooked. The T.T. is still called the International Tourist Trophy Race. Admittedly, a majority of the riders are always British, as are most of the competing machines. But there is always a percentage of oversea entries. Occasionally, foreign machines have been able to score a few notable victories.

This is especially true of the Lightweight or 250 c.c. class. Most British motor cyclists are drawn from the higher ranks of the artisan or *petit bourgeois* class. They can afford a larger and more expensive machine than the 250 c.c. But that size of engine is vastly popular on the European continent, and has there undergone more development than with us, especially in Germany and Italy. Such foreign 250 c.c. machines as the Guzzi (Italian), Benelli (Italian), and D.K.W. (German) are faster racers than our own 250s. It may be that increasing austerity will yet force us to pay more attention to small engines, but for the moment we yield the palm in that neglected field to oversea rivals.

In 1939 we took a sound thrashing from the German B.M.W. in the 500 c.c. Senior class, wherein we had been invincible for years. That was due to two factors. The 1939 international regulations permitted engines to be supercharged, which has the effect of a power rise equivalent to perhaps a 25 per cent. increase in engine size. We had no supercharged racing engines, we were caught napping, and we could not hold the " blown " B.M.W.

Nevertheless, between the wars British journalists who reported motor cycle races all over Europe, normally spent a most heartening time. I recall, for example, crossing the Channel to describe the Dutch T.T. races over the Drente circuit at Assen. Over 100,000 spectators were ringing a 10-mile lap. In each and every class, British riders and British machines secured an almost contemptuous supremacy. As each event finished the massed bands played our national anthem, and our flag was hoisted. This supremacy, with occasional interruptions, characterized motor cycle racing all over Europe between the wars, and survives today, though it is fair to add that for a period Germany was neither permitted to manufacture machines exceeding 250 c.c. nor eligible to compete in international events.

This race-bred quality is not a mere matter of prestige. Very large sums have been earned in the United States since the end of World War II by the export of innumerable British motor cycles. In the U.S.A. the motor cycle market had become small and rather stagnant between the wars. This was due to two causes. The low cost of " gas " and of used cars enabled prosperous artisans to own cars. The American motor cycle had practically shrunk to two factories, neither of which essayed much research or developed much enterprise in a somewhat limited and disheartening market.

Facing a backlog of some 8,000,000 cars after the war, the Americans allowed our machines a generous entry, and the American motor cyclists welcomed our best makes with delirious surprise. Then in March, 1949, some of our racing models entered the great annual American motor cycle race at Daytona Beach in Florida, and our Norton machines won both the amateur and professional classes outright. This dollar influx again stems back to the small handful of enthusiasts who organized the original 1907 T.T. race.

No chapter on racing could be complete without a brief reference to Brooklands. This famous concrete bowl with a steeply banked circuit of 2·767 miles was built by Mr. F. Locke-King, opened in 1907 and finally closed during World War II. Principally renowned for car racing, it also served as the home of the British Motor Cycle Racing Club, who from 1919 onward held on an average eight meetings per year, and gave facilities to factories for individual tests of their own products. It could be lapped by a motor bicycle at a speed of 125 m.p.h. The bowl was usually a scene of frantic activity just before the autumn Show, when makers utilized some speed stunt as publicity for their new models. It was the only place in Britain where really high speed was practicable, with the sole exception of Pendine Sands (where the condition of the beach was always a gamble).

The savagely contested hour record was a recurrent feature of the first importance for many years. Since the track was closed, British makers desirous of exploiting sustained high speed have been driven across the Channel to the Montlhéry track on the outskirts of Paris, though such brief sprints as the flying mile or kilometre records have been possible on certain Continental highways. Neither short, twisty circuits nor the tame perimeters of derelict airfields can replace Brooklands for such purposes. At one period *The Motor Cycle* sponsored annually a great national race meeting there.

Nevertheless, many of the tears shed over its passing were crocodile tears. It was never a comfortable track to ride. At speeds much in excess of 110 m.p.h. it was not particularly safe, and several riders have gone over the edge of its high banking. Its sheer vastness impaired the spectacle of high speed. At the very first meeting a Cockney bookmaker exclaimed in amazement, " Cor! Look at them ——— little beetles creeping round the ——— saucer! " If its huge dimensions dwarfed the feats of monstrous racing cars, motor cycles seemed like ants when speeding over a remote part of its surface.

This spectacular defect limited attendances to gates frequently too small to cover its financial aspects. Nor was it always a comfortable place for the spectator. Much walking was necessary to cover all the coigns of vantage—the paddock, the steeply banked curves, the awkward bumpy sections where the banking flattened out into the straights. In cold weather it was a temple of the winds. In summer heat it became an oven. Traffic jams were the rule on race days over its narrow approaches.

But old-timers will never mention its name without a certain nostalgia. In particular, many motor cycle designers found it an invaluable laboratory. It was naturally ill-suited to the testing of gear boxes. But it certainly furnished an acid test of the sustained maximum revolutions of any engine, as also of tyres, roadholding, steering, and general mechanical stamina. The cost of all technical tests was considerably less than that of a trip to the Continental tracks or to the Isle of Man. Expert officials were always available at reasonable fees to verify performances.

Despite the hammering which any distance records with an unsprung rear wheel inflicted on the unfortunate jockey, many of our semi-professional speed merchants had an affection for it. Moreover, occasions frequently crop up today when designers feel its loss keenly. It is true that on the factory test bench an engine can be subjected to ordeals approximating closely to prolonged laps of such a bowl. But nowadays it is difficult to simulate the ordeal which it imposed on the machine as a whole. The lessons of such ordeals are suggested by the frequency with which our manufacturers now face the far heavier cost of dispatching a team to Montlhéry.

But so far as spectacles for the sporting public are concerned, a much smaller circuit is actually more convincing and more packed with thrills. On such small tracks as Eppynt or Blandford or Scarborough or Cadwell, the spectators are comparatively close to the machines for much of their travel, and similar reasoning applies under more artificial conditions to the 418-yard lap of the Wembley Speedway with the towering slopes of its great bowl seating 93,000 spectators at short range and in physical comfort. (It was for such reasons that during the years preceding the closure of Brooklands, its controllers often substituted a short portion of the track, rendered sinuous by *chicanes*, for plain straightforward " blinding " round the outer circuit of the full 2¾ miles.)

It is therefore questionable whether its technical loss would be acutely felt if, at some future date, a few miles of an arterial highway became available for full-throttle sprints, such as the world records for short distances require.

Indeed, the lamentations so audible when its doom was first announced have almost completely died down. Since Brooklands originally cost nearly £250,000 in an age when the £ purchased far more than it is ever likely to provide in the future, it is unlikely that we shall ever again own a complete speedway of any great size entirely devoted to fast motoring. Should such a possibility arise, the next Brooklands is more likely to resemble the German Nürburg Ring, which embodies a nightmare series of every imaginable type of bend and corner, wedded to ever-varying gradients. Bluntly, Brooklands, though extremely utilitarian, was on the whole rather dull!

Strictly speaking, a tabloid account of motor cycle " scrambles " should be included in this chapter, since they are always fought against the clock. If Brooklands and Silverstone are the Epsom of fast motoring, the scramble is its Aintree, its Grand National. But as the scrambles are run over very short distances, and as yet hardly rank as national classics, they are dealt with in Chapter 20.

Last, but not least in this racing category, the " Continental Circus " must not be forgotten. This small band of cunning racers and deft mechanics borrow their title from von Richthofen's squadron of fighter aces who used to tour the French front in

World War I. Most of them are just one step below top rank in the motor cycle racing world. Equipped with motor vans, packed full of tools and camping gear, they tour the Continent from early spring to late autumn in order to compete at every race meeting which offers starting money and cash prizes.

A merry, courageous crew, they do yeoman service as ambassadors not only of British wares, but also of the British character. At intervals they are reinforced by our fastest stars, who cross the Channel with our best machines to compete in the half dozen selected Grand Prix events, at which marks are annually allotted towards the world road-racing championship. Late in the autumn the minor stars return to England, brown as berries, tough as fencing wire, usually with full pockets. Occasionally, alas, they leave one or two of their number behind in foreign hospitals or cemeteries. They lead a queer, tough, dangerous existence, which they will be sorry to quit when age disqualifies them from their ruthless profession. Meanwhile they make a definite contribution to British prestige.

(*Footnote:*—Space does not permit the inclusion of either the T.T. or Brooklands statistics. Readers who desire to study T.T. history in detail should obtain a copy of *The Story of the T.T.*, written by a former T.T. winner, Geoffrey Davison, and published by him at 9s. 6d. from 106, Bristol Road, Birmingham, 5. Mr. Davison also publishes the stories of the Ulster Grand Prix and the September Manx Grand Prix races. The records of Brooklands have not yet appeared in book form, but are available to painstaking students of the files of the technical Press. The world's maximum speed record figures are set out below.)

WORLD'S MOTOR CYCLE MAXIMUM SPEED RECORD

Year	Rider and Country	M.P.H.	Motor Cycle
1909	W. E. Cook (Gt. Britain)	75·92	994 c.c. N.L.G.
1910	C. R. Collier (Gt. Britain)	80·24	976 c.c. Matchless
1910	C. R. Collier (Gt. Britain)	84·89	976 c.c. Matchless
1911	Jake de Rosier (U.S.A.)	85·38	998 c.c. Indian
1911	Jake de Rosier (U.S.A.)	88·77	998 c.c. Indian
1911	C. R. Collier (Gt. Britain)	89·84	998 c.c. Matchless
1911	C. R. Collier (Gt. Britain)	91·23	998 c.c. Matchless
1914	S. George (Gt. Britain)	93·48	998 c.c. Indian
1920	H. Le Vack (Gt. Britain)	94·79	998 c.c. Indian
1920	E. Walker (U.S.A.)	103·56	994 c.c. Indian
1923	F. W. Dixon (Gt. Britain)	106·8	989 c.c. Harley-Davidson
1923	C. F. Temple (Gt. Britain)	108·48	996 c.c. British Anzani
1924	H. Le Vack (Gt. Britain)	113·61	998 c.c. Brough Superior-J.A.P.
1924	H. Le Vack (Gt. Britain)	119·05	876 c.c. Brough Superior-J.A.P.
1926	C. F. Temple (Gt. Britain)	121·41	996 c.c. O.E.C.-Temple
1928	O. M. Baldwin (Gt. Britain)	124·62	996 c.c. Zenith-J.A.P.
1929	H. Le Vack (Gt. Britain)	129·07	995 c.c. Brough Superior-J.A.P.
1930	J. S. Wright (Gt. Britain)	134·51	994 c.c. O.E.C.-Temple
1930	J. S. Wright (Gt. Britain)	137·32	994 c.c. O.E.C.-Temple
1930	E. Henne (Germany)	137·66	735 c.c. B.M.W.
1930	J. S. Wright (Gt. Britain)	150·74	995 c.c. O.E.C.-Temple-J.A.P.
1932	E. Henne (Germany)	151·86	735 c.c. B.M.W.
1934	E. Henne (Germany)	152·901	735 c.c. B.M.W.
1935	E. Henne (Germany)	159·1	735 c.c. B.M.W.
1936	E. Henne (Germany)	169·016	495 c.c. B.M.W.
1937	E. C. Fernihough (Gt. Britain)	169·786	995 c.c. Brough Superior-J.A.P.
1937	E. Henne (Germany)	173·675	493 c.c. B.M.W.

CHAPTER 20

SCRAMBLES AND ONE-DAY TRIALS

T HE GENERAL PUBLIC KNOW NOTHING of the innumerable " one-day trials " which figure in the annual motor cycling programme, and they care less. Such events are not reported in the national Press, and only a few fixtures of outstanding importance merit detailed descriptions in the motor cycle journals. But for a small coterie of passionate athletes they are almost the breath of life. They possess genuine interest, both sporting and psychological; this interest attaches alike to their origin and their character.

Man is a gregarious animal, and way back at the start of the century each individual motor cyclist—a species then almost as rare as a golden oriole—took pains to trace out other riders, and clubs were formed as soon as a dozen or two of us got together. These clubs were no pipe-and-pint affairs. We wanted to ride together—and a ride implied a purpose. Man is also a competitive animal, and few clubs had existed for more than a few weeks before somebody offered a trophy for competition.

At that date, none of us was ever quite sure whether his machine would go at all on a named date in the future, still less for how long it might consent to keep going. So the first trials were Sunday or Saturday afternoon affairs, and extremely simple. You chose a short length of some fairly level highway, such as the Great North Road, and rode up and down a 25-mile section of it until only one rider retained his non-stop. There was no question of climb or speed—you just had to keep going. Any stoppage put you out, even if it happened when you were trying to turn round in the road at the milestone which indicated the end of the section.

Naturally we very soon learnt how to endow our machines with the ability to cover 100 miles non-stop, whereupon we had to invent some more arduous form of trial. We switched to hillier roads, and borrowed a timekeeper of the rough-and-ready type from the local cycling club. Or we held a speed-judging trial, first depriving all entrants of their watches—there were no speedometers. We organized " passenger " trials for machines pulling trailers, or pushing detachable forecars; " tandem " motor cycles were also admitted. We tried paper-chases with a " hare " dropping confetti at corners. Quite swiftly all these became boring, with the sole exception of hill-climbs.

Those of us who lived in districts insufficiently populous to furnish organized club life had to seek our fun elsewhere. I lived in the north, and some half dozen of us wrote round to all our friends within a radius of 100 miles for news of steep and tricky little hills on by-ways. We would tear off to any such discovery. With single-geared belt drive and a ratio of about $4\frac{1}{2}$ to 1, we could not climb any grade which was both long and steep, but we made astonishing ascents of short, steep hills at which we could get a rush on full throttle, coupled with some frantic pedalling towards the top. If nobody reached the summit, the man who got farthest up put on a swagger.

Small groups of such hill-climbing pioneers formed all over the country. One exceptionally famous trio consisted of Dr. O'Rafferty, from Daventry; Ivan B. Hart-Davies, a Rugby insurance broker, who later set up the final End-to-End record; and Frank Hulbert, of the Triumph Company. This trio, with an occasional fourth or fifth man, devoted many a week-end to visiting distant parts of England, always in search of interesting climbs. By gearing their $3\frac{1}{2}$ h.p. Triumphs down to $5\frac{1}{2}$ to 1 with the aid of adjustable pulleys, they contrived to climb all the notorious main-road hills, and not a few by-road precipices. Eventually, they scrapped their pedalling gears, and climbed on the so-called T.T. Triumph, one of the simplest and most reliable machines ever marketed.

Thus one of the primal male instincts—to achieve something really difficult, and to do it better than anybody else—found special expression in terms of motor cycling. The first result was a crop of speed hill-climbs, tightly administered by famous clubs with professional timekeepers. These were only simple to organize so long as the speeds were not high enough to annoy the police. As soon as accidents began to happen, permission to close a road temporarily became necessary. Such permission was seldom given for roads carrying any appreciable traffic.

One summer I saw Tom Silver on a Quadrant fail to take a corner at high speed—his machine stubbed a quickset hedge, and jammed itself there immovably, while poor old Tom was catapulted far into the adjacent field. Later that same year the Rev. P. W. Bischoff got into a speed wobble at 60 m.p.h. on his Zenith at the top of Kop Hill, and was lucky to escape with his life, though he was a trained acrobat and knew how to fall. Such small incidents made permits almost unobtainable.

So we next switched to hills in private parks, where such could be found. Sir Philipson Stow, a diamond magnate from South Africa, owned a lovely hill near Haslemere, with a little 1 in 4 piece just below a sharp bend through a spinney. I raced up that on a 5 h.p. Vindec with a Phelon & Moore two-speed gear, and attained such speed just above the corner that I ran out of road and miraculously threaded the pine trees for the last hundred yards. The A.C.U. realized that a crop of fractured skulls would do the movement no good, and that hill was never used again.

The historic progenitor of roughriding against the clock was—believe it or not—a *works' outing!* Yorkshire tykes proverbially rank high among the toughs of Britain. The Scott factory is situated at Saltaire, near Shipley. Soon after the first world war, its director, the late A. A. Scott, began to meditate on some new form of staff beanfeast. It occurred to him that his engineers, fitters and mechanics, who were mostly passionate motor cyclists, would enjoy a free-for-all against the clock over their Yorkshire moors and dales. The key principle was the reduction of road mileage to a sheer minimum. A course was to be plotted which consisted almost entirely of boulders, water, gradients, mire, tussocks, terrifying descents and next-to-impossible ascents.

Scott was right—the staff applauded it as the best works' beanfeast ever devised. Its fame spread rapidly, and in 1919 Scott was coaxed to open it to motor cyclists in general under the title of the " Scott Trial ". A year later local A.C.U. officials took it over, and it ranked thenceforward as a sort of motor cycling Grand National, while monied patrons tumbled over each other to present trophies worthy of the course.

Thus, unconsciously, a works' outing begat a long series of " scrambles " against the clock in all parts of the world. The fever spread to the U.S.A. in 1948. The rancour of the Scott parent may be deduced from a few figures relating to its tenth anniversary in 1930. On September 25 of that year, 86 riders started, of whom only a battered 38 ever reached the finish. The gross distance was 55 miles. Let " Promenade Percies " chance a guess at the winner's time before they read on.

It was *three hours, two minutes, twenty-five seconds!* (An average speed of less than 16 miles an hour !)

Of course, the event was a machine-breaker of the first order. As dusk fell, the rescue gangs toiled over the wild country collecting the debris, which might include quite large pieces of motor cycle, not to dwell on those machines which would never again move under their own power until they had undergone extensive repairs. Stretchers and Red Cross men figured in the organization.

Such acerbities must be sharply distinguished from the average " one-day " trial. The Scott might be defined as a revel for he-men; such rough-riding " scrambles " are planned to test the virility both of man and machine to the very edge of despair. They can be quite expensive to the competitor, especially in these modern days when the model possibly cost him £200.

The one-day trial, by comparison, is a test of human dexterity— of the man rather than the machine. It has its mechanical aspects, of course. A typical sample in these days extends to no great mileage—perhaps 80 or 100. There may be time limits, if only to allow the battalion of observers to quit their lonely posts before dark, but there is no emphasis on speed. The basic idea is to confront the competitors with driving tests which just—and only just— fall short of the impossible. The 80 miles may on occasion include as many as twenty " observed " sections. Such sections usually consist of almost unclimbable goat tracks or deep mud.

154

When a hill is very lengthy, its ascent may be split up into perhaps three separate hazards, on each of which marks may be lost for such falls from grace as dabbing with the feet. Occasionally, a really vile hazard will unsaddle the entire entry, or be climbed by perhaps one fortunate expert, and even his performance may not be 100 per cent faultless.

Much naturally depends upon the weather, for on grades of 1 in 3 with a surface resembling the craters of the moon there is a difference between a period of pouring rain and one of long drought. Occasionally two or more of the stars emerge with identical scores, when a special arbitrary test will be employed to find the winner. These deciding tests vary. They may, for example, include a short timed manœuvre, compounded of a sprint uphill, a brake test between tapes, and a re-acceleration.

Needless to say, the design and quality of the machine exert a marked effect on the results. The engine must be the exact opposite of a road-racing engine, which hardly develops any power at all till the revolution meter registers 5,000. In the mountains a rider needs a slogging type of engine, which can tug like a Suffolk Punch at a mere crawl, which will fire dead evenly at minimum revolutions so that its owner can avert wheelspin, which can accelerate like a cheetah when a nine-inch rock step on a single-figure gradient has to be clambered up. Of course, brakes and steering and balance and roadholding are essential.

It would be ungrateful to assume that such tests are not useful in developing roadster machines. Nevertheless, ever since engines began to develop 25 b.h.p. in roadster form, and gear boxes could furnish bottom ratios of 20 to 1 or lower, and chain transmissions functioned calmly under every imaginable condition of motion, the onus in these events was transferred by emphasis from the machine to the man. The machines can with advantage depart from catalogue roadster specification, but they are not freaks. Indeed, as compared with a T.T. mount, they are practically standard.

It is not possible to describe the courses used for such events. Frequently they are narrow strips of an England which is not even familiar to the hiker. Gamekeepers know them. Upland farmers are aware of them as unproductive acreage in the hinterland of their ground. Shepherds may visit them in winter, searching for sheep which have sought refuge from blizzards in deep, narrow folds of the hills. The first key word is gradient. The second key word is an unrideable surface—a moraine, a V-bottomed ditch full of luscious leafmould, a dry torrent bed, a series of Z turns up a goat track—broadly speaking, the kind of place where chamois might congregate if we had any chamois in Britain.

The rough-riders of the organizing clubs devote hours to searching for such places. They even improve upon Nature by damming water to render the awesome track greasy, or drag enormous boulders to hamper an already almost unturnable corner. If the goat track looks reasonably straight, that is, has no corner with a radius of

155

less than two yards, they erect posts and tapes to make the climber swerve more abruptly. They pride themselves on packing the maximum number of hazards into their available mileage, and are only deterred from including 200 distinct hazards into the day by sheer lack of reliable observers to man the course and impose the penalties.

Finance probably served as one factor to increase the vogue of such trials. At one period between the wars the potential output of the entire motor cycle industry exceeded its actual sales. Success in every form of competition was invaluable in the contest for popular favour, and the industry showed itself temporarily liberal to semi-professional or " shamateur " riders. A lad who displayed efficiency in such trials could get a new machine at a special price or, even, free gratis, and also earn a bonus for each success not only from the maker of his machine, but also from oil, tyre, sparking plug and other companies.

Such incentives opened the door to a new profession attractive to athletic lads who sought to escape from the monotonous round of office or factory. The highest monetary awards went to speed, especially T.T. success. Sheer insanity characterized this bonus business at one period, in which one friend of mine received a " retainer " of no less than £800 per annum from an oil company, coupled with very handsome cheques whenever he scored a victory or even a " place " in a major event. (Such rewards were mainly based on road and track racing, but on a minor scale applied also to " chamois " trials.)

Many firms found that a good competition record in road trials was their most remunerative investment. After all, only a very small minority of motor cyclists wish to risk their necks at 100 m.p.h., but most of them desire a machine which can climb any hill or demonstrate reliability over foul going. So today these one-day trials continue in good numbers, attract large entries, and help to sell machines. The skill of the crack riders is literally incredible— comparable with the dexterity exhibited by world-renowned athletes in other sports. The dainty touch of a billiards champion, or of a Cotton flicking a golf ball out of a deep bunker to land a foot from the pin, is not more marvellous than the finger-work of a motor cycle champion operating his twistgrip throttle to coax 3 cwt of motor cycle up a grade of 1 in 3 without permitting his back tyre to stall him by wheelspin.

These men do not accomplish their feats in the brilliant limelight which shines upon a Sam Snead or a Denis Compton or a Tom Lawton. They perform before a tiny audience at the back of beyond and often in pouring rain. But their pre-eminence in the application of brain and body to athletic miracles is every bit as phenomenal as the deeds of men whose names are household words throughout the civilized world.

The outbreak of World War II found the first practical application for their skill. Wars are not fought on asphalt. Wireless has largely replaced the runner, the cavalryman and even the despatch rider as the link between generals and their troops. But wireless can be jammed, shellfire can wreck buried telephone systems, and over much of the frightful terrain of war the motor cyclist retains at least some of his inestimable value in military communications. These trials riders officered motor cycling schools in which the D.R. learnt contempt for every type of natural obstacle.

Actual racing over " the rough stuff " still survives in the form of the " scramble ", the descendant of the original Scott Trial in Yorkshire. These scrambles do not use any roads at all, but are as " cross country " as any equine steeplechase could be. They are possibly less popular than the one-day trial, because they entail more damage to the riders' machines, and incur some personal risk if mainly in the form of sprains and minor injuries. " Moto-Cross " is the name given to the scramble on the continent of Europe. The annual International Moto-Cross attracts entries from five or six nations.

The scramble or moto-cross furnishes a convenient spectacle, since the " lap " may be quite short. The ideal site is obviously a natural " bowl " in hilly country, where the spectators can sit on the grass, and follow the riders round most of the hazards with their eyes.

It is not possible to generalize about either the " one-day trial " or the " scramble ", which may be almost identical in character except that the " scramble " is always timed against the clock. The scramble has also departed from its prototype (the Scott Trial) in that the latter included water hazards, which today are usually reserved for the one-day events devoid of timing. Neither is it easy to account for the popularity of either type of sport.

They have a double interest for the industry, in that they supply good publicity and provide acid tests for engines which develop great power and flexibility " low down ", that is, at low engine speeds. A second motive is that the tough type of amateur rider thoroughly enjoys these knock-about experiences. The harder the going, the better he likes it. One can almost imagine that when all the worst available courses at home grow familiar, an International Moto-Cross may ultimately be organized on the steep tumuli of powdery sand in the Libyan desert, or across the Quattara depression, or even that a gang of enthusiasts might essay to climb Everest on supercharged motor bicycles with caterpillar-tracked wheels! The tough revels in displaying his " he-mannity "!

It is almost impossible to exaggerate the dexterity required to excel in either a scramble or a sober procession through mire and up goat tracks in the 80-mile circuit of a one-day trial. The goat tracks are often places where no car could go, and frequently there is not the width to admit a sidecar. The rider stands poised on his footrests to insulate his wrists and body from the full shock of his leaping projectile, while he daintily operates his twistgrip throttle to prevent wheelspin, on the one hand, and to endow the rear wheel

157

with just enough traction to clamber over a rock step or cope with a grade as severe as 1 in 2.

Some combinations of grade and surface are so vile that the sole hope is to charge them at speed, endeavouring to hold an ever-changing course while the machine is largely airborne. Others, again, must be taken at the most delicate crawl, with both eyes focused on picking the only possible path, perhaps no wider than this page. The water hazards may be so deep that the level almost reaches the machine's cylinder head, nor is there any guarantee that the surface may not screen holes which would enforce a stop plus wet bath.

On emerging from water the brakes are usually ineffective, and the organizer loves to combine the exit with a brief ferocious ascent up which crashing acceleration will be needed, quickly followed by an almost vertical descent, down which sodden brakes may well fail to grip. If Nature herself fails to supply hazards of the requisite severity, pegged tapes condemn the competitor to a succession of short-radius turns against the camber, maybe with rock steps and strewn boulders, or to a stretch of deep leafmould down which a stream is pouring from a diabolical dam built for the purpose a few yards higher up.

Myself no rough-rider, I would chance an opinion that the Highlands of Scotland furnish the cream of natural courses alike for plain rough-riding with Dame Nature as the sole antagonist or for " scrambling against the clock ", though ingenuity can devise some quite incredibly arduous circuits in the Cotswolds.

I shall never forget being set on a drenching day many years ago to climb an interminable Scottish field, confronting us with nothing worse than a single-figure gradient of sodden turf. It was practically impossible to stand on the slimy surface. No man living could have pushed up it. Yet up it we had to go somehow or other. If one came to a standstill, there was nothing for it but to return to the bottom and try again. If I had been prospecting alone and unofficially for the fun of it, I should soon have given the climb best and gone back by the way I came. But the dread of being outshone by others and of actual failure kept us at it, until somehow most of us eventually reached the top.

In quite a different class stands Mamore, which begins with a very long and steep mountain track through straggly woods, round Z-shaped bends, over a surface consisting solely of tumbled stones on a natural bed. If and when the summit is reached in the mists overhead, there remains a plateau which looks much as the Ice Age left it, with, in parts, no road except in the sense of a jumbled litter of stones of every imaginable size. One feels it is just a question whether the machine will fall to pieces before a pounded anatomy cries " Enough! "

With ample leisure on a sunny day, one could take frequent rests to ease aching wrists, and joke with merry companions at the ferocity of the ordeal. But in a cold wind and drenching rain with a silver cup and the dual reputation of oneself and the model at stake, this howling wilderness has to be traversed at high touring speed against the clock. But at long last one dives into bed with even a young and athletic body one huge congeries of aches, wondering as one falls asleep whether the game is really worth the candle, and waking far too early next morning in order to tackle another day of variegated endeavour.

Such ordeals are fine character builders. The manhood of Britain would be a poor and pale affair if it did not revel in such ardours. Such beings may sound crazy to the world at large, but when the natural emergencies of life or the stern crucibles of war require that a man should not flinch, the qualities bred in the artificial arenas of sport come to his aid, and ensure that he shall not fail.

CHAPTER 21

THE END-TO-END RECORD

THOUGH THE GRAMPIAN ROAD ceased to magnetize our faster toughs in 1911, up to that date the Land's End-John O' Groats record ranked as the blue riband of the road. It lost none of its glory from the fact that it was never recognized or supervised by officialdom. Many motor cyclists are still unaware that their pedalling cousins wax every bit as passionate about their muscular records on road and track as motorists become about Brooklands, Utah, Montlhéry, Monza, Shelsley, Silverstone, Goodwood and the rest. Indeed, pedal cyclists possess an extremely live body, the Roads Record Association, with strict laws and able officials, who take great pains to exclude anything phoney from their annals. These stalwarts were the first to recognize the magic of the End-to-End route, which led from the porphyry rocks and cruel seas of Cornwall right up into the northern mists and the land of the midnight sun. Their supreme champion G. P. Mills pedalled its full length many a time on almost every form of cycle—the tricycle, the bicycle, the tandem; indeed, he scorned no type except the fairy cycle, and on all he was victorious.

Such examples tickled the hungry minds of early motoring advertisers. At first, to cover the ground, irrespective of time, was a gigantic achievement. Henry Sturmey, first editor of *The Autocar*, achieved the distance on an American Duryea car. Hubert Egerton, of Norwich, in September, 1901, first blazed the trail by motor bicycle. Quite incredibly, he coaxed a crude and precocious Werner motor cycle, rated at $1\frac{1}{4}$ h.p., over the whole distance—900 miles in four days nine hours, an average speed of approximately 9 m.p.h. This was in no sense a formal record; it was not officially observed and was timed only by the rider. The journey was designed simply to show that a primitive motor cycle could cover the most famous course in these islands. A single mechanical stop near Bristol lasted ten hours!

The cycling world scoffed. They announced their intentions in advance. They rode against the clock. Pansies by comparison, these opulent, knock-kneed motorists kept their departures a secret, saved the £20 fee of an R.R.A. timekeeper, and might be guilty of all kinds of surreptitious cheating.

Stung by such jibes, E. H. Arnott, elected " captain " of the Motor Cycling Club, decided to tackle the run under strict R.R.A. conditions in July, 1902, selecting a 2 h.p. French Werner as his mount. His time was no better than 65h 45m, though, when we

160

allow for the crudity of his machine, the feat was perhaps the finest ever recorded.

In June, 1903, Tom Silver, on a 3 h.p. Quadrant motor bicycle, cut the record to 64h 29m. During the salvage drive for wastepaper during World War II, when we were further besought to clear our attics of all inflammable material with an eye to incendiary bombs, I ruefully sent to salvage a fat wad of typed notes on stiff solicitor's foolscap. It was Tom Silver's " schedule " for the run, which the Quadrant Company generously presented to me a year later when I myself made a futile attack on Silver's figures. Sucker as I was, I utterly failed to recognize that nobody could memorize 900 miles of road and, therefore, considerable assistance from cycle retailers all along the route was essential to success. Tom failed to keep within many hours of his schedule. It proved about as possible of achievement as the General Staff's battle plans for any major engagement such as the Somme battle.

He was supposed to arrive at, say, Perth at 7.29 a.m., when willing Quadrant hands would attend to his machine, while he swallowed some eggflip and a sandwich or two. Racing cyclists would then steer him through any awkward turnings until their calves failed on some flat stretch and he puttered on solo. Similarly, a Quadrant customer would meet him at every dubious road junction, and wave him down the correct arm. All along the route, food, guides and supplies awaited him. Meanwhile his R.R.A. timekeeper, Jack Urry, would be yawning and dosing in the slow trains which would ultimately deliver him at the Land's End hotel well ahead of Tom.

One option was permitted. The potential record-breaker could choose between riding round the two firths which crossed the crow line—Beauly and Forth—or having a boat waiting with steam up to ferry him across. The choice did not guarantee any appreciable difference in time. A couple of steam ferries cost anything up to a further £30, according to the respective bargaining powers of the ambitious factory and the canny Scots mariners. (It is on record that many record-breakers enjoyed the brief relief from the saddle, and that one even undressed and hung overboard on the tail of the ferry during the brief water interlude. Use of the ferries shortened the actual ride by some 20 miles.)

In 1904 I recognized two facts about this record. The first was that even the crude models of that date could knock lumps off Tom's time if they were sufficiently lucky to get a non-stop. So I thought I had better help myself to this record before it suffered a heavy cut from somebody else. Secondly, the tip was to start from Groats at midnight, and *not* from Land's End as others had done. On a June midnight at Groats, if the weather is clear, no lamp is necessary. So all riding in the dark should be reduced to the one short summer moonlit night on the fast roads round Carlisle.

Consequently, I chartered a good R.R.A. timekeeper, D. K. Hall, to guarantee *bona fides*, concluded a good bargain with the Scots ferrymen at both firths, and rode up from Cornwall to Groats in order to memorize all turnings. (Who says, " Poor boob "?) Meanwhile, Arthur Goodwin, the Ormonde manager, feeling a bit above himself because one of his best mechanics had registered 60 m.p.h. in some speed trials with a Paris-Madrid Ormonde model at Phœnix Park, agreed to tune up my Ormonde ferociously, and to go fifty-fifty with me over the expenses.

Shock No. 1 for me was the parlous condition of certain road sections. The Grampian road is now a marvellous highway. In 1904 the long stretch from Struan to Dalwhinnie was no more than a barely visible grass-grown moraine of three-ply formation (two wheel ruts with a central hoof-devastated strip) across the barren moors. Even worse were certain recently " repaired " strips further north. In 1904 a road repair was not entertained until some heavy farm carts had broken their incredibly sturdy wheels over deep subsidences. The " repair " then took the form of dumping a myriad tons of broken stone over the devastated section, which might be several miles in length.

I had next to no experience of rough-riding. I was tough and could stand the frightful bucketing, but no existing motor cycle was fit for such a hammering. However, my arrangements were made, and I could not decently withdraw. But as the Ormonde Company had no cycle branches, and no official retailers, it was not possible for us to organize guides. I must rest content with my two ferry boats, and a few pals at set intervals who joyfully agreed to have food waiting for me—food which I would eat while they filled my tank and gave the model the once-over.

On the way north I doubtless took a lot out of the model— another proof of my suckership. But I decided that the route was not too twisty to be memorized, and I was graduating as a rough-rider. But shock No. 2 awaited me at John O' Groat's house. Entering its bar, whom should I meet but F. T. Bidlake, the famous R.R.A. timekeeper. My sinking heart recognized that somebody else must have simultaneously shared my ambitions, even if he had failed to deduce that a midnight start from Groats reduced the dark riding from two nights to one and had started, instead, from Land's End. " *Who* are you timing? " was my ungrammatical greeting to Bidlake. " G. P. Mills ! " came the crushing reply!

Worse still, Bidlake calmly informed me that the Raleigh people had designed a special bus for the job. This machine was never marketed, but was pedal-less, and distinguished by a simple two-speed gear of the three-chain variety, while my Ormonde had a single-geared belt drive of $4\frac{1}{2}$ to 1 ratio, plus a high pedalling ratio to sustain my climbing speed under " l.p.a." (those initials—the worst under-statement in the history of language—stand for " light pedal assistance "). The Raleigh further boasted a sprung handlebar.

Shock No. 3 was the arrival of Mills in pouring rain next morning in 50h $46\frac{1}{2}$m, a time which chopped nearly fourteen hours off the existing record and imposed a cut of many hours in my maximum schedule. Worse still, the condition of both Mills and his Raleigh sketched in high relief the ordeal which awaited me. Mills was as near the verge of physical collapse as an athlete can well bear. He could hardly see out of his eyes, which had been battered almost to pulp by night hailstorms. He had been slowed by a series of punctures, and during the later stages had repeatedly pumped up tyres leaking from feverish patching. He tottered to bed, slept twice round the clock, and rose as fit as a fiddle.

Meanwhile the weather cleared, and my spirits rose as I started south under a clear sky. The rest may be dismissed briefly. Just two items stand out in my dim memories. Down the Ord of Caithness I was probably doing between 60 and 70 m.p.h. when I ran plunk into a small bevy of sheep asleep on the roadway, invisible as their colour blended into the road surface. A parabola over the handlebars, and I regained consciousness after an interval of x minutes, wondering where on earth I was. I was lying on my tummy surrounded by a tall forest of scraggy heather amid a waste of whitish sand. I rose stiffly, and remembered.

But where was the Ormonde? I was some thirty yards off the road, but there was no sign of my machine. I ultimately discovered it, very little bent, some seventy yards further down the hill, admirably camouflaged in heather. After kicking it straight, I mounted and rode on. So far I had averaged well over 30, and the bends the machine had suffered were not important. But from that point the engine became afflicted with progressive and pernicious anæmia. I was no mechanic, but it did not take long to discover that the valves were barely lifting at all, though the tappet clearances were in order. Deduction: since the heels of the tappets operated direct on the cams, Goodwin's special strong racing valve springs had caused the heels of the tappets to gnaw through the light case-hardening of the cams; the cams were ceasing to " cam ", and were swiftly becoming truly circular.

With much hefty pedalling I staggered as far as Pitlochry, where I ignominiously retired.

Worse was to follow. I was recommended to an hotel to await the arrival of fresh cams from London. Little did I know that in the season this hotel contested with King Leopold's *Chateau des Ardennes* the title of being the costliest caravanserai in Europe. Moreover, the weather was blisteringly hot, and my solitary suit consisted of a special Hoare motor cycle outfit, constructed of thick Harris tweed, interlined with the finest sheet rubber to render it stormproof. So for the next four days I sat ruefully in my bedroom, clad only in my undies, paying the extra house charge for " meals served in guests' bedrooms ", and periodically bribing the hotel porter to ransack the Pitlochry bookshop for volumes which I had not read or might force myself to re-read. (I get through an average novel in 45 minutes!)

From that day till late in 1911 the Grampian road witnessed a series of summer processions, as other toughs took a shot at the record. Only a small percentage of these efforts succeeded, even when seven years' development had exalted the 1904 standards of power and reliability. One poor lad was found wandering about the Cornish lanes in a state of complete amnesia due to exhaustion. Speeds rose rapidly. The police became somewhat excited.

The motor cycling counterpart of G. P. Mills arose presently in the person of Ivan B. Hart-Davies, a Rugby scoutmaster and insurance broker, ultimately killed by a flying accident after he took up aviation with the main idea of setting up an End-to-End record in the air. Hart-Davies was an unusual type. He was no speedster of the T.T. type. But he possessed incomparable stamina and could keep going at an intermediate gait almost indefinitely without fatigue.

Meanwhile Harold Williamson, on a Rex, cut the Mills' figures down to 48h 36m from a southern start, just one month after Mills' success. Williamson held the record until 1908, despite several attacks upon it. Arthur Bentley, a brother of the more famous W. O. Bentley (the originator of the Bentley car and, later, the Lagonda designer) drove his 3½ h.p. Triumph over the course in 41h 28m in June, 1908. In 1909, Tom Peck, on a Rex, accomplished 40h 30m. Hart-Davies' meteoric career began with a 33h 22m dash on a 196 lb single-geared Triumph. In September, 1910, the late Arthur Moorhouse, despite shortening days, rode down from Groats in 32h 13m. His Rex weighed 218 lb including two head-lamps and a heavy kit of spares.

By this time the record was a public infringement of the legal limit, and the authorities began to frown on it somewhat heavily. At an average round about 30 m.p.h., a single rider created no serious peril to the public, provided that exhaustion did not dull his faculties in the later stages. But it was no case of a single rider. The Hart-Davies' technique involved clumps of toughs in snow-white jackets at any area where it was possible to select a false turning. These speedster pals picked up the record-breaker, especially in the night sections or where the route was hard to follow. One of them went ahead. The record-breaker focused his headlamp on his guide's white jacket, and the rest of the gang trailed astern, ready to accelerate to the front if the leader crashed or struck machine trouble. These flying night horsemen amounted to a public menace. So when Hart-Davies, using no ferries, got down from the North to Land's End in the fantastic time of 29h 12m, the A.C.U. called it a day, and thenceforward anybody who lowered the figures and published them was due for excommunication.

No more major feats were attempted, but lightweights and side-cars registered a few comparatively slow rides of real credit considering their mechanical handicaps. For example, in 1910 Harold Cox put a 93 lb Singer of 1¼ h.p. through the trip in 57h 26m, whereupon Eli Clark, on a 2¾ h.p. single-geared Douglas, achieved the miraculous time of 39h 40m. Olsson, on a 7 h.p. Vindec with sidecar, achieved 65h 14m, off which the brothers A. W. and H. M. Bentley chopped 6h 7m on a Rex and sidecar one month later. Then a vengeful Vindec and sidecar, handled by Martin Geiger, cut the passenger time down to 51h 45m.

Not until 1910 were adequate sidecar figures reached when Hugh Gibson forced a 3½ h.p. Triumph and sidecar over the 900 miles in 40h 47m. This was possibly the supreme achievement of the lot, for the outfit scaled 300 lb, plus a live load of 18 stone. It was single-geared, and much of the credit goes to Gibson's passenger, George Wray, whose mournful duty was to hop overboard and trot alongside up many of the steeper hills—or even to chase on foot after the disappearing sidecar and, finally, rejoin Gibson, who waited impatiently for him on the crest.

Hart-Davies crowned his personal fame by setting up a further record with a somewhat primitive 10 h.p. Singer light car.

This picaresque interlude in the story of the motor cycle is certainly worthy of a place in the annals of a sport which has inspired so much courage, skill and perseverance.

CHAPTER 22

SPEEDWAY RACING

FOR LONG YEARS I IMAGINED that modern speedway racing was an accidental product of the use of motor cycles for pacing pedal cycles on tracks. Motor cycles of enormous power were employed for that purpose on French tracks at the dawn of the twentieth century, as were rather smaller motor cycles at Canning Town. But in sober fact there is no more connection between such experiments and the modern speedway than exists between croquet and golf. Motor cycle racing on " dirt " is of purely American origin, and dates no farther back than 1909. My friend " Talmage," of *The Motor Cycle*, has been at considerable pains to excavate the facts, which may be taken as entirely accurate after most careful research.

Previous to 1909, race meetings had been organized on board tracks in the United States by showmen with a yen for money making. Handsome prize money was offered. Large crowds were drawn. Riders of eight-valve Harley and Indian twin-cylinders developed a high degree of skill in fast cornering on hard, unyielding surfaces. But eventually a bunch of machines went over the edge into the crowd and killed eight spectators. This tragedy sounded the knell of organized racing on board tracks. It was evident that natural laws limited the cornering speed on any hard surface devoid of really steep banking.

But the showmen and the riders refused to surrender. Presently they developed a special technique adapted to loose-surfaced tracks, which existed in the States in tolerable numbers, and had been laid down for trotting races with laps averaging between 880 yards and 1 mile. The old board track organization was swiftly transferred to the new medium, and the sport was reborn on a larger scale than the old board tracks had ever known. By 1913 the American record for dirt tracks with a one-mile lap had actually been cut to 43 seconds— a speed of rather more than 83 miles an hour!

The new sport rapidly invaded Canada. Soon a half-mile trotting track at Vancouver became famous for two big meets in each year, dominated by the American cracks from Seattle and elsewhere, who mopped up most of the prize money. One of those Vancouver fixtures in 1913 has a special interest for British motor cyclists. The entry included a sixteen-year-old apprentice to the motor trade, who turned out on a home-tuned Indian machine as an amateur. The pure amateurs threatened to go on strike, so he promptly registered as a professional and, to the general amazement, outrode the American invaders. His name was Alec Bennett, destined to win five Isle of Man T.T. races between 1922 and 1928 (exclusive of numerous Continental road-circuit races) on Sunbeam, Norton and Velocette machines.

From 1920 onward, dirt-track racing spread to Australia. It was now evident that the sport possessed an almost unique " spectator value ". It combined most of the elements which a professional showman recognizes as calculated to thrill the crowds. Its tempo is terrific. It is compact, enabling a giant concourse surrounding a small bowl to enjoy full view of every incident. It embodies the necessary *soupçon* of risk, without exalting peril to such a pitch that the spectators are harrowed or moral considerations are out-raged. It demands a very high pitch of technical skill and genuine courage. In 1928 two contingents of Australian broadsiding champions decided to risk their previous season's winnings on an effort to establish the sport in Britain. There had been preliminary negotiations with British promoters. The money was ready for them, and several tracks were being inspected and prepared.

The first British dirt-track meeting was held on February 19, 1928, on the running track at High Beech, near Epping. From the American, Canadian and Australian standpoint, this meet was a mere caricature. The cinder surface was hard and shallow. The machines were in road-racing trim, equipped with brakes. The British riders had no notion of the necessary technique. Two Australian invaders—Billy Galloway and Keith McKay—could not apply their sliding technique on an unyielding surface. But, with the aid of expertly controlled dry skids, they contrived to make the British competitors look rather silly.

By the following Easter, the High Beech track had been widened and relaid with a softer surface, so that meets on the Saturday and Monday developed a wholly novel atmosphere. The half-mile trotting track at Greenford, Middlesex, was also opened on the Easter Saturday. The Australian, Billy Galloway, gave the British public their first sample of broadsiding at Greenford on the Saturday, and an English rider, Alf Medcalf, on a Douglas 494 c.c. machine, created a similar sensation at High Beech on Easter Monday. A week later further exhibitions thrilled crowds on both tracks. The New Zealander, Stewart St. George, on a Douglas, gave a finished display at Greenford. At High Beech the first British star, Roger Frogley, leapt into fame on a Rudge.

A week later, Blackpool got its first view of the new sport, and the programme included Eric Langton, destined later to captain England in many international Test matches. Sprouts Elder, from the U.S.A., galvanized a huge Scottish crowd at the Celtic track in Glasgow on April 28. Stars of the moment were " Stewie " St. George (New Zealand), and the Australians, Paddy Dean, Geoff Meredith, Billy Galloway and Keith Mackay, among whom St. George was pre-eminent. On May 5 the Australian, Vic Huxley, turned out at High Beech, where he broke the local record on his

English début. Roger Frogley was summoned by public acclaim to attack Huxley's figures and, considering his comparatively brief experience, did well to fail by no more than $\frac{3}{5}$ sec.

Hitherto all dirt-track racing in this country had been in daylight, but on May 5 the track surrounding the Chelsea Football Club's ground at Stamford Bridge saw the inaugural meeting under lamps, an innovation which launched the fashion of huge gates on week nights. The crowd's first impressions were the reverse of enthusiastic, for inspired showmanship held back the stars, and the early heats were contested by English novices, who could achieve no more than a few petty skids on the bends. Then, as dusk drew on, the loudspeakers announced that Stewart St. George would give an exhibition solo ride. He rode four magnificent laps in a hushed, incredulous silence, broken only by the crazy screaming of his Douglas.

When he crossed the final line, the 30,000 fans released their pent-up breath with a roar which rocked Chelsea, as they cast assorted articles from hats to newspapers into the air in such a paroxysm of admiration and wonder as is rare in British sport. When they had calmed down a little, Sprouts Elder brought out his Douglas and produced an even finer display of pluperfect technique. Both men had sprayed great black fans of cinders into the crowd on all the bends. From this moment there was no doubt that speedway racing had come to stay. Financiers connected with the entertainment business opened their purses. Star riders were besieged with offers of fantastic contracts. The crowds flocked.

Naturally, we were all bursting to try our hands at the new sport, none more so than myself, though I was already too long in the tooth to shine at such revolutionary gymnastics. All of us had experience of unintentional skids, both on motor cycles and cars, alike in loose stuff on country roads, on greasy or iced main roads, and through over-braking on hard, dry surfaces. In addition, the more expert among us were not unaccustomed to employing intentional skids to extricate ourselves from occasional emergencies. We fondly imagined, after a few glimpses of the Sprouts Elder technique, that we had only to overcome our dislike of skids to regard a controlled skid as normal instead of as a catastrophe, and we should soon be competing with Americans and Australians on level terms.

I made my first experiment at Stamford Bridge. I was given a few vague hints by an Australian expert, and spent a most humiliating half hour. Maybe my instructor had no intention of giving away hard-earned secrets. Maybe, past memories of skidding made me funk so that I dared not go into a short-radius corner sufficiently fast. Maybe, I was both timid and clumsy. I was thrilled when I churned up a few visible cinders, but though my best pace was a shameful crawl, I fell off repeatedly.

Actually, the technique is complicated and difficult. It is not too readily grasped by a courageous youngster. It is now time to analyse its mysteries.

First, let us consider riding a solo motor cycle round a left-hand bend on a road. The faster the bend is taken, the stronger is the centrifugal force which tries to carry the machine out to the right, and, therefore, the more must the model be banked over to the left to oppose that centrifugal force. Clearly there is a limit to the angle to which the machine may be banked over. That limit is determined by the adhesion of the tyres to the road surface.

The machine cannot be banked over so far on a loose surface without the tyres, and, therefore, the machine, skidding or sliding sideways. The front wheel slides more readily than the rear because, being turned slightly on left lock, the front wheel is canted over more than the rear. Naturally one cannot steer or control the machine with a slipping front wheel. First, therefore, front tyre grip must be regained, and the only way to achieve it is to bring the front wheel nearer to the vertical. This is done by turning the front wheel slightly on to right lock—into the direction of the skid.

On the loose cinder surface of a speedway the whole essence of fast cornering is to take the bend in one long skid or slide. Throughout the entire bend this slide is purposely provoked and, at the same time, delicately controlled by the rider. He can get round faster by power-sliding the machine than by limiting his speed in such measure as would be necessary to avoid sliding.

The speedway bend is approached at a speed which, in view of the loose surface, is apparently suicidal. The throttle is closed, and the model is banked hard over to the left. The front wheel begins to slide and go out of control. The back wheel also tends to slide, but the process builds up a ridge of cinders which blocks its sideways movement. That is the critical moment. Machine and rider will fall flat unless the back wheel is made to slide outwards. The rider opens the throttle sufficiently to spin the rear wheel relative to the track. The spinning wheel clears away the ridge in a cinder plume flung to the rear, and slides outward. Simultaneously, the rider turns the handlebar slightly on to right lock, the front wheel is pushed up and comes right back under control.

By means of the handlebar, the expert can now place the front wheel where he wants it and steer to within fine limits. At the same time he must control the degree of slide of the rear wheel by delicate throttle-work. This throttle control is all-important. The power must be sufficient to keep the back wheel spinning relative to the track, and therefore sliding, all the way round the bend. At the same time, the degree of wheelspin must be the minimum required for the continuous process of flinging away the cinders and keeping the rear wheel sliding. Otherwise the traction or driving force of the rear wheel is reduced and speed lost.

It is a manœuvre most delicate in its essence and may be complicated by the presence of three other riders within very short range of you, all similarly engaged, and the entire quartette racing forward in a thundering roar at the highest speed at which the bend is negotiable.

If the foregoing brief synopsis be re-read, it should be clear that the rider is absorbed in three separate tasks which actually merge into a single complex problem. He must slide, control the slide, and manœuvre for position. The outward slide of the rear wheel is the real genesis of skid, or power-slide, cornering. Although it is spinning relative to the track surface, the rear wheel still exerts a driving force. In other words, traction is obtained. How much traction depends upon the rider's skill with the throttle control. If the throttle is opened too wide, wheelspin is increased, the rear wheel swings out nearly broadside to the direction of travel, the handlebar has to be turned to the right, possibly on full lock, to correct, and traction is lost through the over-slide. (If, in these circumstances, the throttle is suddenly snapped shut, the rear wheel will bite as though meeting an obstruction and impetus may fling the rider to the off side, with the machine somersaulting on top of him. On the other hand, if the throttle is not eased, or is opened more, the overslide develops into a flat-spin which will deposit the rider, usually harmlessly, on the track.)

If you watch an ace on a bend he seems to go round in a smooth and continuous slide, subject to slight corrections necessitated by irregularities in the track surface. With delicate throttle manipulation he tends to build up his speed all the way round. By contrast, the novice goes round in a series of jerks arising from over-sliding one moment and thus having to apply a large measure of correction the next.

Very occasionally one may see a super ace employing immense physical strength to fling his machine into a bend with both wheels sliding. But the incredibly dainty sense of balance and the extreme muscular power essential for this method are rare among mortals, though Vic Huxley, in his heyday, possessed both in an unusual measure.

The run-of-the-mill method, previously outlined, was very soon grasped by the young British recruits who flocked into the sport from 1928 onward. The immigrant aces made admirable tutors, and had the sense to see that their own earnings would steeple in proportion as they helped to equip the new mushroom tracks with an adequate staff of competent riders. Eager apprentices were soon besieging every promoter. The imported aces walked our streets like kings. Some charged high fees for exhibition appearances, and for tuition. All of them pocketed plenty of prize money. The harvest was golden and plentiful.

For a few months all sorts of abuses were rampant. The two main risks were that a number of youngsters might be killed, or that a number of spectators might be hurt if a machine ran wild on a bend and catapulted into the crowd. Fortunately, on the helm there was a very strong hand, that of the Auto Cycle Union, the governing body of motor cycling in this country. The A.C.U. became the ruler of speedway racing rather by common consent than by any formal mandate, much as the Marylebone C.C. governs cricket and St. Andrews lays down the law at golf. The showmen had the sense to see that some impartial dictator was desirable.

The A.C.U. secretary at this critical moment was T. W. Loughborough, not a man to stand any nonsense. He had acquired a unique experience in the control of motor cycle racing at Brooklands, in the Isle of Man, and elsewhere, and was quick to see the inherent risks of the new venture. By 1933 the speedways had become so onerous a burden that the A.C.U. delegated its duties to a newly formed *ad hoc* Speedway Control Board, of which Colonel Vernon Brook is now chairman. The complexity of the organization may be gauged by the fact that its handbook prints no fewer than 583 regulations.

For obvious reasons, the A.C.U. had a tough furrow to hoe during the early years. Safety fences had to be designed and imposed. A high elastic barrier was required to protect the crowds if a machine went out of control on a bend. Since week-night meetings spelt maximum gates, the power stations had to be coaxed to generate the necessary electricity. The wealthy tracks had to be restrained from buying up all the best riders, and so starving the poorer tracks. With the aid of professional showmen, the programme was adroitly framed on similar lines to professional Soccer, so that league championships and Test matches kept interest at a high level, while individual championships added more grist to the mill.

Perhaps no sport in the world demands such firm and close control of its professionals, as a brief study of the actual racing will indicate. First, four men must be got away to a scrupulously fair start. Plainly, the man who draws the starting place next to the inside of the track stands the best chance of securing the inside berth at the first corner. Other things being equal, he then stands the best chance of winning outright, for if he can hug the inside berth all the way round, a rival can only defeat him by travelling considerably faster round the longer, outside line.

Originally, a " rolling " start by flag was employed. This bred plenty of trouble with innumerable false starts as men tried to " jump " the flag. Eventually, a miniature " rising gate " of the type familiar on the turf was adopted, and today the riders line up with engines running and let their clutches in with a bang when the tapes fly up.

Once away, various tactics of a dubious or dangerous type are always possible. For instance, the inside man at the first bend may swing outward, forcing the other three to follow suit, with possibly awkward consequences for the outside man. Or while the first string of a team hugs the inside line, his second string may trail him and hamper his pursuers dangerously. When four men are hurtling round a bend in a bunch, and tempers are high, tricks may be applied to make a formidable opponent crash. So the A.C.U. steward of each meeting is Hitler for the night. He can penalize a rider for dangerous tactics, just as a referee at professional Soccer.

He allows no rider to delay the timetable, and keeps the programme moving in the interests of spectators confronted by a long homeward journey when racing ends at 10 p.m. or later.

So many problems hampered the sport in its earlier chapters that it came near perishing of its own vices, but 1950 found it on the whole in remarkably healthy condition, thanks to the firm hand of the Speedway Board. In view of current controversy anent the transfer of professional footballers, it is worth mention that, when a speedway rider is transferred from track to track, subject to certain conditions he pockets 10 per cent of the transfer fee, plus a further $2\frac{1}{2}$ per cent for each year during which he was licensed to the track which he is leaving.

Female riders are now absolutely excluded. They were permitted for a short period, during which Fay Taylour and Eva Asquith achieved stardom. But public opinion was definitely opposed to the innovation.

Neither rigid control nor firm discipline can wholly exclude accident. A few men have been killed on the cinders, and most veterans have sustained injury at one time or another. The spectators are most adequately safeguarded, and casualties among the participating riders are seldom severe. The men wear crash helmets and other protective devices. The majority of tumbles are innocuous, and the level of riding skill is so high that a fallen rider is seldom hit by his fellow competitors. On the small tracks of this country the actual speeds sound quite absurdly low when compared with other forms of motor racing. Forty-five m.p.h. is approximately a record on the majority of tracks, though the artificial light and the small size of the arena makes it look much faster than it actually is.

Comparisons with Spanish bull fighting are utterly false. Speedway racing is in no sense a " blood sport". While a gala night at a big track may draw up to 90,000 spectators, they do not congregate in the hope of seeing men maimed or killed. They regard injuries precisely as the Arsenal Stadium would feel if the home centre-forward broke a leg. Even the temporary incapacitation of a visiting rider is regretted, as liable to spoil a thrilling match. Every human assembly contains a ghoul or two ; but ghouls are no more numerous at Harringay than at Lord's.

Perhaps the most exciting fixtures are those in the lower divisions of the league. Their riding standards are lower, but four riders of equal calibre are more inclined to bunch. The spectacle of four men broadsiding a fast corner with their wheels almost touching amid black flares of flung cinders will stir anybody's blood. First-division fixtures are dominated by the stars. Since, on an average, some half-dozen men tower above the rest at any given moment, " bunching " is less common in the higher ranks—except at the first bend. Nevertheless, two evenly mounted stars at the top of their form can make the most hardened cynic gasp.

Perhaps the best introduction to the sport is to pay a preliminary visit to one of the smaller tracks, and so acquire a notion of the rudiments. Thus familiarized with the outlines, the student should next attend Wembley Stadium on the night of a World Individual Championship Final—if he is lucky enough to secure a ticket.

This fixture ranks with the Derby, the Grand National, Wimbledon, the Cup Final and an Australian Test Match at Lord's, as one of Britain's supreme sporting spectacles. Indeed, from some angles it outranks them all with the chiaroscuro effects of a starlit night and artificial lighting, the acoustics of a yelling mob concentrated in a deep concrete bowl, and the frenzied tempo at which the programme is carried through.

In the 1949 Championship, 224 original entries had been winnowed down to 16 finalists. Eighteen races ensured that each aspirant should meet each of his 15 rivals in the course of five races. The issue is decided on a points basis, three for a win, two for a second, one for a third, furnishing a maximum of 15 on the five rides. Allowing for a breather at half-time, the eighteen races occupy about two hours. As the gigantic crowd begins to muster in the dusk, the approaches are jammed with every imaginable type of vehicle. The waiting thousands are entertained by military bands and the trick motor cyclists of the Royal Corps of Signals until all ticket-holders have reached their places.

Except when racing is actually in progress, the vast amphitheatre is a sea of faces, brilliantly illuminated. The proceedings open with a parade of riders. Then the A.C.U. steward in his box high up on the grandstand roof assumes control through his switchboard. He touches a light signal, and a bugler summons the four riders listed for the first heat. They ride from the pits to the starting gate, wearing crash helmets of red, blue, white and yellow respectively. As they approach the grid, all the amphitheatre lights are extinguished, and the flood lamps over the track go on.

While the riders travel from pits to grid, four electric lamps in the helmet colours dance a crazy jig in a vertical frame to decide the men's track positions at the starting gate. This taped gate is a miniature edition of those used in horse racing, held down by electro-magnets and jerked up by powerful elastics. When the steward is satisfied with the riders' alignment, their 40 b.h.p. J.A.P. engines roar up on full revs, the tapes fly up, the clutches go home with a jerk which may cause front wheels to rear high in air, and they are off!

As they dash for the vital inside place at the first bend, they are saluted by a reverberating bedlam of noise from 90,000 throats. The spectators are split by three separate loyalties—to individuals, to clubs, and to nations, for Empire and American riders always offer a fierce challenge to our own lads. They go into the first bend at a speed which would cause centrifugal force to whirl them clean off the track, if they did not counter it by heeling over at incredible angles, and by utilizing their peculiar sliding tactic.

As they drift out of the first 180-degree bend, there will usually be some shuffling of positions, with, maybe, a chance for somebody

173

to dart inside the leader, or by coming out of the bend faster, to secure a lead down the straight to the next bend. Since all four men are probably using nominally identical engines (that is, specially designed 500 c.c. J.A.P. single-cylinders with very high compression ratios), any vantage must be based either on perfect engine tuning or sheer riding ability.

Team-work affects the issue in the sense that in the 1,512 yards of the four-lap Wembley heats—a distance which entails eight semi-circular bends—it is difficult enough to pass one man, and next to impossible to overtake two men. Hence, if the first string of a team gets the lead at the start, and his second string can keep close on his tail and a shade outside him, any aspiring opponent will need maximum skill and maximum luck to sneak past the pair within the distance. If a rider emerges from a bend with a modest lead, he can swing outward a little to enter the next bend from a wider angle, but must be careful in such a manœuvre that no rival can nip inside him. Even more important is it to maintain " traction " on his driving wheel while sliding the bends, so that he can come out fast and increase his lead down the brief straights which couple up the bends.

As the winner of a heat crosses the finishing line, a gun fires and every light in the stadium is switched on again. As the shouting dies, the loudspeakers distribute band music for a minute or so, while the results are checked and passed to the announcer. In spite of the size of the arena, the public-address system can claim the tone of a first-class radio set operating in a small room. Mean-while, a tractor hauls a grading machine over the track, and men with rakes smooth the wheel-rutted surface.

In the event of a spill likely to cause any obstruction, red lamps flare out to stop the race. Black flags are used to stop a rider if needful, yellow flags indicate the last lap, and the usual chequered flag signals the finish.

In the 1949 Championship, two of the finest Australian riders—Vic Duggan and Ron Johnson—were absent through injuries. Of the sixteen men to reach the final, three figured in a class by them-selves—Jack Parker (Belle Vue), Tommy Price (Wembley) and Louis Lawson (Belle Vue). The other thirteen, though top-notch riders, were not expected to defeat this trio if luck ran even. Price met and beat Lawson in the fourth heat. In the twelfth heat, Price enjoyed a great stroke of luck, for he was well behind Wilbur Lamoreaux (U.S.A.) when the American's engine seized and let Price in for a win.

By contrast, Jack Parker had one of his heats as good as won when a crash astern of him caused the race to be stopped. On the re-run, Parker got away to an indifferent start and was unable to catch Price, who thus secured the single point which made him champion for a year. It is noticeable that if Parker secures the inside berth early on, it is practically impossible to catch him. He maintains his traction so perfectly through the " broadsiding " that he emerges from every bend with an increasing lead. Many good judges consider that the Australian, Vic Duggan, is a shade better than Parker. Of the 16 finalists in 1949, one was American, five Australian, and ten British.

When the Championship ends, a privileged spectator may be lucky enough to climb to the roof of the Stadium and survey a unique spectacle. Kindly night screens the dinginess of a bomb-hammered suburb. The many thousands of lamps of the vehicles in the huge parks add a fairy glow to the giant panorama. Incidentally, the massed bellow of the Wembley crowd exceeds any other human outcry except the *Sieg Heil* of the Nuremberg Rally when Hitler was at his peak. Even the famous " Hampden roar," when Scotland play England at Soccer in Glasgow, is a pale thing by comparison. This Speedway Final is a function which every sporting Briton should attend at least once in a lifetime.

Be it repeated that there is no organized betting at this famous spectacle. No bookmakers attend. The tote *guichets*, installed at Wembley for dog-racing, are shuttered. The crowd is on an average younger than cricket, football or turf assemblies. Popular aces inspire a *schwärmerei* as frantic as Frank Sinatra's following among the teen-agers of the United States. Incidentally, a speedway ace earns an income ranging from £700 per annum in the lower strata to considerably more for the internationals.

Habitual frequenters of the speedways rapidly become as technically minded and critical as any keen student of cricket or football. The dirt-track ace ranks at least as high in the sphere of athletic achievement as any other champion. No feat in sport demands swifter thinking or daintier muscular control. He resembles the batsman at cricket in that a single slip is fatal to each innings. As a sport, the profession suffers from no more than one defect, namely, that it does not exalt team-work quite so freely as some of its rivals.

The following is a summary of the speedway organization as it existed at the beginning of February, 1950: Thirty-five tracks are licensed by the Control Board, of which nine are graded as First Division, fifteen as Second Division, and eleven as Third Division. Speedway tracks organized 1,023 meetings during 1949. In 1948 there was a total attendance of approximately 12 million spectators. Over 400 riders hold riding licences from the Board. Some half-dozen of the most expert probably earn £3,000 or more per annum, while a Third Division rider may expect to make about £800 in a season.

It is impossible to estimate the earnings with precision, because, when the League Match section of a programme is completed on any evening, private bookings may be available in the second half. Many riders also earn money prizes on grass tracks. The " Points " money varies as between the three Divisions, and additional fees are payable for Test matches, championship races, and so forth. The transfer of riders from one track to another is stringently controlled by the Board, and any transferred rider receives a percentage of any transfer fee.

Fatal accidents are uncommon—there was none during 1949. A benevolent fund exists for the benefit of the dependents of any rider who is killed or incapacitated. Many tracks try out recruits and develop their allotted riders during the winter months, and there is at least one school at which novices may undergo training.

The Third Division is regarded as the natural start for novices. A promising novice may be given his first chance as a reserve in this Division and, if he shows up well, may be admitted to a team, and later transferred to a higher Division. Development is very slow, and it is rare for a beginner to climb swiftly towards the top. Cycle speedways for ordinary pedal cycles have become very popular since 1948, and the managers of the Third Division teams frequent these cycle tracks in order to spot talent. All riders are insured.

The public do not, as some critics imagine, attend a track in the hope of seeing accident. An accident to a member of a visiting team robs the programme of much excitement, while the incapacitation of a home star is obviously a disaster.

CHAPTER 23

BRITISH ROADS

Before the Roman came to Rye or out to Severn strode,
The rolling English drunkard made the rolling English road.

CHESTERTON'S WHIMSICAL EXAGGERATION IS AS PLAUSIBLE as it is untrue. Our roads were begotten by pedestrians, who perforce turned aside when confronted by swamps, dense forests, and ferocious gradients. They were splayed out to a greater width when the horse was domesticated. The invention of the wheel doubled their span. The days of posting with four-in-hands and chaises created a novel demand for firmer surfaces, and gentler ascents and frequent inns to furnish food, shelter and relays of horses. From that date until the dawn of the motoring era British roads remained much the same.

The modern motorist is apt to grumble about our roads, and to compare them with the superb motorways of France, Italy, Germany and the United States. The French *routes nationales* owed their existence to the imperial ambitions of Napoleon and, like General Wade's roads in the Scottish Highlands, were purely strategic in origin. The Italian autostrada was probably inspired partly by a desire to provide employment, and partly for military purposes, and partly to foster the national pride which had been so shaken at Caporetto. The German autobahnen sprang from similar motives in Hitler's mind.

Alone, among modern nations, the United States has been able to face the cost of gigantic national arteries—like the Pennsylvania Highway—complete with elaborate fly-over road junctions, built simply and solely for the purpose of accommodating fast and heavy road transport in real magnitude. Their construc-tions stemmed from Henry Ford's original policy of mass-producing the simple " T " model Ford and selling it at the equivalent of £77 free on rail at Detroit. He converted the American artisan into a motorist, and the consequent need for more capacious roads coupled up to the delivery of goods by road over the immense distances of North America.

British enterprise was not stimulated by any of these spurs, military or industrial. The fringes of all our roads were cluttered by costly vested interests when at long last we realized their congestion and the threat to life and limb which that congestion implied. It follows that all the pioneer motorists suffered from the handicap of following their hobby on the grossly inadequate highways of the

M

four-in-hand coach epoch. Costly as subsequent road developments have been, their sum total amounts to little more than patchwork.

If by some miracle the motorist of 1950 could be transported in time back to 1900, he would instantaneously realize that if our roads today are inadequate, a very great deal has been accomplished. Fifty years ago the average English road was far more attractive from one angle only. Except on the high lands, it often composed a long green aisle, arched with foliage, presenting an ever-changing vista of loveliness and mystery. Its hedgerows were brilliant in spring and summer with wild flowers of a myriad hues and perfumes.

Modern speeds were naturally impossible, for round any of the numerous corners the road might be blocked by a flock of sheep or a drowsy waggoner nodding over his reins. Speed was also extremely uncomfortable, as the surfaces were never smooth unless a section had been newly re-faced, while repairs were not undertaken until the surface had been hammered into a condition which would hardly be tolerated in rural lanes today.

The roads of 1900 were very much narrower than those of today. Traffic was not only comparatively light, but it was also leisurely in its pace. When two vehicles met, it was at a speed which allowed plenty of time for either to pull in towards the hedge, the fence or the ditch. Very few vehicles exceeded an average speed of six or seven miles an hour, though the safety bicycle had raised the rate perceptibly.

When I left my gate on a primitive motor bicycle, I entered a rural highway of considerable local importance, a typical main road of an agricultural county, far better than the secondary roads of the district. Its width averaged about 12 feet between hedgerows. Its surface consisted of water-bound macadam. Three separate excoriated tracks became visible very soon after each re-surfacing. The middle line was hammered out by iron horseshoes, and was visibly punctuated at very brief intervals by the greeny-brown stains of horse droppings in various stages of decay. To each side of this interminable stain the iron tyres of the two-wheeled cart had already begun to disintegrate the macadam. Along both edges of the road a similar process was soon launched by drippings from the boughs overhead.

These boughs only affected the sides of our wider highways. There was no reason why any farmer should fell great trees along the margins of his fields unless or until they became dangerous. They added beauty to the landscape, and provided shade for his cattle in high summer. These survivors of the primeval forests of Britain were long-lived—unless they were elms. Occasionally a winter storm brought down the older monarchs. On one occasion I was brought up short in a gale by a gigantic oak, blocking the entire road, and, reversing my tracks, I found my path similarly blocked in the opposite direction by a tall elm, which had been felled by the gale in the few minutes which had elapsed since I had passed under it.

Landowners and farmers were united in a comprehensible

policy of keeping the rates down to a minimum, and roads were seldom re-surfaced until their condition became really atrocious. They deteriorated far more rapidly than today, for the simple reason that fifty years ago they had not been constructed with sound foundations or proper drainage.

Some readers will still recall the appalling condition of most British roads at the 1918 Armistice, although by 1914 road surveyors had begun to build much heavier foundations beneath most main roads. By contrast, our 1939 roads withstood the heavy traffic of the second World War in quite exemplary fashion.

But at the dawn of the century, when a road required re-surfacing, it was a common practice to dump six inches of fresh road metal full width across the worst sections. As the county was content to employ only a few road gangs, and to make shift with the minimum number of steam rollers, long periods might elapse before this new metal was rolled in and smoothed over with watered mud. Every main road displayed huge heaps of unbroken stone at intervals along its turf fringes. Nearby a shabby pedal cycle stood propped against the hedge. A labourer squatted by the dump of stone and tapped expertly with his hammer all day long, displaying incredible skill in reducing each big stone to the 2½-inch fragments which would pass the surveyor's mesh.

It is easy to imagine the sensations and the curses with which a pioneer motor cyclist met an unrolled strip of new-laid metal extending clean across a steep hill, which he probably could not have climbed in the saddle even if the surface had been tarmac or concrete of 1950 quality!

Imagine further that the luckless motor cyclist was riding on tyres of approximately 2 inch section, inflated to a pressure of at least 20 lb per sq inch ; that his saddle was of the cycle type, small, taut, and insulated only by a couple of small steel whorls at its tail; and that his front fork was utterly devoid of springs! The road surface was always worst at the sharper bends. The heavy carts had no differential axles, and their iron tyres were ruthlessly wrenched round such corners. Moreover, as these corners had been dictated by some obstacle—such as a spinney—drips from the trees were usually at a maximum on bends, and dissolved the soft binding material which had once knit the road metal into temporary smoothness.

High-speed cornering was quite a special experience in those days. The gay recklessness of youth, then as now, provided speed temptations which were even less resistable than today. If the visibility ahead permitted us—and sometimes when it should have restrained us—we went into a corner fast on the line of the middle of the road. The springless front fork began to hop and bob on the corrugated surface, scarred by horseshoes and iron tyres, so that the model was progressing with its front wheel spasmodically airborne. But body balancing is next to impossible in a prolonged series of short hops. So we were quickly hurled off course in proportion to the length and severity of the front-wheel hops, and probably found ourselves jerked across to the outside of the curve, partly by centrifugal force, partly through control weakened by the wheel hops.

Since tree drippings had already broken up the rough finish which the roadmaker had left on the metal bed, the unlucky rider now found himself on the wrong camber with the machine threatening to go out of control, and occasionally the combination of all these handicaps caused him to " run out of road."

The two chief defects of the 1900 type of road have yet to be emphasized. The first was dust. This did not cause a rider any real trouble so long as traffic was light and motorists were few. But on frequented roads, and particularly as the number of motor vehicles began to increase rapidly, the dust was really intolerable. Of course, rain laid it, and high winds swept it out of the cuttings fairly soon. But in a dry, windless summer, such as that of 1949, the traveller rode day-long through thick, gritty mists of grey powder.

I recall a 300-mile ride under such conditions from Cornwall to Surrey in 1902. On the way I had intended to call at the homes of several friends, but literally could not enter one of them. I was in an indescribable condition of filth, filmed deep from head to foot with the loathsome powder, of which pulverised animal droppings were a substantial ingredient. My eyes, ears and nose were full of it. I could not have sat down on any upholstered chair without fouling it. Towards the end of the trip I was refused accommodation at several hotels on a plea of " House full! ", which was certainly untrue.

When at last I found accommodation, although I was half-starved and incredibly thirsty, my first thought was for a bath, and I felt bound to tip the chambermaid heavily, as I could not help reducing the bedroom and the bathroom to a horrible state. Obviously, too, it was wise to carry a complete change, including fresh underclothing, on any such ride, nor was it easy to stack such an outfit aboard a primitive motor cycle, or to proof it against the penetrating powder.

The state of women was far worse, for those were the days when a " woman's hair is the glory of her," and the degree of glory consisted primarily in the *length* of her hair. It was my mother's proudest boast that she could sit on her hair, and one can imagine the combing and brushing essential after a motor trip. The feminine headdress designed for such occasions was peculiar. It consisted fundamentally of a tight roll of light fabric, resembling a narrow cross-section of a gigantic Lyons' Swiss roll; this element was designed to keep the pendant curtain clear of the face and the back hair. From this hung a 4-foot veil of dust-coloured tulle, drawn tight round the neck.

Imagine further the condition of any girl whom we coaxed to accompany us in a trailer—the first (but short-lived) version of passenger motor cycling. She sat silent—a proverbial misery for most of her sex—since conversation was impossible. In her silence she breathed the burnt hydrocarbons emanating from the motor cycle exhaust, and was continuously sprayed with the eddies of fine dust churned up by the rear wheel. If her Jehu was a knightly type, he took special pains to swerve wide of any fresh and smoking heaps of equine excrement, when possible. In rainy weather, the back-wash of the rear wheel towards the trailer was wetter, heavier, and even more noisome.

Rain laid the dust, but it filled the innumerable potholes, great and small, with a nauseating liquor, owing some at least of its colour to the incontinent horse. Moreover, the pioneer motor cycles mostly had tyres which were baldish even when new and, since the machine itself was top-heavy, skids were a constant menace.

For one very brief period I paid allegiance to the Humber Company. Their engineers realized that a tall man could not work the pedalling gear to good effect on a low frame. So they temporarily followed the example of the pedal-cycle factories in offering options in frame height. I believe the height of the standard motor cycle frame of those days was alleged to be 24 inches. But a Humber salesman persuaded me to buy one of his machines built with a 26-inch frame—it may have been a 28-inch frame, but across the gulf of years I will not swear to the major figure.

Moreover, this machine, largely based on Phelon and Moore design, had an all-chain drive, cushioned only by a large spring washer in the front sprocket assembly. It was further disfigured by a " free-engine clutch," which previous to delivery, and on paper, was the dream of my young life, since most machines had no break in their transmission. This clutch consisted of a very wee leather-faced cone, operated by a sturdy side lever working in a quadrant. That Humber would literally lie down in the road at the sight of a small puddle and, if one used the clutch for a restart, it would first rear on to its back wheel, and then lie down!

Since in those days the binding of all road macadam consisted of the local soil, well watered in with hundreds of gallons of water, certain limestone areas—notably the Derbyshire hills and the steeps at the back of Torquay—were notorious for their skidding propensities. In thin traffic an irresistible skid hurts no young man, beyond possible abrasions and gravel rash. But a skid was a major disaster for the pioneer motor cycle, as it either bent or broke a pedal crank. A disorganized pedalling gear deprived you of your only hope of climbing many main-road hills. Should the free-wheel further impishly choose such moments to jam up solid, the efforts of a bent crank to revolve were pitiable to a degree.

Road engineers were naturally aware of all the problems. Most of these gentlemen adopted a somewhat despairing attitude on the whole subject. But about 1905 certain inquiring technicians reminded themselves that as far back as 1845 the Corporation of Nottingham had casually launched an experiment destined to rank as historic. They had attempted to reduce the dust nuisance on the London road in their area by smearing it with tar, and also by using tar instead of water as a " binder " for their macadam.

The Nottingham experiment seems to have been largely still-born, although tar was then an almost valueless by-product of the coal industry, available in far greater quantities than the existing demand could absorb, and on the market in bulk at little more than a penny per gallon. The municipality of Bordeaux, in France, revived the experiment in 1898, adding as a refinement the heating of the tar to render it more fluid and easy in operation. This idea penetrated the brains of our road engineers about 1905 with grati-fying results, and by 1908 Britain boasted 1,269 miles of tarred roads.

This advance was due to a Royal Commission in 1906, followed by a dust-laying competition organized by the Roads Improvement Association in 1907, and by an International Congress called in Paris in 1908 to consider the adaption of roads to motor traffic. Sea water and other chemical compositions were the subject of varied experiments. Finally, the use of tar, of bitumen, and of concrete emerged as the modern remedies, and fathered the magnifi-cent roads available today.

The old waterbound macadam had one merit which tar and bitumen have eliminated. When dry, it facilitated night vision, though this facility was vastly reduced when wet weather darkened the sodden roads. Concrete produces much the same effect as waterbound macadam, but, like its predecessor, reflects rather a trying glare in hot sun. For these reasons it seems that finality in road surfacing has yet to be attained, though a tinted concrete may have possibilities.

1909 brought the establishment of the Road Board, which under-took some degree of central control of the 2,000 separate road authorities which up to that date controlled British roads. As compensation for this sacrifice of local authority, the Road Board was furnished with a large income from motor taxation funds, out of which substantial grants were made to local road authorities. A guarantee was given by the Government of the day that these funds would be exclusively applied to safeguarding and improving the national roadways. But in the repeated financial crises which have hampered Parliament since that date, that promise has gone the way of many another political pledge, and the Road Fund has been callously milked by a long succession of Chancellors.

Nevertheless, unquestionably we have been furnished with a road system incomparably safer and superior to the conditions of 1909. In this brief survey, perhaps only one blunder deserves special mention. In the decade which followed the first World War, some road authorities purchased enormous supplies of various bituminous compounds which were grotesquely ill-adapted for road surfaces. As applied by certain road authorities, they produced an ill-omened surface known to motorists as " black ice." It was excellent when bone dry, but when lightly filmed with moisture, coupled doubtless with oil drippings and rubber dust ground off tyre covers, it generated the most slippery surface known to man, over which the most expert and dainty driving might fail to keep a motor cycle vertical or to prevent a car from sliding helplessly ditch-ward.

Some of these authorities, on discovering their mistake, sold off their supplies of the compound at cut rates to the poorer counties, whose roads instantly developed a high accident ratio. In 1950 only four main complaints can be urged against British roads by a vinegary critic. They are mostly of obsolete design, as compared with the best American practice, a fault pardonable in view of our national poverty. They are inadequate in number, area and form, similarly justified to some extent by the limitations of the national exchequer. They are extremely costly, a factor common to all our modern necessities. The tarred and bitumen roads afford poor night visibility. The concrete roads inflict an unpleasant glare in bright sun. Viewed in relation to the national purse and—in the last instance—the present state of chemical knowledge, these complaints figure rather in the form of dreams for the future than of attacks on the present administrations.

Town and city streets naturally differed vastly from the open roads in 1900. In so far as it is safe to generalize: some wood paving existed in the smarter areas of great cities; setts were the usual street paving in industrial areas; cobblestones lingered in small country towns. Wood paving was highly praised by most road engineers of the period, but could become extremely slippery when filmed with slight moisture.

In such wealthy places as the City of Westminster, street cleaning was most admirably carried out. Wages were low and, as soon as the streets became deserted at nightfall, a host of cleaners appeared like magic, armed with hoses, brooms, horsed sweepers, and other weapons. I doubt whether any other city in the world had its streets cleaned so often and so thoroughly as the statelier parts of London, and even in the provincial cities, watering carts and horsed sweepers with revolving brushes were a common sight. It was not possible to cleanse a thoroughfare like Euston Road so effectively, and its veneer of slime in November was most perilously slippery for cars and motor cycles alike.

South London was even more menacing. Its electric trams were powered by a pick-up trailing through a slot in a metal conduit placed midway between the rails. The middle of the street was thus marked by six parallel bars of metal, inset in stone setts. When this hard strip was filmed with grease, tyre grip touched its absolute minimum. Furthermore, as the middle strip usually stood rather proud of the surrounding road surface, a motor cycle entered it with a bounce, and the rider could expect little tyre grip during the transit.

I remember one greasy November morning about 1905 making three separate attempts to coax a 9 h.p. tricar across the maze of tramlines at the big junction near Kennington Church. On an earlier occasion I hit them with a $3\frac{1}{2}$ h.p. baby Renault car. This car was compared by irreverent cynics to the Holy City as described in the Book of Revelation—" the length and the breadth and the height of it were all equal." When a perfect cube mounted on bald tyres encountered a surface devoid of grip, it just spins! That tiny Renault spun almost like a pantomime columbine.

It was told that Charles Friswell, a famous car retailer, gave a pale young curate a trial run on another cubical vehicle—the early Baby Peugeot—in the Euston Road about 1902. " Do you know, Mr. Friswell," remarked the cleric, " I have never seen a car skid ? " " Haven't you ? " growled Friswell, stamping on the brake pedal. The little car hit about six vehicles before it finally came to rest, facing in the opposite direction after describing a series of circles.

In the heavy industrial areas, streets were often parlous. In the woollen districts of Lancashire and Yorkshire the gradients necessitated steam trams, and the great bales of wool and cotton travelled from rail to mill and back again on steam lorries with iron tyres. The streets were paved with heavy setts. As the foundations were not adequate to stand up to such loading, the setts settled at all sorts of false angles, and the jolting on any vehicle literally made one's teeth chatter, while a very few miles produced aching wrists and " pins and needles " in the leg muscles.

During the " between-wars " depression, when many north-country mills lay derelict, I actually saw in a Lancashire town (which shall be nameless) the *lower edge* of a tramline exposed as it bridged a deep pothole created by some truck knocking one or two setts clean out of the surface. The income from rates at that period was so low that the corporation could not afford to keep their streets in proper repair.

In certain colliery areas—for example, Durham—the local wealth sufficed to maintain really good roads between towns. But the science of road making was not yet well developed, foundations were too light and, if a lump of road metal or a sett chanced to be displaced repairs were not instantaneous. So one night in Durham when my gas lamp was not working too well I rode my Vindec into a hole which was almost large enough and deep enough to trap the entire wheel. I was not going particularly fast, but the tyre sustained a double concussion burst, and the wheel rim was not merely buckled but broken, with about a third of the spokes snapped or dislodged.

That, of course, is a very extreme example of what might happen on our comparatively crude roads early in this century. But such incidents cast into high relief the progress which has been made during the last half century, and further suggest the really colossal expenditure represented by the fine roads and streets of 1950.

In conclusion, although we cannot claim such great motorways as adorn parts of Italy, Germany and, most especially, the United States, it is well to remember that those nations still possess many thousands of miles of really execrable roads, whereas even our subsidiary roads are quite tolerable. We are a small nation, and in the last 36 years we have fought two world wars. The consequent impoverishment has imposed immense handicaps upon us.

We are fully conscious of the defects in our road system, and are as eager as we are alert to perfect our highways. Plans of reform exist against a day when we can afford to perfect what now ranks as obsolete or inadequate. During any such interim we must patiently realize with gratitude that the last couple of generations did their best, and that the results are reasonably creditable.

The factor of congestion must ever remain more severe in Britain than the similar problems affecting other nations. The sole exception to that statement may be found in limited industrial areas of the United States. These islands are small. The fringes of our ancient horse highways remain cluttered up by a myriad vested interests, and even the widening of many roads is hampered by the fact that it entails the sacrifice of acres of agricultural land urgently needed to feed a population too large for our area.

It is not only the private motorist whose vehicle has to be accommodated. Internal communications and supply burden our roads with an immense fleet of commercial vehicles, while many millions of cyclists daily use the roads, since labour must be mobile in so highly industrialized a nation. It is easy to sneer at short-comings in our transport systems. A lively imagination is essential to grasp the magnitude of our problems.

Finally, we may mourn in passing the gradual disappearance of those charming tree-shaded vistas which once made most of our roads so pleasant to traverse. Thoughtless folk may sigh for an imposing linkage of autobahns on the Hitler model. Those of us who have sped with powerful engines over the wide, straight motor-ways of other nations, know how intensely boring such travel can be. They can boast the great merits of safety and convenience, but they rob motoring of much of its ancient pleasantness.

CHAPTER 24

INNS, LARGE AND SMALL

A T FIRST SIGHT, INNS MAY SOUND QUITE IRRELEVANT in a motoring
volume. Yet one of the first discoveries made by every
motoring novice is that from the date of buying his first car
or motor cycle he will spend far more time and money at hotels
than was his previous custom. Indeed, unless he applies stern
self-discipline, he may find he is spending too much money. On
every long trip he eats away from home, and perhaps sleeps in a
strange bed. He cannot sponge interminably on old and scattered
friends. If, in addition, he graduates in any form of competition
riding, he will feed and sleep for weeks in inns of various grades
and sizes. No motor cyclist is so much involved in the hotel world
as a journalist, who may actually in the course of a year spend more
time in inns than at his own home.

In any gathering of competitive motor cyclists, reminiscences
will be placed and dated by the names of inns and hotels sprinkled
all over the map of Europe. A large proportion of sedate tourists,
who never entered a competition in their lives, will find their minds
flitting back to some hostelry where they ate a memorable meal,
or spent an unforgettable holiday. Thus, inns are extremely
relevant in this volume, and my own experiences may stimulate a
host of pleasant memories in the reader's mind.

As a journalist assigned to describe major trials and races, I
have seldom been able to choose my hostelry when on duty, though
my employers naturally paid expenses when fate compelled me to
put up at de luxe hotels. The motor-racing game is played in an
atmosphere of great extravagance. In Hitler's day a German team
of three racing cars, hand-made for a single summer season, might
cost £200,000. Such expenditure is hidden in the research and
publicity columns of the balance sheet. Even a British motor cycle
factory once spent £50,000 on an unsuccessful attempt to win a
single race. Directors and engineers busy with such enterprises
do not frequent cheap inns, and the newspaper man must go where
he will mingle with the men in the know.

Broadly speaking, the smaller inns are more enjoyable than
the palatial resorts. The atmosphere is far friendlier, and the
guest is not surrounded by servile menials whose minds are mainly
focused on tips. I have stayed in the *Chateau des Ardennes*
where there were four waiters to each small table and an electric
bulb was automatically switched on in every drawer of your
bedroom. I have also slept in flea-ridden pot-houses on the

186

Continent where the wine smacked of wormwood and there was no sanitation.

It is not only the journalist who occasionally puts up, perforce, at an hotel rather above his social status. The spectator and the competitor in a motor cycling event often find themselves temporarily housed in unwonted style.

Motor tournaments attract vast numbers of the general public, who will usually overcrowd the complete hotel accommodation of some famous spa. The events are therefore timed " off season ". The municipal authorities of watering places and other resorts contribute substantial sums to the promoters' expense account and prize lists, and even bid against each other to secure the event as a feature of their own entertainment programme. It will usually be timed to extend the natural season either at the spring or autumn end, packing the resort with sightseers a few weeks before the normal season begins or after it is due to end.

Hence the competitors may find themselves in the Scottish Highlands before the salmon or the stags attract, or in Como at the height of summer when the heat would be intolerable for the ordinary tourist. It follows that the professional retinue of photographers and reporters wander almost continuously all over the map of Europe, often staying at palatial hotels where scarlet leather and bright chromium indicate that the tariff will be as mountainous as the scenery.

Many unsophisticated people ask nothing better than to occupy their years in an interminable circuit of such luxurious places. I confess that in youth such gilded surroundings were part of the attraction of the job for me. In my salad days it was an experience to take tea at the Bayerische Hof in Munich, where men in evening dress handed you huge spiced buns at half-a-crown apiece.

But the reaction was rapid and automatic. Sheer luxury very swiftly becomes incredibly boring and monotonous. The process is accelerated by the human atmosphere. The haughty ostentation of the habitués is offensive from the start. On the Continent, personal relationship with the hotel staffs at that level can vary astonishingly. Hall porters, waiters and " reception " are far too well trained and tightly disciplined to betray the contempt which many of them rather justifiably feel for the new rich or the oiled and perfumed darlings of the plutocracy. Their itching palms are hidden behind an impenetrable mask.

Towards humbler underlings like myself, temporarily hoisted by circumstance into such unwonted company, the staff attitude will vary between wide limits. Some of them may tend to be patronizing, aware that the pourboires will not crinkle nor rustle. Others of a sounder quality will feel it a relief to be more natural with simpler guests. But even if they slough their starched formality, and enjoy the chance to offer good service stripped of mercenary motives, they cannot modify the wild extravagance and sham values of the environment. The sheer luxury continues to bore, to irritate and to offend.

187

Be that as it may, the reaction was always identical for the majority of us camp followers. The tournament drew slowly to its appointed end. There came a night when we had completed our descriptions, telegraphed or telephoned the official times, speeds and placings, despatched our photographic plates, and were free to start for home. We tackled the long return trip of 1,000 miles or more to Britain with a resolution to fare simply in simple inns, no matter how generously the London office was prepared to handle our expense sheets. We ignored the famous " recommended" hotels along the return route. With one consent we selected nameless and unknown roadside inns for our midday meals and our night stopping places.

Covetousness might be obvious enough in a village estaminet or mountain albergo, but at least we had shaken off luxury and ostentation. We should be received as men and as brothers. If we were friendly, we should be met as friends. There would be no element of drilled and insincere formality in our welcomes and our adieux. Out of a world of insincerity and monotony and money-grubbing we should step into a world of variety and reality.

If a few examples sound a little ludicrous to readers unfamiliar with the heights on which declassé nobility still struts, remember that their spice was part and parcel of our irritated reactions. One day four of us, riding motor bicycles 400 or more miles a day, were rather late in our race to catch a stipulated boat at Calais. We had risen at 4 a.m. after a largely sleep-less week, gulping a meagre *café complet* before we kicked our dusty machines into life. Early in the forenoon we had swallowed rather a Barmecide luncheon at the top of an Alpine pass, for in six lurid days we had lacked time to enjoy the mountains and this pause was wholly deliberate. None of my companions had ever previously crossed the Channel. I was heading our crazy sprint for the French coast because I alone knew the roads.

Towards 5 p.m., with another 160 miles to be covered before bed, the other three raced up abreast of me, and refused to travel further without a cup of tea! *Tea* of all things, deep in the wilds of Austria! At the next inn they dropped their feet on the roadway, and refused to budge. They invaded the bar, shouting loudly in various English dialects for high tea! The innkeeper's family clustered round us, puzzled and smiling, gabbling some half-German patois which none of us knew. I entered on a lengthy colloquy, partly consisting of signs, partly of bad German, and partly of sketches on the margin of an Austrian news-sheet, explaining our predicament.

Finally, the lovely barmaid comprehended that our throats were full of dust, and that we needed some small snack to stay our tummies for the 250 kilometres ahead. She dragged us into the kitchen, where she proffered beer and cheese, which we all refused. Still laughing, she produced an enormous plum cake and four huge mugs full of a steaming, brown, aromatic liquid quite unknown to us. We finished the cake, washing it down with three mugs apiece of the treacly fluid. We made a mental note that the fluid was called *café kirsch*. The bill was trivial.

Half an hour later I began to wonder whether my front fork was broken, or was my front tyre deflating? I had never been tight on a motor bicycle before. My companions were in similar case. We dismounted, soused our heads in a horse trough full of ice water on a mountain pass, and proceeded unscathed. Rather a contrast with the half-crown buns at the Bayerische Hof!

That night we put up at a small village café in a shabby little French townlet. We enjoyed a rough supper in the huge bar, which gradually filled up with local peasantry. They arrived in families, complete down to babies in arms, and drank nothing but light beer, evidently prepared to make a single *bock* last the entire evening. The glasses were graduated according to the customer's age. Papa had a tall tumbler, Mamma a somewhat smaller glass, and so down to the youngest toddler who sipped a mere toothful from a *petit verre* normally reserved for Pernod.

My three companions, all warm-hearted North-country speed aces, could not bear to witness such parsimonious tippling, obviously dictated by sheer poverty. So we called for a round at the expense of perfidious Albion. This thawed all hearts, and made us freemen of the town for the evening. My companions knew no French, and mine was atrocious, but by some miracle we were all soon communicating freely with the locals, partly by signs and partly in broken English for the men had mostly served in some contact with British troops on the Somme.

Presently matters took a faintly bawdy turn. Madame had a small dog, apparently the product of a liaison between a dachshund and a poodle. It slipped out when a new arrival left the door open. Madame almost went into hysterics, and everybody tumbled out to catch *la p'tite chien*. When it was safely salvaged, I innocently expressed mild surprise that Madame had allowed herself to become so agitated about a little dog. Choking with laughter, she explained that it was the season for the little dog to become *très amoureuse*, and she shuddered to imagine the consequences of such another indiscretion as the union of its own parents. My attempts to explain the joke to two Yorkshiremen and a Lancastrian furnished considerable amusement.

Anon, Madame's little cat similarly darted out through an opened door, and I expressed wonder that Madame was not similarly agitated about her little cat. This roused another gigantic explosion of laughter, as Madame explained that the little cat had undergone an operation which prevented it from becoming *amoureux*.

Such experiences in the small inns of Europe set me wondering whether the little inns of Britain were undervalued in my mind. From that day to this I have missed very few opportunities of sampling our own small inns in preference to the four-star hotels with their impersonal atmosphere, conventional menus and garish cocktail bars. The results have varied between the calamitous and the delightful, but almost invariably have proved utterly unexpected. At least, they have never been so deplorable as to make me change my habit and my principles.

One of the less usual experiences befell me on a wild winter's night at four cross-roads on a bare upland in Gloucestershire. A sudden blizzard drove two of us to seek shelter at a house which we took for one of the old pack-horse inns, since nobody seemed to live in the vicinity. We staggered into the bar, shaking snow off our clothes and massaging our frozen fingers. The Second World War had bred a liquor famine. So when a very smartly dressed woman with a Girton voice came to our rescue, we anxiously asked what we could have to drink. Came the astounding answer, " Anything you like to name! "

My temper being frayed by peering through the snow, I spitefully demanded a double vodka! Without batting an eyelid, she placed a double vodka on the counter within 60 seconds, politely regretting that she was out of caviare.

This inspired my companion to even wilder flights. Something of a connoisseur, he has a strange passion for a horrible liqueur distilled in the Carpathian mountains which he alleges was once a monopoly of the Hapsburg court. It smells like varnish, tastes like turpentine, and is, in fact, a variety of apricot brandy. Ten minutes after consumption, it generates a delightful glow under the lower waistcoat buttons. So he calmly asked for a *barack palinka!* " Touché! " replied our hostess reluctantly, adding, " We finished the last bottle at Christmas. But . . ." (producing a noble flagon) ". . . this is quite a good apricot brandy of another distillery! "

No further introduction was needed. During supper her husband told us that this inn had long been famous for its wonderful cellar. Stranger still, its original inspirer was the village padre. In the days before the Fawcetts and Fabulous Fortune, this vicar had bred and raced champion greyhounds. After any specially notable victory he entertained the whole population at the Pack Horse Inn, and their beverage on such occasions was " white velvet ", that is, a tumbler of champagne, topped with an inch of rich cream.

This is a truly scientific tipple for drinking toasts. Readers who have dined at the Kremlin, or indeed in any Red Army mess, will long remember their first experience of the kind, when the Russians drank our men under the table. Afterwards they learnt that when a Russian faces a wet evening, he absorbs plenty of *butter*. The fat protects the linings of the stomach from the worse effects of strong liquor. Hence the cream topping to the champagne.

After supper our hostess showed us her museum of old glass. Its prize exhibit was the world's finest collection of hollow glass rolling pins. All the best pastry cooks are blessed with very cool hands. If a would-be *cordon bleu* has hot hands, she should roll her pastry with a glass roller full of iced water. In the 18th century such rolling pins could be bought along the wharves of every port in

Europe. They were the favourite purchase of all British sailors looking for a souvenir to bring home to wife or popsie.

The purchase was not entirely unselfish, since the rollers were sold full of schnapps or hollands, and, if slung inside the breeches, might elude the eagle eye of the mate at the gangway when the crew returned to ship. Thus a convention was born that the name and picture of a ship should be painted in colours on the rollers. Alas! many such rollers were smashed in the fo'c'sle orgies which ensued. Moreover, since a drunken crew encounters the maximum perils of the sea, a superstition resulted—it was bad luck to buy a roller bearing the name of your ship; she was certain to founder. So the manufacture of the rollers ceased. They became collectors' pieces, and now are hard to find.

Quite frequently in research visits to our small inns one stumbles on some forgotten fragment of history. One day near Cirencester an inquisitive switch down an attractive lane finished at an isolated inn. Its story, provoked by the apparent absence of any possible customers, was entrancing. When inland water transport was more used than today, Irish labourers were imported to dig a canal uniting Thames with Severn. Irish navvies never enjoyed working "dry" and, when the construction of a tunnel necessitated a prolonged contract, a drink licence was obtained for a small shack.

Today the tunnel is derelict, and many sections of the canal are no more than a necklace of stagnant pools, but the licence remained valid, and is now attached to a fine stone house. It is owned by a family which has long contributed both maids and men to the service of our royal palaces. With good ale, good meals and a bowling alley, it attracts travellers from afar.

On the foothills of a famous Gloucestershire common, history was reborn in strange guises, as I listened to aged men recreating a by-gone age. At school I had learnt how rapacious landlords enclosed hundreds of acres of common land. In this wee tap room we heard how simpler folk also filched public lands. One greybeard had inherited a pleasant little home with fine extensive gardens thanks to an ancient custom which perhaps never claimed full force of law. Squatting was tolerated on the fringes of the common. Provided that the land-less peasant could erect a house and occupy it for one night before the powers that were could interfere, he could remain there.

Some legal dispute naturally arose anent the definition of a "house". It was resolved that a "house" must include a chimney—not merely a nominal chimney, but one which actually conducted real smoke. So the astute squatter would collect a bevy of his pals in readiness for a moon-less and preferably misty night. At dusk they would quietly pounce on the selected site, swiftly erect a fireplace and chimney of local stone, feverishly drape some kind of shack around the chimney, light not too bright a fire, and sleep in the shack. Custom further decreed that a squatter, having thus established his right, was entitled by common humanity to a

191

meagre plot of the surrounding earth, on which he might construct a privy, grow vegetables and keep a pig.

" Not too meagre a plot, either! " I commented, having in daylight admired my new friend's spacious grounds. There were roars of laughter, and I next heard the device of the " rolling fence ". A man's garden must obviously be enclosed, if only to keep his pigs and poultry within bounds. Wooden palings were used for the purpose. A decent interval was allowed, until jealousy concerning the enclosure had simmered down. Then—again on a moonless and misty night—the cronies would reassemble, and the fence would be " rolled ", i.e., cautiously extended a few yards in this direction and in that.

There was no great uproar, since the ground on the slopes below the common was too steep for organized cultivation and all the more enterprising inhabitants looked forward to the squatter's co-operation when they, in turn, should qualify as landowners. Another interval of two or three years, and once again the fence was " rolled " a few more yards. If the squatter lived long enough, he finished up with quite a tidy little property. Nevertheless, it was the general opinion that my friend's famous ancestor had been somewhat over-greedy.

A peculiar strain runs through many of my memories of small inns. One of my professional companions on these motoring jaunts was the sole survivor of a family who had fallen on evil days. His once wealthy sire had owned a superb cellar, and he himself had a taste in wines which he could not afford to indulge. Benighted at a small coaching inn in his thirties, he discovered that the landlord still possessed a good cellar, stocked with sizeable relics of the fine port, claret and brandy which his forefathers had maintained for fastidious and wealthy travellers in the old posting days. Moreover, the landlord had no conception of their value.

At dinner my friend sampled a bottle. Greatly excited, he then inspected the cellar. No pirate, he communicated his expert knowledge to the landlord, bought an option on the entire contents, and sold the surplus at current prices, paying 75 per cent of the value to the grateful innkeeper. Having thus founded a good cellar for himself, he began to ransack promising inn cellars all over the country, just as others searched cottages for antique furniture. In the course of twenty years he made numerous similar discoveries, sometimes in posting inns which had lost their wine-drinking clients when the railway superseded the coach and the chaise, sometimes in premises located near some historic mansion, which now stood derelict or had passed into the hands of new owners with no great interest in vintages.

Naturally he encountered tragedies, where bins of magnificent hocks and moselles had withered into vinegar. But he unearthed much port, claret and brandy of unusual age and quality. Today his cellar book would make the mouth of a Simon or a Sainsbury water, while the cost of his bins has been ludicrously small.

A striking speed impression of R. L. Graham in the 1949 Senior T.T. He led almost all the way on his twin-cylinder A.J.S., but had to retire on the last lap

Racing on the Scarborough circuit. A pack of three-fifties at the Mere hairpin soon after the start

Spectacular sidecar work in the 1925 Sidecar T.T., showing Jimmy Simpson "jumping" Ballig Bridge on an A.J.S. outfit

WINNERS
of the
Senior
T.T.
1907—1949

(Above) Rem Fowler (Norton) winner of the twin-cylinder class in the T.T. in 1907. Speed 36·22 m.p.h.

(Left) C. R. Collier, who won the first T.T. race held in 1907 in the Isle of Man. His mount was a Matchless and his speed 38·22 m.p.h. He also won the Senior race in 1910, his speed being 50·63 m.p.h.

J. Marshall, riding a Triumph in 1908, won the race at 40·40 m.p.h.

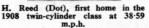

H. Reed (Dot), first home in the 1908 twin-cylinder class at 38·59 m.p.h.

F. A. Applebee, who won the race 1912 on a two-stroke Scott at 48 m.p.h.

H. A. Collier (Matchless) winner of the race in 1909. Speed 49·00 m.p.h.

C. G. Pullin, who averaged 49· m.p.h. on a Rudge in the 1914 T.

O. C. Godfrey averaged 47·63 m.p.h. on an Indian in 1911 when the present mountain course was first used

H. O. Wood rode a Scott in 1913 and won at 48·27 m.p.h.

T. C. de la Hay, whose speed was 51·79 m.p.h. in the 1920 race. His mount was a Sunbeam

H. R. Davies who, in 1921, won Senior event on a 349 c.c. A.J.S. 54·50 m.p.h. He also came first the 1925 Senior at 66·13 m.p riding an H.R.D., a machine of own manufacture

c Bennett, winner of the 1922
ior on a Sunbeam (speed 58·31
.h.). Riding Nortons, he also
a the 1924 and 1927 Senior races
speeds of 61·64 m.p.h. and 68·41
m.p.h. respectively

T. M. Sheard, who averaged 55·55
m.p.h. on a Douglas in 1923

Stanley Woods, the winner of four
Senior races. In 1926 he rode a
Norton (67·54 m.p.h.); 1932, Norton,
(79·38 m.p.h.); 1933, Norton, (81·04
m.p.h.); 1935, Guzzi (84·68 m.p.h.).
He also won five Junior events and
a Lightweight race

J. P. Dodson won the Senior T.T.
1929 on a Sunbeam, averaging
72·05 m.p.h.

In 1930 W. L. Handley, riding a
Rudge, averaged 74·24 m.p.h.

P. Hunt, on a Norton, won at
77·90 m.p.h. in 1931

uthrie won in 1934 at 78·01
. and again in 1936 when his
was 85·80 m.p.h. Both
mounts were Nortons

F. L. Frith rode a Norton to
victory in 1937, averaging 88·21
m.p.h.

H. L. Daniell, a winner (on Nortons)
of three Senior events. In 1938 he
won at 89·11 m.p.h., in 1947 at
82·81 m.p.h., and in 1949 at 86·93
m.p.h.

Meier, winner of the 1939 event
a supercharged B.M.W. twin. His
speed was 89·38 m.p.h.

IN 1907 and 1908 there
were separate classes for
singles and twins on the
short St. John's-Kirkmichael
-Peel course.

Length of the present-day
course is 37 miles 1,290
yards.

Lap record (up to 1950)
set up by G. E. Duke
(Norton) with a speed of
93·33 m.p.h.

A. J. Bell on a Norton won the 1948
event at 84·97 m.p.h.

Where the crowd enjoys the thrill of fine cornering after a fast
straight stretch. A scene at Hillberry in the 1949 Junior T.T. race

Racing on a short circuit. Cadwell Park on Whit-Monday in
1947 showing Nortons in a sidecar event

First man away in the 1949 Junior T.T.
race. Great crowds gathered to watch this
event which was won by F. L. Frith on a
Velocette at 83·15 m.p.h. He also won the
event in 1948 and so had the privilege of
starting first in 1949

Riders at the start of a handicap for private owners at Brooklands in 1934

A pre-war scene at Donington where racing took place in a lovely setting of parkland. Enthusiasm ran high and tremendous crowds gathered to watch the racing

Scrambles on private property are popular, for go sport can be had at comparatively small expense. T scene shows the start of a scramble organized by Wigton M.C.

Where crowds of 80,000 gather to watch speedway racing—a scene at Wembley showing riders getting away in the London Cup match in 1949

A typical trials picture showing how the sidecar passenger (in this case a lady) helps the driver over rough going on steep hills. On Hatch Hill in the Southern Experts' trial of 1948

(Below)
Racing on a disused airfield. A neck and neck tussle at Dunholme Lodge, a course 3·7 miles long. Speeds of around 90 m.p.h. were registered at this event in 1948 which was organized jointly by the B.M.C.R.C. and the Lincoln Club

The famous Scottish Six Days' Trial is always an event of
outstanding interest. The scenery through which the hilly
route passes is of memorable beauty and the hills a real
test for rider and machine. Mamore in the 1949 trial,
showing a leading trials rider, B. H. M. Viney

H.R.H. the Duke of Edinburgh drops the Manx flag, the
signal for A. J. Bell to start in the Senior T.T. race o
1949. Beside Prince Philip is L. H. Lumby, the time
keeper. H. L. Daniell won the race on a Norton a
86·93 m.p.h. Bell came fourth at 85·50 m.p.h.

The charm of these small inns is based upon an aspect of merchandising which is seldom understood. The great stores deal
almost exclusively with commodities which are not consumed on
the premises. There is therefore nothing to fault in a giant emporium
like Macy's, in New York, where under a single roof one may buy
practically all the goods desired by man. Each deal is a mere
private duet between vendor and customer. But the merchandising
of liquor should always be a community affair. Most of it is
drunk where it is purchased, and it is drunk in company. The
solitary drinker is usually not only a boor, but a degenerate.
The true accompaniment of drinking is good company and good
conversation.

The good pub is not so much a shop as a club, wherein mine
host and his friends co-operate in creating a neighbourly atmosphere.
Like an army mess, the tap should have its discipline, albeit silent
and informal. Mine host should seldom be driven to assert his
authority. There is a no formal boycott of undesirable intruders.
But the habitués, together with the landlord, combine to impose
standards which cannot lightly be ignored or challenged.

With these small happy coteries one might contrast the chance
congeries of ill-assorted individuals who throng the giant saloons
of huge suburban gin palaces or the vast beer gardens of Munich.
There is nothing cosy or intimate in such places. A small table
may accommodate some small group of friends or fellow travellers,
but the broad atmosphere has no connecting links closer than those
of the refreshment rooms at Paddington or Euston.

The famous " long bar " at Shanghai, in spite of its immensity,
can boast a real unity, since all its denizens are European exiles in a
foreign land and sustain a rough compression due to the eternal
pressure of the Chinese millions upon their tiny enclave. That is a
special case. Any man who has drunk there remembers it. But
his memories can never be so warm, personal and cosy as those of a
peasant or a traveller who is always welcome in the tap of a small
English country inn.

Perhaps the true function of all the stronger liquors is not so
much their gastronomic pleasantness, nor their exhilarating effect
on a tired and thirsty man. It is rather that they dissolve the shy
reticence and the sour suspicion which attack so many Britons
when they are stone cold sober—defects proof against tea and coffee
and lemonade, but soluble in response to even a modicum of
alcohol.

Chesterton always held that the wine-growing nations are
happier than the abstinent and the beer-drinking nations. Two
modern invaders of the small bar have not contributed to neigh-
bourliness. The introduction of the darts board and the football
coupon have artificially channelled conversation into narrow
conduits, whereas in nobler days it ranged widely over the whole
sphere of man's major activities from religion to politics.

So much for the ideal. The ideal was in fact quite frequently realized in an older period, especially if the assembly were mostly natives of the parish which pivoted on the church, the manor and the inn. The " foreigner " entering such an inn was always conscious of his responsibility, for at first entry he usually paralysed the atmosphere for the moment. If he was a new settler, it behoved him to be modest, forthcoming if accosted during the initial stock-taking noviciate, and hopeful of acceptance. As a wanderer, mine was too often the difficult problem of accelerating the " vetting " process. My efforts occasionally failed—no man is hastily found worthy in such places.

An exception may be made in favour of inns in Britain's Celtic zones, where local curiosity often conquers our national hostility towards aliens. The Celt is never so shy or tongue-tied as the Saxon, so in Wales or Cornwall the initiation may be quite speedy.

I remember one such struggle when I was a one-night guest in a small Northumbrian inn. Conversation froze to dead silence when I entered the bar after supper. When the ice began to thaw, I fumbled for a gambit. After several failures my eye spotted a Hercules humped on a settle in a dark corner. His barrel chest was adorned by a huge silver albert, strung with large medals. Aha, I thought, here is the captain of the local football team. I began talking futba'. It was coldly received. At last, in perplexed despair, I accosted Hercules. Wasn't he interested in fut'ba? All I got was a surly " Noa ".

" In wrestling, perhaps? "

" Noa."

So I commented on his fine medals.

" Oah, *them!* Our *lodger won they with his rabbits.*"

Nobody even smiled. I nearly went to bed in despair, but a sudden brainwave suggested homing pigeons, and instantly I graduated as a man and a brother. We were still hard at it at closing time, but when the local constable peered suspiciously through the smoke, we dragged him into the torrent of talk and did not adjourn till midnight. Even then I made a rare discovery. If you were interested in racing pigeons, you could attend church, but *not* chapel. Pigeons were inseparable from beer and betting, and the Primitive Methodists would have no truck with such.

One of the old wool townlets in Gloucestershire is the pubbiest place that I ever entered, and thereto also hangs a tale. Its population has probably never exceeded 2,000 souls, but the sergeant of police told me that, in the days when one could obtain a drink licence as easily as a postage stamp, the town of N. contained 40 licensed premises—some " off ", some " on ".

Although, in those far-off days, a glass of beer or a tot of gin cost a mere twopence, the folk were not drunken. The plethora of pubs was due to the covetousness of the local employers. The tap-room had long been the customary rendezvous for the weekly-wage payments. Naturally, a good slice of the wages went straight into the publican's till. It soon dawned on the employers that if they owned the inns, a percentage of the wages handed over at noon would be back in their pockets by 1 p.m., including the profit on the ale.

A notorious exploiter of this fact was still remembered, though he had been dead for half a century. He ran two separate businesses, one in N., the other in S., five miles away. He paid his N. staff in his pub at S. and vice versa! Since all his men had to travel five miles to obtain their pay, his rake-off—especially in high summer— was considerable, for there were no buses in the land at that date.

Believe it or not, there are still many English villages which do not contain a single inn. A certain Cornish parish housing some 500 inhabitants boasts five chapels, but no inns. Forty years ago the oldest inhabitant told me that his grandfather could remember a day when the parish contained two " bush-houses ". Ivy being sacred to Bacchus, a spray of foliage over the door was once the traditional sign for taverns, hence the proverb that " good wine needs no bush ". The dead grandfather had been a trifle vague about the precise liquors obtainable at these bush-houses, but my informant named smuggled cognac, red French wines from the same luggers, potent cider from the local orchards, and particularly strong home-brewed ales.

The brew-houses were even then in existence, though not in use. The larger farmers built their own brew-houses, with which they reconciled underpaid labourers to working long overtime at harvest. John Wesley was responsible for converting the Cornish to total abstinence. When the first fine furies of revivalism died down, teetotalism was fostered by the Rechabite friendly societies, whose members forfeited benefits if the accursed thing passed their lips. So in this 6,400-acre parish, the entire population were signed teetotallers with the exception of two ungodly farmers, who served the ancient parish church as its wardens.

One of these farmers will be remembered a thousand years hence. It fell on a day in the First World War that a Spanish vessel was torpedoed off the coast, and hundreds of enticing barrels floated ashore. The coastguard—perhaps deliberately—were tardy in mustering on the porth. But the bulk of the parishioners, in the spirit of their wrecker ancestors, were waiting to meet the barrels. The first cask to be broached contained an unidentifiable brown liquid. They sent in haste for churchwarden Sam. When he hurried down across the dunes, they proffered a blue delft mug containing a couple of pints. Sam sipped at it cautiously. " Tesn't ale! "

" Try 'un agen, man! "

Another sip.

" Tesn't whiskey, nother! "

A third sip.

" Dang me, tesn't port wine, nother! "

" Why then, Sam, if 'er bain't ale, whiskey nor yet port wine, tes surely all right for we! "

When the coastguard eventually arrived, the entire beach was littered with the sons and daughters of Rechab, supine, glassy-eyed and stertorous, for the casks contained an excellent sherry of high alcohol content and none of them had previously tasted anything stronger than hob-stewed tea. Sam, straddling a barrel and still firmly gripping his blue mug, was practically the only conscious Cornishman on the porth. History does not relate what the board of the society did about the scandal. But on the following Sabbath the local preachers excelled themselves from the pulpit.

I sometimes wonder how many of his peculiar names Charles Dickens acquired from public-house signboards. My own pluperfect example was culled from a small tavern in Wilts, which half a century ago was administered by one Euphemosia Tulkinghorn. Dickens can never have passed that way or the lady would surely have earned immortality.

Some of the heaviest drinkers in Britain were the northern coal miners in the period when beer and spirits were cheap and plentiful. Nor is the fact recorded to their shame, since their dirty, comfortless pit villages were devoid of any amenity other than the inns. Fifty years ago they crowded the scarce inns of the once agricultural villages and, in fine weather, overflowed on to "long bars" consisting merely of a sheltered bank of earth under shadowing trees, every man bringing his own supplies of liquor. A new era dawned when they found all-weather accommodation in working men's clubs. Thereby hangs many a tale.

In one such village the miners resolved to emulate a neighbouring village which already boasted a fine licensed club. Puzzled about the financial aspect, they consulted the local financier—the owner of their general shop, one of the few parishioners who could read and write. A sum of £4,000 was decided upon. Old Bill was wasted on a village. He offered to lend them £4,000 at 7 per cent, pointing out that the security was weak. They accepted. Ten years later they discovered that Bill had borrowed his £4,000 at 4 per cent and had thus drawn a gross profit of £1,200 before he was pilloried. He had to fly for his life.

Naturally, the atmosphere of such a huge club never achieved the cosiness of a village tap. But it operated almost wholly for good. The womenfolk had never frequented the superseded taverns. It was not thought reputable, and anyhow most of the wives belonged to the strait and narrow religious sects. But there was no harm in women going with their husbands to the club. They made a point of trailing their husbands thither on " pay " Saturdays, and they saw to it that the men did not liquidate all their fortnight's wages.

In fact, the club was a considerable financial benefit to the place. Previously, there was hardly any saving. The simple folk were too suspicious to put much in the Post Office Savings Bank—they did not trust " Lunnon folk ". There was no local building society, since entire villages might suddenly be emptied and derelict if a coal seam ran out. But their own men formed the club committee, and paid high interest on the shares. Many a family turned thrifty owing to the building of these clubs.

Perhaps these memories contain one explanation why the British working man is not enthusiastic for nationalized inns. He may approve the nationalization of many industries, but he is suspicious of any tampering with his inn because his inn is really his club.

CHAPTER 25

THREE GREAT MOTOR CYCLISTS

W E BRITONS ARE OFTEN DERIDED BY OTHER NATIONS because we exalt our champion athletes into national heroes and pay our best entertainers higher salaries than a prime minister, a general or an archbishop. Elements of absurdity probably exist in such contrasts. Nevertheless, we are not quite so crazy as the indictment implies. The balance is at least partly corrected if we remind our critics that we feel a unique pride and affectionate respect for a Churchill, a Montgomery, a Cavell, and that such gratitude is not necessarily expressed in terms of cash.

We love a great entertainer like Gracie Fields because she has so often ministered to our weariness and lifted us out of the depressions of exhaustion. A Denis Compton counts his fans by the million partly because he is a great entertainer in a different field from stage or screen, but far more because he represents a peak of personal success which owes nothing to luck or favour. He started at the bottom, seized all his opportunities and, in so doing, displayed those qualities of courage and resolution which are hallmarks of the British character and are especially admirable when coupled with sincerity and modesty.

Every sporting journalist learns to admire the technical skill of any great athlete. Moreover, he soon realizes that such skill is not always linked with courage, resolution, modesty and sincerity. When he encounters these five qualities combined in a single personality, and especially in an individual who climbed to the top by his own efforts, he recognizes a great man.

Such superb athletes are far more numerous than a Churchill or a Cavell. The services which they render to humanity are valuable and amply merit such small rewards as come their way in terms of fame or popularity or wealth, even though no balanced mind ranks their contribution to our common life with that of a Montgomery, whose genius transformed the trend of a battle for freedom, or of a Churchill, whose faith supported our failing spirits on a day when all the world deemed us lost.

Subject to such distinctions, the writer, as a sporting journalist of long and varied experience, passionately supports the claims of three separate types of motor cyclist to high pedestals in the world of sport. Their claims need support because motor cycling is a pastime confined to approximately 1 per cent of our people. We are at this moment a nation of 50,000,000 persons, of whom few more than 600,000 are motor cyclists. Our champions do not exhibit their skill, as professional footballers do, before a weekly audience of 1,000,000 spectators. The vast majority of Britons have still to see a great motor cyclist in action, for only one of our activities—racing on the cinder speedways—is conducted in large towns and cities, and even that is mainly attended by certain definite strata of the population.

Moreover, the daily newspapers, hard pressed for paper, necessarily cater for majorities and devote the barest minimum of their space to any of our activities. A Compton century earns the headlines. A Cotton round of 67 is a national event. On foreign soil I have seen a hundred thousand Dutchmen leap to their feet and cheer to the echo five British motor cyclists who won all five classes in an afternoon's motor cycle racing, whilst Dutch bands played our national anthem fortissimo. This wild, spontaneous tribute was awarded to our boys in spite of the fact that they had publicly outclassed all the best riders in Holland. But the British daily Press ignored this British triumph.

In fifty years of motor cycling, the men who have ranked in that field on the same level as a Compton, a Lawton, a Cotton or any other sporting hero, have been numbered by the hundred, and a catalogue of their names would be a tedious affair. So for present purposes I shall attempt no more than an analysis of the virile qualities which made such men worthy heroes in their restricted sphere, reminding readers that in other lands their feats have always received much ampler recognition than on their home soil, and that their names are household words not only in British motor cycling circles, but throughout the Empire, and equally in France, Austria, Italy, Germany, and other lands where we are not especially popular.

These supreme athletes automatically divide themselves into three classes: the T.T. winner, who races all over Europe on road circuits; the " chamois " type of acrobat, who rides neatly and confidently over such broken country as might dismay a mountain goat, unless that animal was scared to the verge of desperation; and the speedway champion.

As a preface, one curious feature of such athletes must be recognized. In other sports, youth is an essential ingredient. In them, technical skill must be wedded to superb stamina, with heart and lungs sufficiently youthful to maintain muscular accuracy at its zenith when exhaustion impends. Ninety minutes of high-speed professional football, 36 holes of golf for six consecutive days, the long strain of a Wimbledon tennis championship when the player must remain eternally almost as nimble as the ball he pursues, the stress of 15 three-minute rounds in a heavyweight boxing fight for a world title, 60 overs for a demon bowler under burning sun on ground like concrete—these ordeals can only be surmounted by the frame of a young Hercules.

The most severe motor cycling tests impose no such strain on heart and lungs, since the engine is mainly responsible—not solely, but mainly—for the endurance aspects. A champion motor cyclist will not ordinarily be hampered by the galloping pulse or the struggling, breathless lungs, which afflict any athlete who is solely propelled by his own bodily mechanism. But he must be physically strong and be in perfect training to ensure the co-ordination of bodily and mental faculties which his task demands.

The motor cycling champion must produce a judgment and a courage far beyond the demands of other sports. Alone among world athletes, he competes literally at the risk of his life. Golf links, rivers, Lord's and the Arsenal Stadium are not strewn in imagination with the dead bodies of men who have struggled thereon. Every motor racing circuit maintains sad memories of the men who have died at this point or that. This factor more than counterbalances the share taken by steel and rubber in our champion's achievements.

The purely physical burden in motor cycling is thus tolerable to a later age. In football or cricket a man borders on the veteran age early in his thirties. Many motor cycling champions do not reach their peak until nearly forty, and may win in the best company several years later. Very, very rarely does a lad in his early twenties qualify for real stardom—it takes longer than that to perfect the delicate judgment which permits an average of about 90 m.p.h. to be maintained round so searching a lap as the Isle of Man T.T. course, with its hundreds of varied bends and its demand for literally hundreds of gear changes in the 37-odd miles of a single lap. (Seven circuits, or approximately 264 miles, constitute a T.T. race.)

THE T.T. ACE

The T.T. races are normally held early in June, just before the real holiday season opens in the Isle of Man. There may be upwards of three separate events for engines of different sizes, but the climax is the Senior Race, for engines of 500 c.c. cylinder capacity, conventionally rated (in the old days) at $3\frac{1}{2}$ h.p.; the actual brake horse power may be 50—until recently the highest power ever extracted from an engine of that size by any engineers in the world, except with superchargers, in which case 90 b.h.p. would be possible. The total entries for the week will depend upon national prosperity, with 150 as a typical figure.

In 1950 the Senior Race attracted 75 starters (the permissible maximum). Fifty-two of them completed the seven laps. The winner, Geoffrey Duke, is a youthful genius, still in his twenties, and probably destined to rank as a world champion for years to come. His average speed was 92·27 m.p.h. over the most testing course on earth, and his fastest lap was covered at 93·33 m.p.h. His unblown Norton was 2·89 m.p.h. faster than the previous best, registered on better fuel by a supercharged German B.M.W. in 1939.

Wind resistance increases as the square of the speed. It is therefore essential to sit on a cushion over the back wheel and flatten the chest on a pad fixed to the top of the petrol tank.

The neck is bent upwards just enough to furnish a view of the road ahead. The arms, wrists and hands are condemned to an unnatural posture by the need to minimize wind resistance. This cramped position must be continuously maintained for three hours, except during a single hectic stop of some 25 seconds at the half-distance to replenish the fuel and oil tanks.

The Manx course is a " rider's course ". At no point does the road permit a clear view for even one mile ahead. The route writhes and twists in an incessant tangle of corners with ever varying radii. At two of these the machine must be braked almost to a standstill. Others may be taken by an expert at speeds up to 100 miles an hour. When preliminary practice is complete, the tarred road surface is marked by an endless polished " tape ", perhaps 18 inches wide, indicating the roughly correct line into and out of each of the hundreds of bends.

Since the entries are drawn from riders who have served some sort of novitiate in the Manx Grand Prix or on the short tracks of the homeland and elsewhere, most of these aspirants possess an approximate notion of the best way of tackling any given corner. But only a select minority know, by genius or experience, what is the absolute maximum speed at which a man can, first, get round a corner without crashing and, secondly, emerge from that corner in the ideal position to tackle the next corner ahead.

In other words, a round of the Manx circuit has affinities with a round of golf. At Hoylake it is by no means enough to stand on a tee and drive the ball 300 yards. That ball must finish on the correct spot to ensure that the second shot on to the green will be simplified and safeguarded. One might, in fact, split up the 37-odd miles of the Manx circuit into, maybe, 400 sections, each of which has to be knitted into the next to form a pluperfect tapestry. Naturally, the whole of this complex creation is complicated by the presence of other riders. One is frequently hampered by the presence of slower men who have to be overtaken.

Nor is the race a mere matter of human *v.* human. Engines demand the most sympathetic consideration. Their design is a compromise, dictated by three separate considerations. First and foremost, they must be designed to last at least 270 miles at an average speed bordering on 90 m.p.h. It would be a blunder to make them so sturdy that they could last unimpaired through 1,000 miles at 90 m.p.h. Perfection is attained when their stamina is trustworthy over the requisite distance.

Secondly, they are driven not by reference to a speedometer, but by reference to a revolution indicator. On the dial of that instrument is a red line at (perhaps) 7,000 r.p.m. The rider will normally keep the revolutions below that danger zone. But if glimpses of his more formidable opponents, or secret signals from his manager at the pits, inform him that some rival is ahead on corrected time, he must accelerate somehow. In all probability he cannot save time by more lurid cornering. He is probably already taking every rational risk in his corner-work. To increase his lap speed in emergencies he must, therefore, flog his engine beyond its possible bursting point, and he will effect this principally by making greater use of the lower gear ratios in accelerations out of the corners and up steep gradients—the circuit crosses a shoulder of Snaefell mountain at an altitude of over 1,400 feet.

Thirdly, since the rider must average close on 90 m.p.h. for the distance, inclusive of very marked and definite slows for the worst corners, the engine is designed to develop maximum possible power and this means that its power is " high up ". At ordinary street speeds the engine may be almost unmanageable—it will sputter and misfire and develop hardly any power at all. It is probably rough and miserable until the indicator registers at least 5,000 r.p.m. Thus, from the start, the rider must continuously use his wits.

Since the road is comparatively narrow, the men are started either separately or, perhaps, in pairs at half-minute intervals, according to the number of competitors. On the latter basis, with 60 starters, No. 60 is dispatched 14½ minutes after No. 1. The rider therefore cannot personally watch his most threatening opponents. It is up to his pit manager to keep him informed of his position, and no speech is possible between them except at the half-distance fuel stop in the frantic hurry of refilling tanks and changing goggles bespattered with dead flies or rain.

The pit manager in turn is hampered by the starting-time intervals. He may know, for example, that the ultimate winner will come from six men, who started respectively as Nos. 1, 9, 27, 38, 49, and 59. He keeps tag on his five principal rivals and, as soon as he himself can work out the sums created by the starting intervals, he is ready to signal his own man.

The usual system is to hold up a small blackboard, on which the salient fact is chalked, perhaps *en clair*, perhaps in code. The message might be " 3—28 ", which, being interpreted, means " You are lying third, 28 seconds behind the leader ". Or it might assume a simpler form, such as " Keep going as you are ", or " Quicker " or even " All out! " The rider receives such advice, usually at one of the points where the road compels him to slow down a trifle, and he reacts accordingly. If he has already kept as near the red line on his rev. indicator as possible, he must now begin to ignore that red line wherever practicable.

Suddenly, a breakdown or a substantial acceleration on the part of one of his chief rivals may transform the whole situation, either alarmingly or encouragingly. In other words, it is no mere matter of squatting low on the tank and using the twistgrip throttle, the brakes and the gear pedal. The rider's brain is perpetually in swift and desperate action. Years of experience may have rendered his cornering semi-automatic, but he must never permit his brain to drowse even for a split second.

Naturally, overtaking slower men, some of whom he will even " lap ", creates a succession of acute problems, and may often compel him to take extreme risks, as, for instance, where a slower man is swinging wide on corners or is on his " line ". The necessity to pass a bunch of two or three slower men who are keeping close company may develop into a veritable nightmare. Sometimes, again, he may utilize a formidable rider almost as a windshield, sit in the other fellow's slipstream for a time and, perhaps, try to tease him into displaying his real maximum.

Often a team of three riders may be able to apply team tactics, especially if one of them starts close to a dangerous opponent. Then A. of the A.B.C. team may try to tempt Y. of the X.Y.Z. team to go too fast and break up his engine, so that B. may slip through to win. The whole race, on this and other points, may be a continuous mental exercise no less than a violent physical effort.

Apart from the problem of space, I am reluctant to mention names, because the ordeal confronting the 1926 winner was so fundamentally different from that faced by the 1950 winner. In 1926 the Senior was won at a mere 67·54 miles an hour, i.e., some 25 m.p.h. slower than in 1950. It does not by any means follow that Stanley Woods, who won in 1926, displayed any less prowess than Geoffrey Duke, who won in 1950. In 1926 the road surface was grossly inferior; this, the comparatively crude forks and the lack of rear springing forced Woods' machine to jump about a good deal, and the physical punishment was then so severe that many a rider finished completely exhausted and was only fit to go straight to bed after a hot bath and massage.

Again, a man like C. R. Collier, who won the first T.T. over the " short course " of 15–16 miles in 1907, had only one gear, a crude and not wholly dependable machine, and poor brakes. He had to reinforce his weak engine by hearty pedalling on the milder hills of that obsolete circuit. His total effort is probably quite comparable with Duke's ride of 1950 on a modern machine of fantastic power and general efficiency.

This analysis furnishes the material to match the feats of a T.T. winner against similar eminence in all other sports. As a footnote, the reader unfamiliar with motor cycling history should realize that the T.T. is only one—if the most difficult and the most celebrated—of a long string of similar races. During the summer months, every other week contains a roughly similar fixture in Ireland, France, Belgium, Italy, and so on. To all of these British makers despatch their " travelling circus " of star riders and star mechanics. Between the wars Britain was almost monotonously invincible and it has been much the same post-war; for example, in 1949 her riders and machines won the 350 and 500 c.c. solo and 600 c.c. sidecar international road-racing championships.

THE SPEEDWAY ACE

Second on my roll of honour for motor cycling champions stands the cinder ace. Like the T.T. star, age does not wither him. Long experience is similarly required to graft pluperfect judgment on his physical qualities. Both alike require the courage, the determination, the judgment and the physical qualities (including a greased lightning reaction period and an abnormal sense of balance) which mark all motor racing men of quality.

But these faculties are employed under sharply contrasted conditions. The speedway ace rides at several brief races in the course of a single evening programme, but each brief sprint lasts no more than a minute and a half or thereabouts. He fights in unpleasantly close company. The starting gate lifts. He must get his clutch engaged with a madly racing engine in a microscopic fraction of a minute, yet with sufficient restraint to prevent the machine rising vertical on its rear wheel like a rearing horse.

He must at all costs fight to snatch the inside berth at the first corner and, having secured it, hug that berth at the inner edge of the cinder track so lovingly that there is no room for a rival to nip inside him, and so fast that his fleetest opponent cannot ride round him on the outside. It is not his luck to steer a vertical machine on a straight line. Twice at least—in each separate lap—he must throw his quivering steed into a turn and hold the slide for about 100 yards, while leaning over at an angle of less than 45 degrees with the " dirt ", hemmed in, perhaps, by three other men of equal skill similarly engaged within a few feet of his shoulders or either skidding wheel.

All the time, he is fully aware of accidents in which his personal friends—or himself—have crashed, been rammed by another rider. All the time he is conscious that any defect of skill or courage may lead to his being dropped from his team and joining that great company of " has-beens ".

Here the reader without experience of such feats may easily visit his nearest speedway and gauge the skill of the stars for himself. I advise him to do so. By contrast with the comparatively quiet atmosphere of Lord's or the Arsenal Stadium, he may form his own impressions of athletes whose deeds are less publicized. I warrant he will go home gasping and full of disturbed admirations.

THE " CHAMOIS " MOTOR CYCLISTS

It is less easy to find a convenient opportunity of estimating the merits of the men who win their trophies in one-day trials and scrambles. The dates and venues of the big events are published in the motor cycling Press. Perhaps the finest is the British Experts' Trial, annually held in late autumn, usually in the Cotswold area which abounds in freak goat tracks.

Here may be seen the leading exponents, pitted against the craziest obstacles which Nature provides to prohibit any form of wheeled transport. Some of the observed sections are so vile that the best chance of surmounting what is, perhaps, an almost unclimbable torrent bed is to charge it bald-headed at high speed, steering by body sway as one stands on the footrests of a machine which has both wheels airborne for much of the distance. Others are conquered by daintier methods, the almost imperceptible twitch of the forefinger on a twistgrip which supplies precisely the tiny push of power requisite to clamber over a greasy rock step without generating the wheelspin which might halt the machine. On others, reminiscent of a Wild West rodeo, nothing can succeed except the mastery which ties down a bucking, jumping, rearing machine to the only available 2-inch strip of hard going on which the driving tyre can bite just enough to keep the rider moving.

Hawk eyes—those of the officials—watch for a dabbing foot. Perhaps not a single rider makes a clean ascent of the worst clamber when the weather has been cruel, and most of the entry may fail on many of the climbs, while, perhaps, water—almost saddle deep—defeats others in the valleys, or deep mire seizes and stalls them.

The crux varies in character and severity with each instalment of the truly abominable route. Yet the acknowledged experts conquer most of the tests almost superciliously, and some freak, arbitrary test against a stop-watch may be required to select a winner from the small coterie who, without losing a single mark, have defied the worst which ingenious organizers can devise for their discomfiture. One turns homeward from such an exhibition with a deepened humility and a profound admiration for human achievement.

I wish space were available to tell the story of all these modern champions. But the main purpose of this volume is to take a perspective view of our story as a whole.

CHAPTER 26

SOME FAMOUS MAKES

A.B.C.

THE FERTILE BRAIN OF GRANVILLE BRADSHAW concentrated upon motor vehicles for a few years from about 1912 onwards. Its products included: a small car with basket-work body, driven by an airscrew; a very ordinary 3½ h.p. motor bicycle with a flat-twin engine set longitudinally in the frame; a series of oil-cooled engines with the cylinder barrels almost sunk from view in a deep crankcase sump carrying a large quantity of oil; various simple forms of rear springing; an air-cooled 12 h.p. two-cylinder car ; and a 400 h.p. air-cooled aircraft engine of the radial nine-cylinder type with copper-plated finning. But he temporarily revolutionized the motor cycle world just after the first World War.

The Sopwith aircraft factories were seeking occupation for peace. They began the quantity production of a remarkable 3 h.p. motor bicycle with a small flat-twin engine set horizontally across the sprung frame. It started as a lightweight. The writer was once photographed holding it aloft in his two hands, with the crankcase at chin level. By the time production engineers were satisfied, it had swollen into a mediumweight roadster. It was nevertheless more compact and lighter than its rivals, while built-in legshields and under-tray permitted the rider to wear indoor clothes. A beautiful four-speed gear box, with " gate " control on car lines, was among its merits. The order books filled as half our fraternity howled for delivery.

But a multitude of snags were hit in the effort to produce. Inflation expanded the price to £160. When deliveries at last began in earnest, thousands of orders had been cancelled in favour of other makes which were quicker on to the post-war market. Moreover, the early samples were handicapped by simple faults—the valve gear was unsatisfactory, the kick-starter gave trouble, and so forth. As the result of all these delays and hitches, the company closed down.

Nevertheless, the modified machines were so good that numerous appeals have since been heard for the revival of a potentially fascinating machine. The comparatively small number which had actually been delivered achieved a wild success, and put up some fine performances on Brooklands, while private tourists were charmed with them. A few are still running. If the machine had been produced in normal times and in less of a hurry, the type would almost certainly have survived and ranked high among the very best motor bicycles in the world. It deserves special credit for being the first to standardize a rear-sprung frame.

ARIEL

The Ariel is one of the few factories which has survived all the vicissitudes of the industry from the very start. They produced, in 1898, a gear-driven, air-cooled tricycle which was, in its main features, a copy of the original De Dion, but secured vastly increased comfort by shifting the engine from the De Dion position behind the rear axle to a position inside the wheelbase. This simple change moved the centre of gravity forward and prevented the light front wheel from becoming airborne over every appreciable hump on the road surface.

Moreover, the workmanship was definitely superior to Continental standards, and the machine could claim very reasonable reliability. A. J. Wilson rode one in the Thousand Miles' Trial of 1900. During 1899–1900, fair quantities of this tricycle were sold, and the Somersetshire county surveyor found one invaluable in his work. The firm presently followed the growing fashion, and in 1902 switched to a Kerry-engined bicycle. It has manufactured motor bicycles in immense variety ever since.

The long Ariel line culminated in the famous 1930 four-cylinder "Square Four". This engine achieves compactness by adopting a couple of two-cylinder units with their crankshafts geared together. For comfort, manners and high performance it is still pre-eminent, and is the only four-cylinder to earn and retain a large market. Most of the simpler and cheaper Ariel models have been similarly successful, though the company has not sought publicity by ambitious racing programmes. 1950 found it the only factory in the world simultaneously producing models with one, two and four cylinders.

A.J.S.

The brothers Stevens exhibited an early interest in motor cycles and marketed a lengthy series of excellent machines, among which two models proved especially popular. One was a charming little 2¾ h.p., which in various guises won a host of adherents. The other was a big 800 c.c. vee-twin, once famous for use with family sidecars, which reached its peak fame about 1920–25.

From 1914 until 1930 A.J.S.s remained exceptionally prominent in the 350 c.c. Junior T.T. races, with occasional feats in the 250 c.c. and 500 c.c. classes. In 1921 their stock had quite a boom, for they finished first, second and third in the Junior T.T.

Eventually the factory became merged with Associated Motor Cycles, who applied new blood and renewed energy to the racing game in particular, so that in the 1948–50 period both the 350 c.c. and the 500 c.c. A.J.S. ranked among the champions of speed. Their roadster models are equally eminent in the milder sphere.

207

BARR & STROUD

The sleeve valve, as an alternative to the "mushroom" or "poppet" valve, has had a chequered history in the motoring world. The Knight version figured on Daimler cars for many years, but has long since been discarded. The single-sleeve valve engine, made by Barr and Stroud under Burt-McCollum patents, achieved a limited popularity in motor cycles between the wars and later was adopted as the basis of Bristol sleeve-valve aircraft engines. The motor cycle engines were very quiet, reliable, and pulled well at low speeds. They were ultimately abandoned, possibly because of cooling and lubrication difficulties and their not, at that date, being adaptable to the high rate of revolutions desirable with such small engines as lend themselves to a motor bicycle of reasonable performance.

BAT

The Bat was made at Penge in the first decade, powered with J.A.P. engines, and demonstrated by T. H. Tessier. Its publicity was audacious, for from the very first it dispensed with pedalling gear and optimistic claims were made that it would climb all hills under engine power. It was graced by the first spring frame, consisting of a small sub-frame, carrying saddle and footrests, suspended by springs from the main frame. For some years it was a great favourite with sporting riders. Ridden by men like H. H. Bowen and the Bashall brothers, it often put up a couple of sensational laps at the start of a T.T.

BENELLI

Chiefly known as a beautiful little Italian 250 c.c. racer, which won the 1939 Lightweight T.T. in the hands of E. A. Mellors at 74·25 m.p.h. and, with Dario Ambrosini in the saddle, the 1950 Lightweight T.T. at 78·08 m.p.h. The engine is a single-cylinder with the twin overhead camshafts driven from the crankshaft by spur pinions.

BLACKBURNE

In 1902, Geoffrey de Havilland built himself a 499 c.c. motor cycle, possibly the first to incorporate a mechanically operated inlet valve. The cylinder barrel was cooled by coils of copper wire. The compression ratio was 4 to 1, and an outside flywheel was used. In 1904, Alick and Cecil Burney bought the rights. In 1912 they took Harold Blackburne into partnership, and thenceforward the engines were marketed under the name of Blackburne.

The Burney brothers left the company in 1914 to join the first detachment of motor cycle despatch riders in France. But the manufacture of Blackburne engines up to 450 h.p. continued until 1937. The make was chiefly famous for smooth roadster engines of medium performance, though many successes were scored in the T.T. races.

208

BROUGH SUPERIOR

Designed and ridden by the irrepressible George Brough, and built in Nottingham, the Brough Superior was always in the limelight. His father, W. E. Brough, was also a designer and manufacturer, and an early flat-twin Brough belt-driver was ridden through a Scottish Six Days' by George on a single gear with great *éclat*. Almost every Show produced some new Brough Superior sensation, including a model incorporating an 800 c.c. Austin water-cooled four-cylinder engine and a " Golden Dream ", with an embryo transverse four.

The pride of the Brough stable was the world-famous S.S.100, often described as the two-wheeled Rolls-Royce. This had a special 1,000 c.c. overhead-valve J.A.P. vee-twin engine, supertuned, with heavy transmission. Inquirers who visited the factory could see it touch 100 m.p.h. on the road, possibly with the demonstrator riding hands off, or approaching similar speeds with a de luxe sidecar attached. Lawrence of Arabia was its best-known enthusiast. He used to average 50 m.p.h. on it, and was eventually killed when riding it.

Being practically hand-made from special parts, its price between the wars was £180. So far it has not been revived since the war, presumably because under conditions of inflation its cost would be fantastic. Many of these machines are still running well.

B.S.A.

This factory supplied cycle components of the best quality to the trade from 1880, and in 1910 produced its first motor cycle—a $3\frac{1}{2}$ h.p. belt-driver. In 1914–1918 military models were supplied to Russia. After the armistice a constant stream of new designs were marketed, of which the more famous were the 1920 6/7 h.p. sidecar outfit with enclosed chain drive and the famous 493 c.c. overhead-valve " Sloper " of 1926.

Racing was abandoned after an unlucky T.T. experiment in 1921, but the firm's roadster models were best sellers until 1939 and this is also the case post-war. Several other *marques* are now made by associated firms, for example, the post-war Sunbeam (q.v.), the New Hudson autocycle and the Ariel. There is an exceptionally full range of B.S.A. types, among which the " Bantam " and the vertical-twins are prominent. B.S.A. machines have a splendid record in reliability trials. The firm is perhaps especially far-sighted in paying particular attention to the 125 c.c. " Bantam " model during present financial stringencies.

D.K.W.

This German two-stroke has repeatedly been very formidable in the Lightweight T.T. Ridden by E. Kluge, it won the 250 c.c. event

o

in 1938 at an average speed of 78·48 m.p.h., including a record lap at 80·35 m.p.h. This average speed, accomplished with forced induction, was not beaten until 1950. On the Continent it dominated the 250 c.c. racing class for two or three years before the war. The touring-type D.K.W. owes its efficiency to a special system of porting, for which the patent has now expired. It is not certain that this patent was ever valid, but nobody challenged it in the courts.

DOUGLAS

This factory has changed hands more than once, but has always been devoted to the horizontal twin-cylinder engine. The original parent of the clan was successively known as the Barter and as the Fairy, and burst upon an astonished public in the A.C.U. End-to-End Six Days' of 1906. We had never seen an engine which started so easily, ran so smoothly, and pulled so well for its size, while its ridiculously light weight was a giant asset. At that date it was little more than a " motor-assisted bicycle " and its power-to-weight ratio was high.

When certain crudities had been pared off, its popularity further increased, until in 1912 it created a positive furore by securing first, second and third places in the Junior T.T. (" mountain course "), W. H. Bashall finishing first at 39·65 m.p.h. By this time it had blossomed forth with a neat countershaft two-speed gear and a chain as the primary element of a " chain-cum-belt " drive. Even the popularity of the Triumph was threatened. In the First World War it was unhesitatingly selected for large military orders.

Since the 1918 armistice the company has undergone sundry reorganizations, and between periods of stress has produced several very charming machines. Somehow it has never quite attained the pre-eminence which its fundamental merits might have justified. The management has not always been blameless. The city of Bristol does not possess so large a pool of skilled mechanics accustomed to light engineering duties as Coventry or Birmingham or Wolverhampton can claim.

On at least one occasion a Show caught the board napping with a positive avalanche of short-dated orders, far beyond their works' capacity. They accepted these orders, and farmed many components out to sub-contractors. As the machines reached the customers, they gave heaps of trouble, and the firm issued free replacements, which ate into profits.

At the present moment the factory is concentrated on a most attractive flat-twin with torsional rear springing, and its future will be watched with deep interest. This type of engine, though awkward to house in a cycle frame, is probably the smoothest twin-cylinder in the world. Overshadowed at the moment by the " vertical " twin, it may yet come into its own, especially in the 350 c.c. class. An engine of this type powers the German B.M.W., which holds the world's record for the fastest land speed on two wheels, and

210

which—in a supercharged version—beat our best unblown 500 c.c. engines in the 1939 Senior T.T.

EXCELSIOR

This make was eminent among the very first quality British motor cycles. Around 1902 its 2¾ h.p. model, fitted with an M.M.C. copy of the De Dion engine, was possibly the best on our market. It had coil ignition, surface carburettor, automatic inlet valve, belt drive, and rigid fork, but was very well made, and capable of 45 m.p.h. The trademark still survives in different hands, which of recent years have produced many excellent lightweights, including several very fast racing models which figured splendidly in the Isle of Man T.T. For the 1950 season it marketed a vertical twin-cylinder two-stroke with rear-sprung frame.

F.N.

These initials are the title of the Belgian equivalent of Woolwich Arsenal, situated at Liège. From the earliest days, F.N.s have produced fine and original motor cycles. Their most famous production was a shaft-driven, line-ahead, four-cylinder, designed by Paul Kelecom, whose engines at one time competed with the Minerva engines for adoption by small British assemblers.

FRANCIS-BARNETT

It is seldom that a really original brain remains in the service of a small firm content to manufacture low-priced lightweight motor cycles. There are many such models on the market, and a carping critic might be tempted to describe them as " much of a muchness ". That does not apply to the Francis-Barnett, now merged with Associated Motor Cycles. As far back as 1923 they marketed a 147 c.c. model with a frame bolted up from standardized steel tubes and, as such, easily repairable by owners resident in lonely places. Presently they flanked this with their famous " Cruiser ", a totally enclosed model of 250 c.c., rideable in ordinary clothes and suited for hosing down after a run in filthy weather.

Side by side with these, they produced a family of first-class lightweights designed to assist the graduation of a pedal cyclist, e.g., an elderly man or a district nurse. The range starts with an auto-cycle furnished with pedal gear, and ascends through slightly more complex designs up to a fully equipped roadster of 197 c.c.

GILERA

The Italian Gilera four-cylinder machine is probably the fastest 500 c.c. road-racing motor cycle in the world. In 1950, it won both the Belgian and Dutch Grands Prix. While its record of victories is not especially impressive, this may possibly be ascribed either to its being ridden by riders just below the top class or to the machine as a whole not being too well suited to circuits embodying plenty of bumps and corners.

GUZZI

The Guzzi factory beside Lake Como earns its bread and butter mainly by turning out thousands of lightweight motor cycles with tiny engines and an amazing performance. In addition to these, and to 250 c.c. and 500 c.c. roadsters and to a three-wheeled commercial vehicle, the factory produces racing machines of 250 c.c., 350 c.c. and 500 c.c. Its racing machines are always very light, and capable of quite fantastic speeds : with a little more stamina, they could have monopolized these classes during the last few years.

Ridden by Stanley Woods, a 500 c.c. Guzzi startled the world by winning the 1935 Senior T.T. with four seconds to spare, and the make has been very threatening in several later Seniors. The 250 c.c. Guzzi won the Lightweight T.T. in 1935, 1937, 1947, 1948 and 1949. Since the British industry does not seriously concern itself with the 250 c.c. machines, the Guzzi has had little to beat in that class other than, in pre-war days, the D.K.W. and, especially in 1950, the Benelli. But if we began to challenge its 250 c.c. supremacy, it would not be easily dislodged.

HUMBER

This honoured firm played a leading hand in pioneer days. In 1898 they evolved their " Olympia tandem ", which later partly inspired the frantic tricar boom of 1905–1907. Fundamentally, it was a tricycle of the single rear wheel type, with an upholstered, spring-mounted seat slung between the two front wheels. A small air-cooled engine was mounted on a skeleton outrigger frame of steel tubing protruding behind the rear wheel, which was chain-driven.

Pennington was, in part, the originator of this queer layout and, subject to shifting the engine, it may have inspired J. van Hooydonk to build his famous Phœnix Trimo some four years later. It is not on record that it sold in any quantity.

Humber then proceeded to adopt the Phelon & Moore chain drive under royalty, and they sold a number of motor bicycles, including a machine which had one of the first free-engine clutches, actuated by a long side lever working in a ratchet quadrant. In 1902, when motor tricycles were dying, they built probably the best motor tricycle ever made, with girder fork, two wheels astern, all chain drive and a single geared version of the P. & M. layout. They continued to coquet mildly with the motor cycle industry for many more years. Their failure to generate a more passionate enthusiasm is perhaps ascribable to their reputation for manufacturing the world's best bicycles, plus a similar absorption in the expanding car industry.

They sang their swansong about 1912. Three-speed hub gears, in which they were interested, had begun to boom in 1911, when out of the blue Humbers suddenly produced some charming little 2¾ h.p. three-speed motor bicycles, on one of which the late P. J. Evans won the 1911 Junior T.T. by over 9 min from H. A. Collier's Matchless. Had they elected to follow up this surprise success, they might have bulked high in subsequent motor cycle developments. But they gradually lost interest as their car production expanded.

INDIAN

This imported American machine claims attention here because of its profound influence on the British industry for a few years from 1911, when, shrewdly managed in this country by W. H. Wells, it secured the first three places in the Senior T.T. For a short period British designers had every reason to fear it in speed events, and the sensation of 1911 was principally due to the makers' early adoption of all-chain drive with a countershaft two-speed gear box.

History brings strange revenges. The Indian machines practically disappeared from our market, partly owing to our imposition of heavy tariffs, partly to stagnation in the American motor cycle industry, created by the irresistible competition of cheap mass-produced cars.

After VE Day our manufacturers exported thousands of our post-war machines to the U.S.A., where they entered a stagnant market, in which only the Indian and Harley-Davidson models had survived. Both had crystallized in the form of rather out-of-date big-twins.

JAMES

One of the oldest firms in the industry, which has in its time produced some delightful machines in many classes. A 3½ h.p. vee-twin and a 5–6 h.p. twin, designed mainly for sidecar work, are particularly memorable. Nowadays it concentrates exclusively on its light-weights, which have a great reputation.

LEVIS

This Birmingham factory was never large enough to tackle production on a modern scale. Its memory must not be allowed to die, because over a long term of years it equipped happy users with first-class two-stroke lightweights and also with 250 c.c., 350 c.c. and 500 c.c. four-stroke models of mild originality, excellent quality and of rather a sporting type.

The writer's family for many a year used a wee 2¼ h.p. belt-drive Levis two-stroke as a utility hack, often in the hilliest country. When rusty with age, it served to teach Boy Scouts the rudiments

213

of riding in large fields and served as their D.R. machine in many successive camps. For several of these Scouts it paved the way for subsequent employment as chauffeurs.

McKENZIE

Mr. McKenzie deserves to be remembered, for, although his vigorous effort failed, he very nearly scored a remarkable success. His standpoint was that a majority of cyclists would much prefer motor-assisted bicycles to unlimited pedalling, if only they realized the possibilities of a wee engine, that a majority of this majority could afford to buy a miniature power model and that it was hopeless to approach this vast public through motor cycle retailers or the motor cycle Press.

He therefore designed a simple little motor-assisted bicycle, and expended his not inconsiderable capital in advertising it in the national dailies and in the county weeklies which permeate rural areas. His carefully planned efforts received a minimum of support from local traders. He could not sell his machines at a really low price if he paid a substantial commission to the retailers. Local salesmen were not interested in a small commission, since a motor cycling ignoramus is a terrible nuisance to his supplying dealer.

McKenzie nearly got away with his ambitious project. One of the reasons why he failed was that the quality of his goods was hardly high enough. Nevertheless, I know of one which he sold as far back as 1925 and which, thanks to capable maintenance by an intelligent owner, is still in daily use.

MATCHLESS

The Matchless is one of the pioneer makes, as old as the industry and always taking a leading part in its progress. In 1907, ridden by C. R. Collier, it won the first T.T. (over the " short " course) at 38·22 m.p.h. For the next five years the Collier brothers were invariably formidable in the T.T., winning again in 1909 and 1910. The Plumstead firm was still only a small concern, but on numerous occasions it met and beat many of the larger factories. During the decade previous to the First World War it was perhaps especially famous for its sidecar outfits with J.A.P. engines, as also for its 500 c.c. roadsters fitted with short-stroke overhead-valve J.A.P. engines.

After the armistice, it continued to turn out in great quantity a steady variety of first-class models. Two of these, produced some ten years later, were more than distinctive, though they failed to achieve a permanent market. The twin-cylinder Silver Arrow was a worthy forerunner of the 1949 LE Velocette, being vibrationless and silent, while a child of ten could start its engine. The four-cylinder Silver Hawk was as good a four as has ever been made.

The firm ultimately took over A.J.S.s and one or two other

concerns, under the name of Associated Motor Cycles Ltd. Today it manufactures Matchless and A.J.S. machines at Plumstead and Francis-Barnett machines in Coventry, commands an enviable world market, and wins at least as many important races as anybody else. After VE Day it standardized a 350 c.c. racer for general sale, a machine on which its customers have won innumerable speed awards, while its 500 c.c. " works " racers secured the 500 c.c. World Championship in 1949.

Not the least service rendered by Matchless to motor cycling was their introduction of the hydraulically controlled telescopic front fork, a principle later also applied to rear suspension. This system was not, perhaps, completely new, as it has affinities with an early Scott fork and also with the forks of the pre-war German B.M.W. machines. But the Matchless people can at least claim to have perfected the principle and initiated the fashion. It notoriously transforms previous standards of roadholding and comfort.

MORGAN RUNABOUT

Designed by H. F. S. Morgan for his private use in 1909, the first Morgan had a 7 h.p. Peugeot vee-twin engine and was assembled in the Malvern College workshops. Patents were obtained in 1910, the drawings being made by a youthful apprentice who is now Sir John Black, of the Standard Motor Company. Two single-seater models were exhibited at the 1911 Olympia Show. These were fitted with J.A.P. 8 h.p. twin- and 4 h.p. single-cylinder engines respectively. The first public award was a gold medal in the 1911 London-Exeter Run.

Two-seater models were shown in 1912 and secured so many orders that attempts were made to interest some large manufacturer. When these failed, Morgan built and equipped his own plant at Malvern and formed a company with his father, Prebendary Morgan, as chairman. After the 1914–1918 war rising orders compelled a further enlargement of the factory, and output rose to 2,000 per annum.

The mass-produced cheap car almost drove three-wheelers off the market between the wars, but the sheer genius of the Morgan chassis has kept it in production for 40 years. It remains an object lesson to all designers in its stark simplicity, with weight and cost pinned down to an absolute minimum. From that angle it deserves close study wherever it is exhibited.

MOTOSACOCHE

A rough translation of this name would be " engine in a handbag ". The firm is Swiss, and during the second decade they evolved a beautiful little motor which was encased between sheet-metal panels, flared at their fore ends to catch the cooling draughts. It could be bolted to a sturdy pedal cycle, and drove the rear wheel via a raw-hide, twisted belt, tensioned by a jockey pulley clipped to the seat-pillar tube. They also built larger engines for roadsters which were used in this country by Matchless and one or two others. They deserve to be mentioned, since they were almost the only firm in the industry's first quarter century to succeed in cultivating the " motor-assisted bicycle."

NER-A-CAR

The Ner-a-Car appeared in June, 1921, and secured a considerable vogue. It eventually perished, possibly because its makers refused to yield to the sporting fashions of the age, but one still hears occasional demands for its resurrection. Its high quality and unique features induced owners to continue riding it long years after its manufacture had been abandoned.

Fundamentally, it corresponded with its name, being con-structed as a low, flat chassis on car lines with all its mechanism encased. The low chassis permitted a large comfortable saddle to be mounted level with the top of the rear tyre. The side-members of the chassis extended forward in the form of a U, and carried at the front a pair of sprung and pivoted arms bridged by the axle of the front wheel, which was steered by a side-arm. The front wheel was shrouded in an enormous mudguard, so that the model could be ridden in ordinary clothes. The layout was described as skidproof, possessing unusual stability largely due to the very low centre of gravity.

The drive of the early two-stroke model was by friction. The flywheel rotated across the chassis frame, and was faced with a removable phosphor bronze disc. This disc was engaged at right angles by an aluminium wheel, faced with fibre. The latter could be moved by a lever across the flywheel disc, and a notched quadrant provided five different gear ratios. The weight of the machine was 196 lb.

Several years after the demise of the company, its machines remained in daily use, especially by professional women living in country districts—midwives, village organists, etc.

NEW IMPERIAL

There is at least one bright jewel in the New Imperial crown. At the 1901 Stanley Show this firm exhibited the first wholly British machine of 500 c.c.! Its engine was incredibly mounted above the front wheel, which it drove by twisted belt. Half a dozen were made. One was sold! The remainder were ridden by members of the staff.

But the engines must have been sturdy, for nearly forty years later one of them was still in use—on a chaff-cutting machine! Manufacture continued until shortly before World War II, the company turning out a steady stream of good medium-weight roadsters and racers. It secured many high honours in the T.T., where it was always formidable in the Lightweight and Junior events.

NORTON

The Norton clan are the racing machines *par excellence*, as befits a factory which won the twin-cylinder class of the first T.T., in 1907, with a 5 hp. model ridden home by Rem Fowler at 36·22 m.p.h. A Norton ridden by Geoff Duke beat all comers in the 1950 T.T. at 92·27 m.p.h. (Duke, by the way, first competed on the Isle of Man Course in 1949—in the Manx Grand Prix races—and 1950, therefore, was his first T.T. He also holds the all-time record for the fastest T.T. lap, which he rode at 93·33 m.p.h. Nortons have won a total of 24 T.T. races and an incalculable number of Grand Prix and other major races all over the Continent. In the spring of 1949, two of their machines, ridden by Americans, won both the amateur and the open speed events in the American championship races at Daytona Beach, while a Canadian won the 1950 open event. Old " Pa " Norton, the bearded enthusiast, who originated the family, lived for motor cycling, but unfortunately died before the firm attained its full stature.

Such racing supremacy by no means implies that the factory's touring machines are rough or rampant, and for many years past they have not only been probably the most popular choice among speed enthusiasts, but enjoy a fine reputation for ordinary private use in sedate touring.

Many honoured names are omitted in this volume for reasons of space, but one name must be included,. The engineering wizard mainly responsible for the speed of Norton machines is one, Joe Craig. When he first extorted 50 b.h.p. from an unblown Norton engine, he could claim to have wrung more power from a 500 c.c. cylinder than any of his predecessors.

PHELON & MOORE

As far back as 1902, the P. & M. engineers pinned their faith to all-chain drive, which they manufactured at their Cleckheaton factory. They further used a sloping engine as an integral part of the front down tube of the diamond frame, thereby securing a balanced weight distribution and ensuring a rigid bed for the engine. The Humber Company used this design under licence for some of their earlier machines (see " Humber "). Until this day the P. & M. machines, now called Panthers, retain an unsullied reputation for first-class craftsmanship and high reliability. The original layout is employed on the big single-cylinder, the Model 100.

In reliability trials their record bears comparison with the whole world. They have also claims to have introduced the first satis-factory change-speed gear. This employed two primary chains of different ratio, the rear sprockets being clutched to the countershaft by an expanding device based on metal wedges. The design became obsolete when the single primary chain, leading to a countershaft type of gear box, became popular.

PHOENIX

Phoenix machines, using Minerva engines, were prominent during the industry's first decade, and owed their quality to J. van Hooydonk, a manufacturer who was also a passionately keen rider. He was among the very first to produce a variable gear (a two-speed hub) and a practicable tricar—the famous " Trimo." Since both his capital and works were small, he failed to weather one of our depressions and, to the universal regret, went out of business.

QUADRANT

This make, like the Excelsior, almost dominated the hobby for a few years from 1902 onwards, thanks to a rugged simplicity and excellent workmanship. Ridden by Tom Silver, a Quadrant set up a notable End-to-End record in 1903. One of the attractions for the motor cycling novices was Quadrant's famous " single-lever " control. A short radial lever on the tank top controlled the ignition switch, the ignition advance, the valve lifter and the throttle.

The firm also produced a light 2 h.p. belt-driven tricycle (with two front wheels) and a dual-engine tricar, on which one engine was kept in reserve for high speed and hill climbing! They also marketed one of the very earliest spring forks, utilizing small coil springs between the spindle ends and the fork slots. One model challenged the supremacy of the 1911 3½ h.p. Triumph in popular favour, but later financial difficulties ensued and the name ultimately perished.

RALEIGH

The Raleigh factory was early in the field with a motor cycle which had its engine mounted above the front wheel. The drive to the rear wheel was by a belt crossed in X fashion, which furnished a better grip on the front pulley than the direct arrangement. In June, 1904, G. P. Mills slashed many hours off the End-to-End record with a most attractive pedal-less two-speed machine. The sales department failed to exploit this success with any vigour. A stream of charming models followed in due succession right up to the 1930's, including a beautiful little tricar known as the Raleighette.

But somehow the directors' hearts never seemed to be in the motor cycle business, from which they ultimately withdrew in order to concentrate on the pedal cycle. They were doubtless disheartened by the repeated vicissitudes of the industry, but their customers held so high an opinion of their design and workmanship that, with the aid of energetic sales campaigns, they might have ranked among our leaders.

REX

These Coventry-built machines enjoyed a very considerable vogue during the first two decades of the sport. They were always early with new designs, including the spring fork, the free-engine clutch and a primitive two-speed gear. Their sales owed much to fine riding by Harold Williamson, who held the End-to-End record for four years. They flung themselves into the tricar boom with great energy, producing a variety of models. One of their more eccentric ideas was a neat " beehive " silencer on the cylinder head, which hardly improved the cooling! They ranked among the best sellers during the second decade, and survived the first World War only to fall victims, with many companions, to the between-wars depression.

RILEY

The Riley firm built one of the earliest motor bicycles, but did not persevere with it, although its engine displayed workmanship of a quality rare at that date. They presently switched to tricars, starting about 1905 with a sturdy $4\frac{1}{2}$ h.p. water-cooled engine, backed by a two-speed gear and chain drive, and rapidly advancing to a very successful model with a 9 h.p. vee-twin engine and three speeds. They next tried this same engine in a small car, mounting it low down on the right-hand-side running board within easy reach of the driver. This seduced them into the car field, whereon they abandoned motor cycles for ever.

ROC

The Roc works at Guildford, controlled by A. W. Wall, earned three titles to fame before succumbing in one of our periodic slumps. They produced one of the first free-engine clutches (in the rear hub, with a separately spoked belt rim) and an early two-speed gear. The " Auto-wheel " was an ingenious power unit for attaching to a bicycle, the entire mechanism, including a tiny petrol tank, being contained in a third wheel, which was hinged to the pedal cycle and pushed it along. Sir Arthur Conan Dolye was interested in the company.

ROYAL ENFIELD

This Redditch firm can claim a distinction shared only by Ariel and the long-extinct M.M.C. firm. One of its models—a quadricycle—competed in the spring of 1900 in the Thousand Miles Trial, entered by Edward (now Lord) Iliffe and driven by Walter Grew, first editor of *The Motor Cycle*. From that day to this, Enfield machines have been prominent in practically every famous trial, and the number of their models has been legion. The most distinctive of all, perhaps, was the 6 h.p. chain-driven vee-twin, with handle starting, a tough, durable design, widely popular over a long term of years for sidecar work, with especially honourable records in rural transport.

Immediately after the first world war, the writer owned a house in a remote part of Cornwall, five miles from a railway station of the two-train-a-day type, and equally far from a doctor. Both doctor and post were brought to his door on Enfield sidecars, which mocked at the Cornish hills. The company has always shown a mild interest in racing, but can boast a specially remarkable record in reliability trials of every type. Incidentally, the Enfield designers were among the very first to adopt all-chain drive and variable gears. Their " Flying Flea " lightweight was used in great numbers by paratroop divisions in the second world war.

RUDGE

Rudge-Whitworth pedal cycles have been renowned since the early days of the cycle movement. The company entered the motor cycle industry with great energy in the second decade, missed a Senior T.T. victory by a hairsbreadth (5 secs) in 1913, and won by 6½ minutes in 1914. It built some first-class tourist machines in 250 c.c., 350 c.c., and 500 c.c. classes, together with a fine " big single " for sidecar work. Its " Multi " gear—a special version of the controlled variable pulley—was possibly the most efficient version of that drive ever conceived. Its " all black " machines, substituting a durable film of black plastic for the then normal nickel plating, made a great appeal to lazy owners, who disliked spit and polish. It won both the Senior and Junior T.T.s in 1930 and the Lightweight T.T. in 1931 and 1934.

Eventually, adverse balances caused the company to be sold and only bicycle manufacture continues. To this day some of the last motor cycles from the factory continue in daily roadster use, and others even win occasional speed victories.

SCOTT

No Scott has failed to achieve outstanding originality. Their founder, the late A. A. Scott, probably owed much to education at a freak school (Abbotsholme), whose headmaster firmly believed that the main function of the educator was to teach lads to think. Comparatively few people know that the original Scott was built about 1902 (at Saltaire, Yorks.). It embodied a tiny two-stroke twin-cylinder engine, jammed against the sides of the steering head and driving a large rear pulley by belt; this pulley drove the rear wheel by chain.

In 1908, Scott flung a bombshell into trade circles by winning three classes of the year's main hill climb near Daventry with an utterly revolutionary machine, comprising a twin-cylinder, water-cooled two-stroke engine, open frame, twin primary chains controlled by friction clutches on a countershaft (operated by rocking pedal), and a kickstarter on the rear spindle. Unfortunately for the cause of progress, the machine did not appeal to everybody. It is characteristic of the simple two-stroke engine that it is inclined to " sputter" (four-stroke) when running free or under light load, and it is slightly more extravagant of fuel than the four-stroke types of similar size.

220

Moreover, as normal engines were developed to generate considerably more power, the Scott engine proved incapable of similar tuning, and lost its 1912 and 1913 ability to win T.T. races.

Just before the 1939 war, after Scott was dead, his successors were busy experimenting with a three-cylinder two-stroke engine. The present writer rode it on two occasions, and found it the equal of a six-cylinder four-stroke engine in many respects. The factory manufactures one of the very best small engines for autocycles.

The famous Scott "crab" was a three-wheeler arranged on side-car lines, but with a two-seater body, windscreen and hood. Its framework was a bolted assembly of standardized tubes, adapted for repair in colonial regions. Unfortunately its lop-sided appearance proved fatal to financial success.

SINGER

The Singer played a minor part in the industry during the early decades, but was more than prominent for a few years from 1900 onwards, when it applied the famous Perks & Birch " motor wheel " to beautifully finished bicycles and tricycles of its own manufacture. The wheel contained the entire mechanism, and won adherents mainly by dint of a Simms low-tension magneto (with make and break *inside the combustion chamber*). This short-lived ignition was wildly popular for a brief period, as it was free from the perpetual worries of primitive coil and battery ignition. Later the firm deserted us in favour of motor cars.

STARLEY

Very few enthusiasts have so much as heard this name, but about 1902 Mr. Starley produced a few experimental machines which substituted shaft and worm drive for the belt. Born long before their day, they never went into production, but, in a sense, rank as the pioneers in a field later exploited by F. N., Sunbeam, Velocette, and others. It is still quite possible that shaft drive may ultimately supersede the chain.

SUNBEAM

In the heyday of the pedal-cycle boom, three makers ranked as monarchs—Beeston-Humber, Lea-Francis, and Sunbeam. Any of these three could charge up to £25 for a de luxe pedal cycle. Sunbeam's " little oil-bath " chain-case basked in world renown. It followed that when they condescended to build motor cycles, their machines would be good. For a time they toyed with the job. I first encountered their work in the form of a curious little car known as the Mabley, which resembled a tiny canoe on wheels. Anon they hurled their energies into first-class motor bicycles, displaying in every detail their famous quality of workmanship and material.

On tne road they maintained their enviable reputation. But in days when competition was acute, they just failed to establish the sort of reputation which ensures record sales. They used racing for publicity purposes, but were generally cruelly unfortunate in the T.T. George Dance, their star jockey for many years, was literally hunted by the worst luck. Repeatedly when the race seemed to be in his pocket, some trumpery item—perhaps a valve spring not of their manufacture—let him down. H. R. Davies was 2nd in the 1914 Senior T.T. T. C. de la Hay won the Senior in 1920, and Alec Bennett won in 1922.

Afterwards they rather faded in the competition sense, until 1928 when C. J. P. Dodson won the Senior, a feat he repeated the following year. On the road they dwindled to just another motor cycle. That dull period was to end. In 1946 Sunbeams suddenly emerged with a completely original specification, deservedly called " the car on two wheels." There is no space here to detail its specification, but the photograph in the photogravure section reveals its claim to high honour. It is obvious that we shall hear far more of Sunbeams from now on.

TRIUMPH

At the dawn of the century the Triumph Company enjoyed an enviable reputation for turning out one of the very best British pedal cycles at the lowest price consistent with first-class quality. Its directors, led by M. J. Schulte, early cast a critical eye on the primitive pioneer motors. Schulte, a keen-witted engineer of sound judgment and great caution, actually investigated the German Wolfmuller motor bicycle before the Emancipation Act of 1896, and imported one for test on the Coventry cycle track before the law permitted him to exceed 4 m.p.h. on any public road.

About 1901, Schulte imported Minerva engines of $1\frac{3}{4}$ h.p., clipped them beneath the front down tubes of specially reinforced bicycles, and tested them painstakingly over Midland roads. By 1906, he felt the times were ripe for a plunge, and built the first small Triumph engines, eventually deciding on a 3 h.p. model, vertically mounted in the middle of the frame. This engine was quiet and reliable, but suffered from the lack of suitable materials for such highly-stressed items as valves and piston rings. He instituted research, procured tougher valve steels, and in 1907 manufactured the first samples of his $3\frac{1}{2}$ h.p. model, destined to achieve unique and abiding fame.

In 1908, this type finished first and third in the T.T. at 40 m.p.h. and, from that date onward, Triumph machines have usually come near to dominating the motor cycle world. No profession is immune from jealousies, but magnates associated with rival firms have often frankly confessed that Schulte saved the industry from possible extinction in its early days, when a limited body of customers were growing somewhat weary of roadside trouble, weak climbing and the marketing of so many inadequately tested designs.

Schulte's caution made him occasionally slow to move with the times, but a sturdy conscience forbade him to market any commodity of which he was unsure, and he seldom put a foot wrong. During the long clamour for variable gears he refused to launch any transmission change without thorough secret tests. Repeatedly he sent the writer and others machines which never qualified for public sale, and demanded the frankest reports from us all.

Before the First World War he marketed the $3\frac{1}{4}$ h.p. with a multiple-disc, free-engine clutch. A little later he modified it to a three-speed countershaft gear box with primary chain and secondary belt drive, and this model was easily the best used by the Army in 1914–1918. Some of the despatch riders, finding it dangerous to remove a hand from the bar on the vile surfaces of Flanders and France, bent the gear lever downward and operated it by foot. Some folk consider that this makeshift was the real genesis of the modern foot change. But all the time Schulte was scheming to eliminate the troublesome belt drive, and in 1920 he marketed with pride a new Triumph with all-chain drive and a three-speed countershaft gear box of Triumph manufacture.

Schulte has long since gone to his rest, but his successors preserve his ideals and, in the years immediately preceding the Second World War, they once more initiated a policy to be widely imitated, when they produced their world-famous 500 c.c. " vertical " or " parallel " twins.

VELOCETTE

This firm has never made a bad machine, though it marketed its first model in 1909. Three of the machines have been exceptionally famous—the small two-strokes rated at approximately $2\frac{1}{4}$ h.p.; the 350 c.c. overhead-camshaft from 1926 onwards; and the LE 149 c.c. introduced in 1948. They were the first factory to build racing machines of the " works " type in numbers and sell them to the public. Their overhead-camshaft KTT model is perhaps the prettiest and neatest racer ever produced. First raced in 1925, it was released for public sale in 1928, has scored innumerable speed successes all over the world, and ranked as official champion of its class for 1949 in the hands of F. L. Frith and 1950 (A. R. Foster).

The LE model is unique in the world at the time of writing, and follows the general lines known as " Everyman " type. It has a silent, flat-twin, water-cooled engine; fore and aft springing; shaft drive; and lever starting from the saddle. A main aim of its design is a 20,000 mileage without repairs or adjustments. It is more fully analysed in Chapter 27.

VINCENT (FORMERLY " VINCENT H.R.D.")

The H.R.D. firm was founded after the First World War by H. R. Davies, who had raced successfully on Sunbeams and A.J.S.s. Some years later a wealthy undergraduate bought the name and goodwill and added the prefix Vincent. Since VE Day the company have principally concentrated on powerful 998 c.c. machines of the vee-twin type and on high speed. Their quality is superb, and they have succeeded to the niche vacated by the Brough Superior. They build the fastest production machines in the world.

VINDEC

Although the Vindec disappeared from the market before the First World War, and embodied a French engine (the 5 h.p. Peugeot vee-twin), it deserves mention in this select list, because it did much to keep the sport alive in the first decade. It was faster than most machines of the day, and adorned by one of the best of the early spring forks—the French Truffault. Its moving spirit was W. H. Wells, who dropped it when he secured the British agency for the Indian machines manufactured by the Hendee Company, of Springfield.

WERNER

This French machine was the first practical motor bicycle, making its British début in 1900. The first model was front-driven by twisted raw-hide belt, with tube ignition and surface carburettor, a specification which induced frequent skids often followed by fire. Its designers rapidly switched to a layout with a vertical engine immediately in front of the bottom bracket, the forerunner of modern practice. Their fertile brains toyed with all kinds of innovations, few of which stood the test of experience—leather-faced pulleys with flat belts, carburettor inside the tank for protection against dust, and so forth.

About 1904, they built the first vertical twin-cylinder, rated at 4 h.p. Their British sales shrank, as we began to produce sound designs. They were the first engineers to realize that a motor cycle required front forks very considerably stronger than those of pedal cycles. A front-wheel-drive model can be inspected in the South Kensington Museum. Ridden by E. H. Arnott, a 2 h.p. Werner set up the first motor cycle End-to-End record in July, 1902 (880 miles in 65 h 45 m).

WOOLER

A highly original design, introduced in 1911. One of the first to standardize a spring frame. It also utilized a special type of variable-pulley gear. The front pulley swung radially on a gear wheel driven off the crankshaft, and operated by pedal. The gear reduction made a large engine pulley possible, and the swing mounting enabled the belt tension to be maintained on all ratios. Owing to the shape and colour of the tank the Wooler became affectionately known as " Flying Banana ". Manufacture was suspended during the post-war depressions, but an experimental four-cylinder was staged at the 1948 Show.

ZENITH

In the second decade, the Zenith was one of many machines largely assembled from standard components and fitted with J.A.P. engines. In its 8 h.p. form it was a favourite with the speed brigade. As the demand for variable gears became acute, its designer, F. W. Barnes, produced his famous " Gradua " gear. This employed (*a*) a variable engine pulley, of which the diameter was varied through a " coffee-grinder " handle on the top tube, and (*b*) a simultaneous correction of the belt length through sliding the rear wheel to or fro in the rear-fork slots. This did not really solve the gear problem, as the lowest available ratio was only about $5\frac{1}{2}$ to 1, while the maximum of 3 to 1 was of very limited practical use.

However, the facility of suiting the ratio to a gradient enabled the Zenith to win plenty of speed hill-climbs, and in ordinary road-work the arrangement was preferable to any fixed gear. Consequently, the Zenith was presently barred from single-gear classes in hill-climbs, a ban skilfully exploited for sales purposes by the company. Later, when variable gears and chain drive were improved, the Zenith lost its chief claim to fame.

Note: Numerous other machines of various dates are still affectionately remembered by their quondam owners, and others again continue to be made and marketed with success. Space forbids a " potted biography " of them all, and this selection has been reluctantly based on such as appear to the author to have played a notable part in the developments of the earlier period, or to have evinced high quality and some originality in the later stages. The majority of the exclusions were either short-lived or were light-weights of good quality but no fundamental originality.

CHAPTER 27

THE MOTOR CYCLE OF TOMORROW

ENGLAND IS A DEMOCRACY. Her individual citizen enjoys at least as great a degree of personal freedom as any modern state grants to its nationals. This freedom is of no recent creation. Our forefathers fought for it through many centuries. We inherited their bequest. Its main effect is to make us a nation of individualists. We carry this sturdy individuality into all our activities—even into our sports.

It persists vigorously within the confines of each separate sport. For example, football is really a very simple game. It consists fundamentally of attempts to make a leather-cased bladder pass between two sets of wooden posts at opposite ends of a small field. Nevertheless, our individualism prevents us from ever agreeing on a universal version of this simple hobby. Some prefer a round ball, others an oval. Some think it should be handled, others only permit the use of the feet. Some insist on amateurism, others encourage professionalism. The oval ball enthusiasts are split into two separate camps, whose adherents refuse to play with each other.

Hence it is hardly surprising that nothing approaching unanimity exists among motor cyclists concerning the ideal design. Their ranks include, at one end, the fans of the motor attachment for bicycles, which weighs about 20 lb, costs about £20, emits much the same kind of noise as a leviathan mouse might emit behind the skirting-board of a Brobdingnagian dwelling in *Gulliver's Travels*. At the other extreme, there is a club confined to the owners of Vincent motor cycles—which means, chiefly, the 998 c.c. twin-cylinder. This weighs about 460 lb, costs in 1950 about £400 including purchase tax, and is eager to travel at well over 100 miles an hour. These two extremes are separated by at least half a hundred types, varying enormously in price and in design, each passionately supported by its own clientèle.

Such chaotic opinion in 1950 plainly cannot produce any kind of unanimity in 1955. Should we fail to solve our current financial problems, the percentage of motorists to population might dwindle considerably, or we might have just enough money to afford standardized motors of a very austere type. Short of such disasters, we shall long remain as individualistic as we are today.

Thus the title of this chapter, " The Motor Cycle of Tomorrow," can only be interpreted by the author as an individual, and along the lines of British individuality as it appears to his gaze.

If we assume that motor cycles develop in an atmosphere of freedom, most existing types will survive. By " freedom " we mean opportunity for the designer to construct machines to his desired specification, and sufficient money for the individual buyer to select from a wide market a pattern which most appeals to him. If such " freedom " exists, current individualisms will survive with it. Almost every existing type of motor cycle will survive, continue to be manufactured, and undergo developments similar to those which slowly transfigured its predecessors. In a free market, the Buyers' Guide of 1970 would catalogue a range from the 25 c.c. " motor-assisted bicycle " right up to the equivalent of a 998 c.c. Vincent, with modernized samples of all the intermediate types which today occupy the gap between these two extremes.

The precise nature of such " development " is probably a far more controversial matter. The thesis of this chapter is, therefore, controversial. It lays down certain desirable qualities which can be incorporated in roadster machines, with very few exceptions indeed. These qualities are:—

1, Absence of vibration due to the engine.
2, Absence of vibration due to the road.
3, Absence of mechanical noise.
4, Absence of the " tinny " noise, due to the " ring " of existing air-cooled cylinders.
5, Ease of engine starting.
6, Accessibility of all components liable to demand periodical attention.
7, The lowest possible weight consistent with the technical requirements.
8, The lowest price consistent with rather an exacting specification.
9, A minimum working life of 20,000 miles before any major reconditioning, such as decarbonization or a cylinder rebore, becomes necessary.
10, A good standard of speed and climb, in proportion to engine capacity.
11, A flush surface area to simplify cleaning.
12, A reasonable degree of protection from weather.
13, A shaft transmission.

Reflection will indicate how these thirteen ideals can—in theory—be incorporated in the design of any roadster. A brief note on each item in the table drives home this claim. For example—No. 1: By the adoption of a well-balanced engine, devoid of a noticeable vibration period. The horizontal twin is an example. Other types are possible. No. 2: By efficient fore-and-aft springing, coupled with a comfortable seat and fairly large tyres. No. 3: By a combination of design and first-class workmanship. No. 4: By liquid cooling. No. 5: By the combination of a multi-cylinder engine and the substitution of a pull-up lever for the acrobatic and awkwardly placed kickstarter. No. 6: By proofing certain components against the possibility of petty trouble (for example, protecting the carburettor by an adequate fuel filter); by such a two-unit construction as figures in the LE Velocette; and by careful location of items like the clutch adjuster. No. 7: By design and by the use of light alloys. The minimum weight must clearly depend upon the decisions taken concerning ideal No. 9. No. 8: The price must always vary with the general financial status of the nation, but can be reduced by scientific production methods, by design and, perhaps, by restricting the output of a factory to a single model with one or two major options. No. 9: A matter of design and of workmanship. No. 10: This already presents no difficulties. No. 11: This point has yet to receive adequate attention. It can be secured by (*a*) enclosure or (*b*) intentional design (most existing designs are far " cleaner " than those of 1930). No. 12: Weather protection is the thorniest item on the list. But a combination of legshields and footboards, with detachable windscreens and detachable handlebar shields (" muffs " of aluminium, possibly?) could effect a vast improvement. No. 13: Shaft drive, already entirely practical, is becoming slowly but steadily popular.

Subject to one conditional exception, the ideal machine for the general roadster purposes of tomorrow already exists. It is not yet so acclaimed, for only a small minority of motor cyclists have ridden it. Moreover, it will make no violent appeal to the majority of existing riders unless or until one item in its specification has been revised, with consequential effects on other components, for its engine is considerably smaller than the rank and file of motor cyclists approve.

The claims which I advance for this exciting prototype of future designs are based upon a single undeniable fact. It is entirely proof against *all* the criticisms which have been advanced against practically every motor cycle in the world by practically every man and woman who have ever ridden them. In every particular (except one) it touches the peak of every motor cycling dream.

Incidentally, it was designed especially with an eye to flow production, i.e., the system originally introduced by Henry Ford in America, a system which enables labour to reach the maximum production, and enables capital to market a commodity so produced at a minimum price. Whether England sinks or rises, that system is likely to prevail. Although other motor cycles have undergone slashing alterations from the production angle, and other factories have been modified to incorporate such methods, it is probable that no other factory is so efficiently tooled and arranged from this viewpoint, or so adapted to concentrate on a large output of a single model. (The majority of factories still produce a variety of widely different models, a feature which probably hampers cheap production.)

Turning to the design of this dream machine, consider the basic faults figuring in the indictment brought against motor cycles by their devotees and by the general public.

The first is noise. On this the public are unanimous. They agree that motor cycles emit, on an average, far too much noise, and that the staccato character of this noise, peculiar to the pauci-cylinder engine is a peculiarly irritating form of noise. Our x machine is so nearly mute that strangers suspect it of being propelled by steam or electricity, although, in fact, it is powered by a petrol engine of tolerably normal design.

The second clause in the indictment is *engine* vibration. Actual users accept this, because it is not easy to fit a genuinely smooth type of engine within the narrow confines of a cycle frame, while a four-cylinder engine—regarded as the minimum for car use—is slightly more expensive to construct and " has more bits to go wrong " when exposed to the weather. (Car engines are sheltered under a steel bonnet, but several problems beset the notion of enclos-ing a motor cycle engine: weight, drumming and inaccessibility, for instance.)

The public exaggerate the vibration common to all single-cylinder motor cycle engines. It is not really annoying. But John Citizen sees that few cars tremble visibly when parked by the kerb with their multi-cylinder engines running on a tiny throttle opening. Equally, he notices that when a motor cyclist straddles his stationary machine with its engine running, its entire anatomy is trembling very noticeably. He falsely imagines that a long motor cycle trip spells several hours of perpetual dithering.

Riders phrase it differently. They confess that " my engine suffers from a ' period ' at (say) 38 m.p.h. in top gear ". But they have grown case-hardened to these mild " periods ". (Of course, they would like their engines much better if they had no vibratory " period ", but they do not really resent the defect.) Our x machine does not suffer from engine vibration. You may balance a penny on edge on any of its flat surfaces, just as you can balance a penny on the radiator of a Rolls Royce car.

Third in the indictment stands *road* vibration. It is common knowledge that the springing of motor cars has undergone almost incredible improvement during the last half century. The com-bination of large, soft tyres with costly upholstery and elaborate metal suspension can almost cause the seat cushions of a high-class car to slide forward at a constant level over quite rough roads. Such jerks and impulses as penetrate to the bodies of the occupants survive only in a mild and gentle form.

By contrast, the motor cyclist is still visibly a prey to physical shocks. The suspension of his machine, like that of the motor car, has advanced mightily with the passing years. Today he rides over large tyres on a big saddle embodying long springs. His hydraulically damped·telescopic front fork rules out minor bumps in incredible fashion. Nevertheless, it is plain to all eyes that he does not loll with quite the cushioned ease of a film star in the back seats of a Rolls.

One of the explanations is the usual absence of any springs for his back wheel. (Such rear suspensions are on the market in quantity. But they add about £20 to the cost of his mount, and swell the list of components which, being liable to wear, must sooner or later add to his maintenance costs. As most motor cyclists work to rather a tight budget, only a small minority of them afford this additional luxury.) Our x machine possesses a very original, cheap, and efficient form of adjustable rear springing, in conjunction with a most excellent front fork and a first-class seat.

The fourth clause in the anti-motor cycle indictment is unreliability. Bluntly phrased in one word, that accusation is untrue. The motor cycle was slower in attaining high standards of reliability than the motor car. Today it has attained them. If I were starting out this minute to ride to John O'Groats or to Geneva on a motor cycle, I should make no more preparation than if I were making the same journey in a Rolls. I should neither expect nor encounter more trouble with it than with any good car.

The accusation was true in the past. Motor cyclists were frequently seen " tinkering " by the roadside, long after the spectacle of a car in trouble by the kerb or the hedge had become unusual. One element in the contrast was that the motor cyclist attends to his own petty adjustments, whereas many car owners have such jobs tackled at a service station by professional mechanics. A second element was that certain components of a motor cycle were deliberately designed to require regular attention, usually because such design spelt economy.

Take the final drive of the car and of the motor cycle as an example. Cars are driven by shaft. Apart from replenishing the back axle with lubricant, such a shaft may run 100,000 miles without attention. The final drive of a motor cycle is almost invariably by an exposed chain. In the broad sense, that chain is as dependable as the propeller shaft of a car. But it requires occasional adjustment for length—an affair of a few minutes. It also needs periodic cleansing and dressing with lubricant. (The propeller shaft of the car receives such attentions in the garage—replenishing the differential and, perhaps, lubrication of one or more universal joints.)

Omitting tedious detail, our x machine has a final shaft drive concealed in one of the steel tubes forming the rear frame. That item is characteristic of its entire layout. From stem to stern, the machine is designed to demand no attention, except the filling of its tanks for 20,000 miles. One sample of the meticulous care devoted to this ideal is worth mention. It is common knowledge that the thread-like passages and jets of a carburettor for a very small engine are liable to be choked by impurities in the petrol. This nuisance affects both cars and motor cycles. Our x motor cycle has its fuel supply guarded by a filter which traps obstacles no larger than a thousandth of an inch in diameter.

A fifth charge against motor cycles was that their mechanism is inaccessible. The mechanism of a car is distributed over and under

230

a flat metal platform which may measure as much as 5 × 15 feet—a total area of approximately 8 square yards. The mechanism of a motor bicycle is mostly crowded into a small vertical panel, barely amounting to 2 square yards. Donald Heather, joint managing director of Associated Motor Cycles, Ltd., once opined that, if a motor cycle was to appear handsome, the vertical panel of its frame should be so crowded with mechanism that it would be impossible to " spit through it "!

It follows that some details of the complex mechanism are inaccessible. I have owned machines from which a sparking plug could only be removed by a special tool. Our x machine is admirably laid out from this point of view. The backbone can be removed with a simple spanner by a clumsy amateur in 30 minutes, whereupon all the components are as ready to hand as if they were spread out upon a bench. This " reduced accessibility " is justified by the design which renders them all safe for 20,000 miles.

The sixth hostile clause concerns engine starting, a feature in which car owners have usually had the laugh over motor cyclists. It is a familiar sight to see a car owner swing comfortably on to his cushioned seat, adjust a choke, touch a button, and have his smooth engine purring like a happy kitten within 30 seconds. By contrast the motor cyclist has to employ—often in public—bodily contortions for which the human frame is exceptionally ill-designed. After straddling his mount, flooding the carburettor and setting a variety of levers, he props up the heavy machine with his left foot and attempts to administer a hefty swinging movement with his right foot to a steel bar placed at an awkward height below and behind his right knee. Sometimes the engine responds immediately. Sometimes quite a series of ungainly " kicks " may be required to extort an answering roar.

This picture is not wholly fair. Every car owner recalls tragic episodes in the privacy of his shed, especially on frosty winter mornings, when his battery ran down without coaxing a mutter from his engine. Finally, he had to get a heavy starting handle out of the tool-kit and swing the engine until he was bathed in sweat. Those tragedies are suffered in private, whereas the motor cyclist's humiliations are often public at the kerbside.

On our x machine there is no kick-starter. A radially mounted lever, perhaps 18 inches long, is located conveniently by his right hand. When he is ready to move off, he pulls gently on this lever, and the engine promptly responds—so silently that the indicator provided is necessary to assure him that it is actually running.

The seventh accusation against the motor cycle is that it is far too heavy. Any weak or lazy owner must surely flinch from the effort of turning a full roadster motor bicycle round in its narrow garage, or from any form of manhandling it during stoppages on an interrupted journey. Our x machine scales 240 lb. The rider does not support it during stoppages, for it keeps itself vertical by means of a readily operated prop-stand. It is, in fact, a lightweight

231

machine—at least, no ideal specification is yet possible at a lower weight.

The eighth accusation is that motor cycles are very dirty, very difficult to clean and, further, expose the rider to the weather to an unpardonable degree. The x machine is delivered fully equipped with footboards and legshields. Its mechanism is designed to eliminate oil leaks, and is sufficiently enclosed to present a series of smooth metal panels to the weather—panels capable of being hosed down in a very few minutes. If the rider cares to add a plastic windscreen, he can enjoy as much protection from the weather as is possible on any two-wheeler, a protection comparable to that furnished by an open sports car. He will not need to have his shoes cleaned after a ride in bad weather.

The fuel consumption is over 100 miles to the gallon. The oil consumption is approximately 5,000 miles to the gallon. It will take a heavy rider up steep main road hills with ease and certainty, if not very fast.

This eulogy may conceivably create an impression that the little Velocette will drive most rival designs off the market. There is no prospect that any single design will ever establish a monopoly. We Britons are a nation of individualists, and this foible is nowhere more marked than in the motor cycling field. The sponsors of the new Velocette cherished no such hopes.

Three separate ideals mingled to furnish their inspiration. First, they desired to attract thousands of new customers into the hobby by offering them a model comparable with the Rolls Royce car in the four-wheeled sphere—silent, comfortable, absolutely durable and trouble-free, easy to start, and low in weight, though not claiming the Rolls speed performance. Secondly, they expected—and with reason—to captivate thousands of existing motor cyclists who in the past were forced to ride far less suitable machines for " utility " purposes. Thirdly, they felt that the principles underlying their design could be extended to render the lustier types of motor cycle more attractive to a good many owners who lay a definite emphasis on really high speed.

They were—and are—completely aware that the LE is not everybody's meat. Many a typical motor cyclist prefers two wheels to four for the sake of the ravishing performance obtainable from a high-powered two-wheeler. It enables him to register the high cross-country average of a sports car at ten times the price, for, if its maximum speed can seldom be utilized on the level along English roads, it will storm up steep hills as fast as the bends permit. A 50 m.p.h. maximum, coupled with a modest speed on the upper reaches of such a climb as Porlock, has little appeal for such owners.

Again, the LE is definitely expensive, as lightweight, low-powered motor cycles go. One of the worst headaches concerning its introduction was the fixing of its price. Two distinct policies were open. One was to have pinned the figure to a minimum and spread over a period of years the heavy cost of re-tooling a large plant for mass production. The other was to recoup this expenditure—possibly some £100,000?—in the first year or two, and slash the price later, should circumstances permit.

Costs after the conclusion of a world war are always full of question marks. In 1919 I paid £650 for a 10 h.p. Singer car when inflation was at its height. A few years later an 8 h.p. Morris car was marketed at no more than £100. Was that experience of the inflation-deflation cycle to be repeated after World War II? The makers wisely decided to run no formidable risks.

The design is definitely costly, just as champagne costs more to make than beer. For example, its efficiency and durability partly depend on a free use of ball bearings. So far from attaining rapid and substantial deflation (as in 1920), inflation has increased in the first five post-war years. The cost of the LE has risen to match, and at the moment of writing stands at £116 16s, plus £31 10s 9d purchase tax!

Yet another factor hampers this most attractive design from leaping to world-wide favour in a few months. Between the wars a good number of riders switched to new makes, or later models of their favourite make, as often as every spring, or at least every other year. As a class we motor cyclists are not particularly well-to-do. Peace found us owning machines which were mostly at the very least six years' old. The majority of the industry's output since 1945 has been earmarked for export. The small percentage available for the home market has been catalogued at prices which would have seemed fantastic in 1939. In 1939 we could buy roadsters of fair quality for £50–£75. In 1950 a typical price is £160.

When a lad has scraped that sum for his first post-war machine, he is seldom in a position to switch to a newer introduction. A slab of the £160 represents purchase tax, which he will never fully recover on resale. A further deduction must be made for the fact that the model now ranks as " used ", even if its running efficiency is every whit as high as when he bought it.

These considerations obviously tend to limit the sales of the Velocette. The most effective deterrent is the limited performance in terms of really high speed, alike on the flat and up steep and prolonged gradients. The machine already enjoys an astonishing demand in the teeth of the arbitrary handicaps imposed by post-war conditions. Within a measurable period it will doubtless have to contend with other novel and thoughtful designs, many of which will probably be partly inspired by its basic principles.

In my personal opinion, we shall shortly see those principles embodied in more powerful chassis. Such a design will confront its constructor with some formidable problems. Several Velocette features depend intimately on its water-cooled, horizontally opposed, twin-cylinder engine. This type of engine is eminent for extremely smooth running, remarkable silence (given a suitable exhaust system) and very easy starting.

But an increase of its cylinder capacity to 500 c.c., or even 350 c.c., immediately creates housing problems. Those problems were admirably overcome before the war in the famous German B.M.W., but they are nevertheless formidable. Whether such a development is ultimately tackled by the Velocette or by some rival company, radical re-tooling would be inevitable, with its concurrent capital outlay.

At the moment several tolerably dogmatic comments are possible. The LE has proved certain claims. It is possible to divorce motor cycling from vibration and from the " tinny " ring which has hitherto characterized all air-cooled engines. It is possible to endow a motor cycle with a transmission which demands no frequent or regular attention. It is possible to rid a motor cycle of uncertainty and exertion in engine-starting—to achieve in sober fact the " tickle-starting " which had long been a hazy dream. It is possible to invest a motor cycle with a Rollsian silence, both mechanical and gaseous. It is possible to eliminate most of the petty items which formerly imposed excessive maintenance jobs. We can confidently expect these ideals to be incorporated in the heavier and lustier types.

All this transformation will constitute a great debt which the motor cycling world will largely owe to the Velocette designers, just as we originally in a distant past owed reliable ignition to Simms and Bosch, satisfactory carburation to men like Longuemare, good brakes to Ferodo, good transmission to Armstrong, Sturmey-Archer, Renold and others.

In sum, we are now entering upon a new era, so far as motor cycling is concerned, and the Velocette has blazed the trail over which the wheels of tomorrow will flit. It is no exaggeration to say that the present popularity of the Velocette is as nothing compared to the craze which may yet salute the appearance of a 350 c.c. machine embodying its excellencies.

One aspect of the LE has not even now received the consideration which it merits. Without doubt, many potential motor cyclists still stand aloof from our ranks because they regard the motor cycle as an essentially *unstable* machine in the sense that they are afraid of skids, especially on greasy roads in urban traffic. It is the universal experience of LE owners that this smooth, light model requires no conscious " holding up " under such road conditions. It seems to possess a marked stability hitherto foreign to most two-wheelers in unpractised hands.

The factors underlying that stability still await analysis, although the *fact* of the stability is admitted and recognized. No doubt it is in part due to the low weight, which removes the sensation of a demand for considerable muscular power. It owes much to the remarkable smoothness of the engine and its great controllability at low speeds on a low gear ratio, as contrasted with the tendency to jerks experienced with a rortier type of engine.

Weight distribution and a low centre of gravity may enter into this success, as does the clinging of an admirably sprung rear wheel to uneven road surfaces, contrasted with the wheel-hopping of a rigid rear frame. It feels safer and easier to steer than the autocycle or motor-assisted bicycle at half—or less than half—the total weight.

In these senses it deserves to be rated as the " motor cycle of tomorrow." I regard it as destined to beget a noble breed of new models, many of which will assuredly carry other transfers and nameplates. It is in sober fact one of those revolutionary motor cycles, which like the original Douglas, Triumph and Scott machines exerted so marked an influence on design at the now distant dates of their respective débuts.

INDEX

*Other books published in conjunction
with "The Motor Cycle"*

MOTOR CYCLES AND HOW TO MANAGE THEM

31st Edition. This is an authoritative, comprehensive guide to motor cycles, their care and maintenance. Written in a simple, understandable style, it is full of valuable hints and tips. *4s. 6d. net.*

MOTOR CYCLIST'S WORKSHOP

5th Edition. This is a complete guide to workshop practice for the ordinary motor cyclist. A special section is devoted to tuning for speed and efficiency. *3s. net.*

TWO-STROKE MOTOR CYCLES

10th Edition. Designed to help all owners of one of the most popular types of motor cycle on the road today, it affords a complete understanding of how a two-stroke functions, its construction, maintenance and upkeep. *3s. net.*

SPEED FROM YOUR MOTOR CYCLE

6th Edition. The author's wide experience and his ability to present his knowledge simply make this book of immense value to the motor cyclist who is interested in tuning for speed. *3s. 6d. net.*

YOUR AUTOCYCLE and How to Get the Best From It

A helpful, up-to-date guide giving hints and tips in easily understandable form on every aspect of autocycle ownership. *2s. 6d. net.*

DORSET HOUSE, STAMFORD STREET, LONDON, S.E.1